A View of THE NATION

A View of THE NATION

an anthology
1955–1959

EDITED BY
HENRY M. CHRISTMAN
INTRODUCTION BY
CAREY McWILLIAMS

GROVE PRESS, INC./NEW YORK
EVERGREEN BOOKS LTD./LONDON

Fitz Memorial Library
Endicott Junior College
Beverly, Massachusetts 01915

Copyright © 1955, 1956, 1957, 1958, 1959, by *The Nation*

Copyright © 1960 by Henry M. Christman

First Printing

Library of Congress Catalog Card Number: 60–7638

A View of The Nation is published in two editions:

>An Evergreen book (E–233)

>A cloth bound edition

Manufactured in the United States of America

CONTENTS

Introduction, *by Carey McWilliams* · 11
Original Prospectus for *The Nation* · 13

ARTS, LETTERS, AND CULTURE

THE AMERICAN WRITERS

The Ruins of Memory, *by Josephine Herbst* · 19
Novelists of Two Wars, *by Joseph Waldmeir* · 25
The Neglected Henry Miller, *by Kenneth Rexroth* · 31
The Age of Wouk, *by Maxwell Geismar* · 37
The Lost Dreams of Howard Fast, *by Stanley Meisler* · 40
Salvo for William Carlos Williams, *by M. L. Rosenthal* · 46
J. D. Salinger: The Mirror of Crisis, *by David L. Stevenson* · 56

POPULAR CULTURE

Sophistication in America, *by David Cort* · 62
The American Theatre: Show Business Is All Business,
  by Richard Hammer · 69
Hugger Mugger in the 57th Street Art Galleries,
  by Walter Goodman · 72
Newsstand Strip-Tease, *by Milton Moskowitz* · 76
The Uses of Religion, *by Robert Hatch* · 79
American College Life: My Crusade Against Fraternities,
  by Wade Thompson · 81
Who's On First: The Great American Sports Ritual,
  by Edward L. Rousseau · 87
The Happiness Rat Race, *by George P. Elliott* · 94

ISSUES OF THE DAY

SOCIAL, ECONOMIC, POLITICAL

THE RANGE OF SOCIAL PROBLEMS

Four Myths Cripple Our Schools, *by Myron Lieberman* · 105
The Question of Food: Brannan to Benson to Brannan,
  by Reo M. Christenson · 121

Housing: How to Build a Slum, *by Timothy J. Cooney* · 126
Leaderless Decency: The South Stalls Its Future, *by Harry Golden* · 130
Young Jim Crow, *by C. Vann Woodward* · 135
Narcotics: Congress Encourages the Traffic,
  by Alfred R. Lindesmith · 140
Too Many Sex Laws, *by Karl M. Bowman, M.D.* · 146
He Never Had a Chance, *by Fred J. Cook and Gene Gleason* · 152

WAR, PEACE, AND THE MILITARY

The Arms Race: Count-Down for Disaster, *by Walter Millis* · 169
The Airpower Lobby, *by Al Toffler* · 176
Small Business and the Cold War, *by Carey McWilliams* · 191
The American Legion Dies Laughing, *by Harvey Glickman* · 199
The Military Reserves: Learning the Cannoneer's Hop,
  by Richard Elman · 204

THE ECONOMICS OF LIFE

Recipe for Prosperity: "Borrow. Buy. Waste. Want."
  by Kenneth Burke · 210
Siobhan McKenna at the N.A.M., *by Dan Wakefield* · 216
Madison Avenue Jungle: Admen and Madmen, *by David Cort* · 222
Sex As a Selling Aid, *by Eve Merriam* · 230
The Credit Card Millionaires, *by Richard Schickel* · 237
Myth of the Powerful Worker, *by Harvey Swados* · 243
TVA: The Unlearned Lesson, *by Lloyd Armour* · 258
Planning for the Year 2000, *by J. Bronowski* · 264

CONTRIBUTORS

LLOYD ARMOUR is on the staff of *The Nashville Tennessean*.

KARL M. BOWMAN, M.D., is Professor of Psychiatry Emeritus at the University of California School of Medicine. As Director of the Langley Porter Clinic, he was instrumental in preparing a report on "California: Sexual Deviation Research," an important document in its field.

J. BRONOWSKI, distinguished British scientist and man of letters, is the author of "Science and Human Values," which appeared originally in *The Nation* of December 29, 1956. He is also the author of "The Face of Violence," "The Common Sense of Science," and "William Blake, a Man Without a Mask." He is the Director of the Coal Research Establishment of the British National Coal Board.

KENNETH BURKE, poet and critic, is the author of "Permanence and Change: An Anatomy of Purpose" and many other books.

REO M. CHRISTENSON, author of "The Brannan Plan: Farm Politics and Policy," teaches Government at Miami University, Ohio.

FRED J. COOK, one of the country's best-known crime reporters, is the author of "The FBI" (*The Nation*, October 18, 1958), which won the New York Newspaper Guild's Page One Award for magazine features. He was co-author with former Senator Robert C. Hendrickson, first chairman of the Senate Subcommittee on Juvenile Delinquency, of the book "Youth in Danger"; his latest book is "What Manner of Men." He is the author, with Gene Gleason, of "The Shame of New York" (*The Nation*, October 31, 1959), from which "He Never Had a Chance" is taken.

TIMOTHY J. COONEY, author of "Ultimate Desires," works for New York City's Commission on Intergroup Relations.

DAVID CORT served as associate editor of *Vanity Fair*, book review editor of *Vogue*, was foreign editor of *Life* from 1936 to 1946, and is the author of numerous books, his most recent being "Is There an American in the House?" The item here included is to be found also in the latter book and is reprinted with special permission of The Macmillan Company and the author.

GEORGE P. ELLIOTT is the author of "Parktilden Village."

RICHARD ELMAN is the author of "A Coat for the Czar," a collection of stories.

MAXWELL GEISMAR is the author of "Rebels and Ancestors," "The Last of the

Provincials," and other studies of the American novel, the most recent being "American Moderns: From Rebellion to Conformity."

GENE GLEASON was winner, with Fred J. Cook, of the 1957 Page One Award for the best local news reporting (subject: the wiretapping of a union headquarters during New York's subway strike).

HARVEY GLICKMAN, co-author with H. H. Wilson of "The Problem of Internal Security in Great Britain," is an instructor in the Department of Politics at Princeton University.

HARRY GOLDEN is editor of *The Carolina Israelite* and author of "Only in America" and "For 2¢ Plain."

WALTER GOODMAN is articles editor for *Redbook* magazine. The item here included appeared in his book, "The Clowns of Commerce" (Sagamore Press), and is included with special permission of the publisher and the author.

RICHARD HAMMER has written on the theatre for *The Economist* (London) and other publications.

ROBERT HATCH is the literary editor of *The Nation*.

JOSEPHINE HERBST is the author of "Satan's Sergeants," "Somewhere the Tempest Fell," and other novels; also "New Green World: John Bartram."

MYRON LIEBERMAN is on the staff of the Educational Research Council of Greater Cleveland and is educational consultant for *The Nation*. His most recent book is "The Future of Public Education."

ALFRED R. LINDESMITH, author of "Opiate Addiction," is Professor of Sociology at Indiana University.

CAREY McWILLIAMS is the Editor of *The Nation*.

STANLEY MEISLER is a Washington newspaperman and occasional contributor to critical and political journals.

EVE MERRIAM, whose most recent book of poems is "The Double Bed," last year won one of the CBS $5,000 prizes—the Cowan Prizes—to work on a poetic script for television. She is at present working on a book.

WALTER MILLIS, author of "The Road to War" and "Arms and Men," is one of the country's most acute students of the political aspects of modern war.

MILTON MOSKOWITZ is senior editor of *Advertising Age*.

KENNETH REXROTH, poet and critic, is the author of "Bird in the Bush" (New Directions), in which the item here included appears. It is used with the permission of the author and publisher.

M. L. ROSENTHAL is the poetry editor of *The Nation* and Associate Professor

CONTRIBUTORS

of English at New York University. Two books of his will appear this year—"A Primer of Ezra Pound" and "A View of Modern Poetry."

EDWARD L. ROUSSEAU is on the faculty of Marquette University.

RICHARD SCHICKEL is on the staff of a national magazine.

DAVID L. STEVENSON teaches contemporary literature at Western Reserve University. He is the author of "The Love-Game Comedy."

HARVEY SWADOS is the author of "On the Line" and "False Coin."

WADE THOMPSON, on the faculty of Brown University, is currently preparing a book tentatively titled "Sacred Cows," which will extend his satiric analysis to other sacred American institutions. He is also finishing a novel with a Broadway background, based on his gallant attempt as a one-time trade union organizer to organize the Radio City Rockettes.

AL TOFFLER, former labor reporter, is a newspaperman specializing in the Washington scene.

DAN WAKEFIELD, a staff contributor to *The Nation*, is the author of "Island in the City."

JOSEPH WALDMEIR teaches English at Michigan State University.

C. VANN WOODWARD, Professor of American History at John Hopkins University, is the author of "The Strange Career of Jim Crow" and other books on the South.

INTRODUCTION

A merger of the somewhat divergent but related interests of three men was largely responsible for the founding of *The Nation*, today this country's oldest weekly journal of opinion. The men and their interests were: James Miller McKim, the Philadelphia philanthropic abolitionist, deeply concerned with the welfare of the recently emancipated Negro freedmen, E. L. Godkin, whose primary interest, perhaps, was in reforming journalism, and Charles Eliot Norton, the Harvard scholar, who was, of course, concerned about cultural standards and the level of taste and opinion in America. These were the moving figures in the new venture and the initial support centered primarily in Boston, New York, and Philadelphia. All told, forty stockholders provided a capital of $100,000 and Volume I, No. 1 duly appeared on July 6, 1865. After putting the first issue to bed, Godkin dashed off a note to Norton in which he said: "No. 1 is afloat, and the tranquility which still reigns in this city, under the circumstances, I confess amazes me." But he need not have been so rueful; down the years *The Nation* has on more than one occasion disturbed the peace and its history has been anything but tranquil.

Before the first issue appeared, Godkin issued a seven-point prospectus which was essentially a statement of broad principles. To this seven-point prospectus, however, he added a few statements which are relevant to his theory of the function and quality of a journal of opinion. He said, for example, that *The Nation* would "make an earnest effort to bring to the discussion of political and social questions a really critical spirit, and to wage war upon the vices of violence, exaggeration, and misrepresentation by which so much of the political writing of the day is marred." This was followed by the covenant that "the criticism of books and works of art will form one of its most prominent features; and pains will be taken to have this task performed in every case by writers possessing special qualifications for it." Considerably later, one of his colleagues, C. C. Nott, suggested the theory underlying *The Nation's* editorial policy when he said that it was "a leaven in the lump of American journalism . . . an external conscience of other publications."

Still another colleague of Godkin's, A. G. Sedgwick, stated his idea of the publication in this way: "It was understood from the start," he wrote, "that *The Nation* was to be essentially different from other publications. . . . Its object was to be the cultivation of reasonableness. Its tone was to be that of the clarion which inspired the generation awakened to battle by *Sartor Resartus*. . . . The onset sounded by it was that of the critical, the scientific, the enlightened, the sound, the cosmopolitan, the rational." *The Nation's* purpose, Sedgwick said, was to evaluate critically the American achievement; to pronounce an informed judgment on "books and men and movements." But its special purpose, he added, was to seek out and expose "the absurdity of the fallacies underlying the extreme view on either side—the faculty of seeing through the Idols of the Tribe of which only highly trained minds were capable." The policy of the paper was "the policy of attack . . . a policy that preserved it from the popularity for which, of course, it never made the smallest bid." To the same point, Godkin once said that *The Nation* was edited for "the remnant," meaning the select minority who have a relish for dissent and a well-founded appreciation of its uses and values.

Years later the late H. L. Mencken, for years a contributing editor, had some things to say about *The Nation* which were quite in spirit with the original intention and the philosophy underlying it (Baltimore *Sun*, July 6, 1925). "*The Nation* is unique in American journalism for one thing: it is read by its enemies. . . . That is, the more intelligent of them— the least hopeless minority of them. It is to such minorities that *The Nation* addresses itself, on both sides of the fence. It has penetrated to the capital fact that they alone count—that the ideas sneaked into them today will begin to sweat out of the herd day after tomorrow. . . . Editorial writers all over the land steal ideas from it daily; it supplies, indeed, all the ideas that most of them ever have. It lifts them an inch, two inches, three inches, above the sedimentary stratum of Rotarians and ice-wagon drivers; they are conscious of its pull when they resist. . . . It is my contention that *The Nation* has led the war in the reform of American journalism—that it will be followed by many papers tomorrow, as it is followed by a few today. . . . Its politics are often outrageous. . . . It has no sense of decorum. . . . It is sometimes a bit rowdy. . . . But who will deny that it is honest? And who will deny that, taking one day with another, it is generally right—that its enthusiasms, if they occasionally send it mooning after dreamers, at least never send it cheering after rogues—that its wrongness, when it is wrong, is at all events, not the dull, simian wrongness of mere stupidity?"

This theory of its function is *The Nation's* prime capital, indeed its only capital. It is as sound today as when Godkin first articulated it. He never believed for a second that the stock of shibboleths would ever diminish, in any future society that he could imagine, to the point where exploding them would no longer be a function of critical journalism. He would have agreed with Kingsley Martin that "When a very great many, very important pundits all agree that something very terrible and mysterious will happen if we depart a hair's breadth from orthodoxy, the time has come to say, 'Oh Yeah,'" The myths might take new forms but there would always be a function for the journal of opinion that would, so to speak, challenge the dogmas-of-the-week, the Idols of the Tribe. Incidentally, it should be noted that Godkin steadily insisted that the journal of opinion should not deal exclusively with recondite matters. He was forever saying that it should be interested in "the matters which were passing before everyone's eyes, and which at a given moment occupy the thoughts of his neighbors."

The selections that appear in this anthology were made by Henry M. Christman, not by the editors, and the subject-matter arrangements are his, not ours. But we are, I should hasten to add, pleased with his selections. They are representative of the range and quality of *Nation* articles for the period covered and exemplify its basic editorial philosophy and journalistic style. They constitute, I feel, an admirable introduction to a publication which, now as always, is edited for "the least hopeless minority ... on both sides," a minority which, happily, is considerably larger than it was in 1865 and is growing all the time.

CAREY MCWILLIAMS

ORIGINAL PROSPECTUS FOR THE NATION

THE NATION

A WEEKLY JOURNAL OF POLITICS, LITERATURE, SCIENCE, AND ART WILL BE PUBLISHED JULY 6, 1865.

Terms:—Three Dollars per annum, in advance; Six Months, Two Dollars.

ITS MAIN OBJECTS WILL BE

First.—The discussion of the topics of the day, and, above all, of legal, economical, and constitutional questions, with greater accuracy and moderation than are now to be found in the daily press.

Second.—The maintenance and diffusion of true democratic principles in society and government, and the advocacy and illustration of whatever in legislation or in manners seems likely to promote a more equal distribution of the fruits of progress and civilization.

Third.—The earnest and persistent consideration of the condition of the laboring class at the South, as a matter of vital interest to the nation at large, with a view to the removal of all artificial distinctions between them and the rest of the population, and the securing to them, as far as education and justice can do it, of an equal chance in the race of life.

Fourth.—The enforcement and illustration of the doctrine that the whole community has the strongest interest, both moral, political, and material, in their elevation, and that there can be no real stability for the Republic so long as they are left in ignorance and degradation.

Fifth.—The fixing of public attention upon the political importance of popular education, and the dangers which a system like ours runs from the neglect of it in any portion of our territory.

Sixth.—The collection and diffusion of trustworthy information as to the condition and prospects of the Southern States, the openings they offer to capital, the supply and kind of labor which can be obtained in them, and the progress made by the colored population in acquiring the habits and desires of civilized life.

Seventh.—Sound and impartial criticism of books and works of art.

The Nation will not be the organ of any party, sect, or body. It will, on the contrary, make an earnest effort to bring to the discussion of political and social questions a really critical spirit, and to wage war upon the vices of violence, exaggeration, and misrepresentation by which so much of the political writing of the day is marred.

The criticism of books and works of art will form one of its most prominent features; and pains will be taken to have this task performed in every case by writers possessing special qualifications for it.

It is intended, in the interest of investors, as well as of the public generally, to have questions of trade and finance treated every week by a writer whose position and character will give his articles an exceptional value, and render them a safe and trustworthy guide.

A special correspondent, who has been selected for his work with some care, is about to start in a few days for a journey through the South. His letters will appear every week, and he is charged with the duty of simply reporting what he sees and hears, leaving the public as far as possible to draw its own inferences.

The following writers, among others, have been secured either as regular or occasional contributors:—

INTRODUCTION

Henry W. Longfellow, James Russell Lowell, John G. Whittier, Samuel Eliot (Ex-President Trin. College, Hartford), Professor Torrey (Harvard), Dr. Francis Lieber, Professor Child (Harvard), Charles E. Norton, Judge Bond (Baltimore), Edmund Quincy, Professor W. D. Whitney (Yale), Professor D. C. Gilman (Yale), Judge Daly, Professor Dwight (Columbia College), Judge Wayland, Frederick Law Olmsted, Rev. Dr. McClintock, Rev. Dr. Jos. P. Thompson, Rev. Phillips Brooks, Rev. Dr. Bellows, C. J. Stillé, Henry T. Tuckerman, Bayard Taylor, C. A. Bristed, C. L. Brace, Richard Grant White, William Lloyd Garrison, Sydney George Fisher, Theodore Tilton, James Parton, Gail Hamilton, R. H. Stoddard.

130 Nassau Street, N.Y.

JOSEPH H. RICHARDS,
Publisher.

ARTS, LETTERS, AND CULTURE

THE AMERICAN WRITERS

THE RUINS OF MEMORY / JOSEPHINE HERBST

What seems to be missing in a good deal of contemporary writing is a sense of the world. The world around us. For some time we have had so many writers trailing their own nervous systems, premonitions, fantasies and horrors that perhaps the time has come to dig up man, the guilty worm, and to see him in relation to an actual world. It has gone so far that the word "actual" may start an argument. I mean it, just the same, in its Jane Austen sense, its Flaubert sense, its Tolstoian sense. To insist on this point of the actual is, practically speaking, avant garde. One thing is certain, we have no avant garde to flutter anybody at present. The one we had got stuck some time back in the pages of the little magazines when they went academic. Then the critics took over. This has been a long period for the critics and editors. The great authors to come up since the Second World War have mostly been dead a long time. Kafka, Melville, Hawthorne, Henry James should be with us always but their resurgence in the forties presaged more than recognition of their stature. It signified also a genteel retreat from a period too complicated to confront easily. The writings of the detached past became a kind of smokescreen to conceal the present dilemma, and the ruins.

But a ruin can be as good a point of departure as any. There is usually new life in the ruins as anyone who ever saw a population react from a bombing can testify. But the picker-uppers are not trying to salvage tender mementos only. They usually are looking for bricks and firewood.

In the twenties writers seem to have been valued above critics and when a critic really got under the skin he was apt to be a writer. If you were a young writer then and read Ezra Pound in the *Little Review* or *Poetry Magazine* you were fired to write to the limit of your skill. Today if a young writer reads too much criticism he may feel that there is no use manning the ship which is overmanned already and besides will the captains care for his particular skill?

If past history is any guide, the present phase that tends to the compulsive presentation of people as isolated moral atoms without any sensible relation to society or the ideas of their time ought to have departed before this.

For literary epochs come and go but this wave seems to have frozen in the cold war. In the freeze more is paralyzed than anyone cares to admit; perhaps more than the writer dares admit. But there is no such thing as a writer untouched by his time. Even the most inner experience is a response to some outside. That response may lead Kafka to explore the dark region beyond human experience or explanation in *The Castle* or Sean O'Casey to write from a sense of mission *Red Roses for Me*. In a favorable period when the atmosphere is fluid there will be many varieties of response to experience and what emerges is creation in full flower. Not without flaws, the decade of the twenties approached such a time of creative flowering if only because it was relatively hospitable to the new and diverse.

Every period takes stock of the one preceding it and the past that was good enough for the fathers never seems good enough for the children no matter how idyllic it may seem to the great-grandchildren. Writers in the twenties reacted not only to the shock of the First World War but to the values held dear in the nineteenth century. The stock responses of good will and progressive enlightenment as an explanation of human behavior had failed Dreiser and Sherwood Anderson even before the First World War. The new attitudes were expressed not only in the realm of ideas but were implicit in the texture of the work, its language, its style, even in what came to be tagged "lack of style."

If the values of the nineteenth century failed the writers of the twenties they collapsed utterly in the thirties. What could liberal belief in rationality do against the irrationality which was spreading over Europe? In a period of demoralization and terror it was no bad thing to try to act, however mistakenly or inadequately, as the conscience of the age. If you can bear to lift the black cloth placed over the thirties by the revisionists, some of whom seem more infatuated with the revelation of their own private sense of guilt than in the situation as it *then existed*, you may be surprised to discover work not entirely marred by "innocence" nor requiring the afterthought of "shame." The reaction in the forties, the Second World War, the new cynicism, the new prosperity and the new smugness put the thirties, its work and the sources of its potential, into a time capsule where it has been effectively isolated. But the fact remains that work marked by vitality and venturing did emerge in the arts, the theatre and in the writing of that decade and found a new dynamic.

It is a new dynamic which is now conspicuous by its absence. Material prosperity can never answer the questions, why do we live, what does it mean? When the notion spreads that getting along may be the ultimate aim of man's efforts, the surface hardens and the writer, by nature more of a rebel than he may choose to admit, tries to burrow somewhere for a hidden meaning. If the rigidities set up make it dangerous truly to look at the world around us, the writer may be driven to look only at himself, unrelated to the actual world. But writing *should* be dangerous; as dangerous as Socrates. There should be no refuge for the writer either in the Ivory Tower or the Social Church.

Gissing, whose work Henry James admired, said that in all character there sits a mind, and that the mind of the dullest is not dull because, at its lowest, it will at least reflect the social dilemma. Perhaps the writers in the thirties were so hard-pressed by the immediacy of the dilemma that they scratched around for characters to explicate it. But it was no longer a time when the Nick Adamses up in Michigan could feel the question of the hour as merely a choice between freedom or that "fat married look." Straws in the wind, out of jobs, out of luck, the Nick Adamses of the thirties might well ask, freedom for what? It was a time when the feelings of the individual might seem haphazard, trivial, inconsequent compared with his feelings experienced as a member of a particular group. As an experience this was not new; soldiers in war know it; European literature has reflected it, but in the thirties it seemed to have had special significance for a nation dedicated to individualism. Some of the writing of the decade reflected this special kind of comprehension. Not every writer was obsessed with "the way out" or the idealized "worker," but as man had become a political animal, whether he liked it or not, the writers most sensitive to the temper of the time were bound to reflect it.

When you read *Let Us Now Praise Famous Men,* you realize that James Agee was feeling his way into the lives of poor and rejected people from whom his normal fate as a writer might have isolated him. There was discovery here that reminds us of the nineteenth-century Russian literature when Tolstoy attempted to understand far beyond the boundaries of his estate, and the affairs of Dr. Chekhov informed the writer Chekhov.

It takes a true writer to show us what has been missing in our lives. No one can give the writer an assignment that his own impulse has not bespoken but more than his security should inform him. "The pen," said Kafka to Janouch, "is not an instrument but an organ of the writer's." But what if that organ suffer a fatty degeneration and come to resemble the diseased liver of a Strasbourg goose? What has a writer to say if he agrees that this is the best of all possible worlds and all of our major problems have been solved on a miracle time belt of endless prosperity? Aren't all the Nick Adamses of today fairly courting that "fat married look"? The routine may become boring, and the writer who in his life may batten happily on his role in a priggish status quo, may revert in his writing to the exotic and cash in on a kind of romantic nihilism which never attempts to deal with more than the desperate *sensations* of a felt or imagined experience. Don't our modern Stavrogins tend to wallow luxuriously in their dreadful predicaments? Seen without any surrounding pattern to light the actuality, they emerge as little more than case histories. One pathological case confined to its pathology is not a subject for literary work. Dostoevsky's Stavrogin also struggled against his doomed nature; he killed himself because he had a vision of a human world, not because he saw inhumanity triumphant with himself in a stellar role. His reaction implied more than a blighted ego.

How did we get where we are? Perhaps if beating the breast in public confession had not become *sine qua non* we might find out. Guilt is real, it is serious, but when it becomes also a fashion, there is corruption. No one can seek for new clues or discover the actual world when it becomes clouded with the smoke of penitents burning the past.

We are not only what we are today but what we were yesterday and if you burn your immediate past there is nothing left but ashes which are all very well for those heads that like nothing better than to be sprinkled with ashes. But are these ash-covered heads really the spokesmen of our conscience? For conscience implies constant vigilance, inquiry, challenge, seeking, wonder. A conscience larded with complacency and self-righteousness is no longer a conscience. And we may well ask what has come out of all this in the way of writing and where and how is the writer facing up to the consequences of his knowledge. Are these frequent stories of innocents whose baffled illusions are made to seem important, oh far more important than life itself, really the expression of man's fate? Is the eccentric really our man of the hour? Life is shown up as a little shabby in comparison to some of this starry-eyed frustration. In fact, many writers seem intent on what D. H. Lawrence called "doing dirt on life."

May a conscience be time-clocked and serve one decade and not another? It is all very well to have pursued with vigilance the psychopaths of "radical conformity," minds hardened against any human plea or valid idea embarrassing to the Party. But a mind can harden while manning a power post, any time, any place, whether in politics, government, Hollywood, the university or an institute of art and letters. It can harden while it succumbs to prevailing fashion under any banner.

If the social criticism of the thirties seemed able to analyze the roots only by disparaging the flower, the new detective-critics seem able to admire the flower only by pulling it to pieces. Between the opposing factions of this modern War of the Roses the flower is victimized, and the writer, without whom there would be no flower, seems relegated to a Nobody. If behind the leaders of one faction waved the banners demanding a deterministic construction of man's role, behind the leaders of the opposing faction rose the misty phantoms of a Southern feudal aristocracy. Excesses in one direction turned to excesses in another; in both instances we seem to see looming above us the stern father image of an arbitrary authority. It is not only in politics that the age has been thus marked.

The language of our new critics was seductive, called us to account on many basic literary issues; and since we were fed up with too much democracy in the thirties, the notion of an aristocracy, if only in the arts, made a telling point. Form and precision of language are all-important but there is also a point of view and one may well ask in what origins it arises. What assumptions are made from which the elegant flower is to grow? It is not coincidence that most of the writing to please the new detective-critics came from Southerners, most of whom were emigrés living in the North, getting their livings in Northern cities but with all feeling, knowledge and creative source in the South.

If it is our privilege to admire a body of brilliant writing by Southerners, worthy of a lasting place in our literature, it is also pertinent to ask why, in general, it has become so static. If it succeeded in producing a renascence for which we should be grateful, why did its influence effect a stalemate and degenerate into the picturesque, the bizarre and the exploitation of the eccentric? The insistence on perfection may produce a Rimbaud, revolutionary in form *and* content, but it may also settle for an inverted romanticism, a kind of snobbish chastity, implying that the hurly-burly is really not good enough for these particular garments. Then the will to perfection without the valid idea may proliferate into mere decay and tedium, descending into the language and the thought of journalism, relying finally on the violence of the "you-gotta-knock-'em-dead" school. The secret prince and dreamer of perfection may become lost in the glitter of honor, and his talent may then make of him an actor for life.

There is a distinction to be made between the actual writing of the group that produced the renascence and the effects which followed in its train. This is no challenge to that body of writing; its writers had their aim and had to fulfill it by the inner secret processes of all creative work. But it also seems true that the sights were set toward a traditional past to the extinction of a prevailing present and as a result precluded a dynamic for writers to follow. From the richest section of this country in the sense of a literary potential we have arrived at a dead level of little studies of general decay. But the fact is that the South is not so much decaying as *changing* and it is fair to ask what use other writers in other countries in other epochs made of similar situations of transition. And it seems also to the point to suggest that of all the Southerners, Faulkner, who has mostly stayed put, has been able to gouge deeper, range more widely and feel more intimately the pressure of Southern change and responsibility, and to be, so far as I know, the only writer of the South willing to put himself on record on the murder of young Till. As for earlier epochs the writer did not have to applaud in order to respond knowingly; Balzac, attached to the feudal past, could take in what was going on around him with everything thrown in; Stendahl could write of the business-king Louis Philippe so incisively that *The Green Huntsman* could not be published in his life-time. A response to change was inherent in every line of Jane Austen. As for the Russians whose serfs were liberated in the same decade as the Civil War, what did they *not* do?

This discussion would fail to make its point if it appeared to set up new goals for more authority instead of more freedoms. The writer has suffered more than the Wars of the Roses in this period. He, like everybody else, seems to have been atomized and a waif on his own, to be shut off from many of the sources of knowledge more freely come by at an earlier period. If his road leads to the university and conformity, it is not altogether by choice, but by grim necessity in a society where the writer has never been a culture-hero. Roving was good for the writer; to have been a reporter undoubtedly informed Ring Lardner, Ernest Hemingway, Stephen Crane. To know far more than he may ever use is imperative for the writer.

We should not have to choose between Dreiser or Henry James. A writer must follow his bent but there are situations when pressures from without press so strongly that he hardly knows if he is bending to his own inner impulse or to some compulsive outside. In these days of specialization, when the scientist may be immured with his experiment without knowledge of what is going on in other laboratories, when he may even be in ignorance of the whole meaning of the cultural processes of which he is a part, it seems to me that the writer too is running a risk of falling back into his own little corner where his very isolation within himself is aiding a sterilization of creative powers. Or in another category, that he too often refuses to confront the implications of his own work, and intending to show the menace of the violent, secretly champions the force he would deplore. If we believe with Henry James that any theory which prevents a writer from seeing is a wrong one, we might also meditate on the words of Rilke: that "everything is gestation and then bringing forth. To let each impression and each germ of feeling come to completion quite in itself, in the dark, in the inexpressible, the unconscious, beyond the reach of one's own understanding, and wait with deep humility and patience the birth-hour of a new clarity; that alone is living the artist's life—in understanding as in work."

NOVELISTS OF TWO WARS / JOSEPH WALDMEIR

John Dos Passos' *Three Soldiers* and Ernest Hemingway's *A Farewell to Arms* are the two American World War I novels which have retained, and even enhanced, their stature over the years. That the novels were ideological, expressing a particular attitude toward the ideas and principles which motivated the war and the actions of individual soldiers, probably accounts in large part for their continuing critical and popular appeal. This is not to discount their considerable literary merit. Thomas Boyd's *Through the Wheat*, William March's *Company K*, Humphrey Cobb's *Paths of Glory* and Dalton Trumbo's *Johnny Got His Gun* are at least as eloquent ideologically; it is perhaps in the very intensity of their ideology that they fall short of Hemingway's and Dos Passos' artistic achievement. However, these novels also come more readily to mind than the fictitious diaries, the combat-adventure stories, and the sentimentally propagandistic pieces of World War I.

Primarily for these reasons the ideological novels of the Second World War merit more serious critical consideration than the non-ideological novels. A practical, secondary reason is that, over the past fifteen years, so many war novels have been published that any discussion which is not extremely selective will degenerate into a mere list of titles and authors. It should not be inferred, therefore, that the novels excluded from this discussion are necessarily inferior, as novels, to those included. Some of them are—such sentimental, pseudo-ideological potboilers as Elliot Arnold's *Tomorrow Will Sing* or Paul Gallico's *The Lonely*, for instance —but not the fine combat-adventure stories like Harry Brown's *A Walk in the Sun*, Lawrence Kahn's *Able One Four*, or Peter Bowman's *Beach Red*; nor the penetrating studies of self-consciousness and war neurosis: Prudencio de Pereda's *All the Girls We Loved*, William Hoffman's *The*

Trumpet Unblown, and Vance Bourjaily's *The End of My Life*. But considerations of art aside, the seriously ideological World War II novels are the ones most likely to attain permanence.

As soon as one speaks of permanence in connection with war novels, a question is almost automatically asked: Where is the Hemingway or Dos Passos of the second war? The answer is simple, but its implications are extremely important: There aren't any; there never can be any. There is a Shaw and a Mailer and a Hayes and a Burns and a Heym and a Myrer; there is even a Wouk and a Cozzens. But there is no Hemingway or Dos Passos or Boyd or March or Cobb or Trumbo; neither is there a "Bury the Dead" Irwin Shaw nor an Alfred Hayes who was once a poet in the pacifist John Reed Club. These were two entirely different wars and they were fought, as far as the novelists are concerned, on entirely different premises.

Cynicism, pessimism, disillusion, constitute the negative ideology of the serious World War I novels. They portray war as vicious and hateful, stupid and cruel; a foul trick played by man upon himself. Nothing could be more preposterous than a war that was fought for no reason and which therefore neither side could win. Essential values—patriotism, democracy, traditions, sacrifice—embarrass Frederic Henry and embitter John Andrews, because they are both the cause and effect of the preposterousness. Thus, in some of the most bitter iconoclasm in literature, the values are hacked at, demeaned and destroyed. Hemingway's and Dos Passos' heroes desert the fight with few qualms; Hicks, in Boyd's *Through the Wheat*, like the heroes of March's *Company K*, gradually loses all illusions as he fights on. Cobb's five heroes are executed as cowards; and Trumbo's Johnny, a horribly pitiful basket case, with no arms, legs, stomach, face, or identity, is frustrated—in the name of patriotism and good taste—in his one faintly optimistic desire to be placed on display as a pacifist lesson.

The World War II novelists still see war as hateful, brutal and cruel—the brave, like Noah Ackerman in Irwin Shaw's *The Young Lions*, still are destroyed; so are the honest, like Lieutenant Hearn in Norman Mailer's *The Naked and the Dead*; the good, like Sergeant Byng in Stefan Heym's *The Crusaders*, Danny Kantaylis in Anton Myrer's *The Big War*, and Moe in John Horne Burns's *The Gallery*; and the gifted, like Alan Newcombe in *The Big War*. They too refuse to be misled by the grand abstractions; they refuse to over-simplify motivations, and they castigate those who do.

Nevertheless, there is an essential difference between these novelists and their World War I counterparts. The World War II novels are optimistic and positive. They were written in the conviction that fighting the war—and winning it—was a worthwhile objective. Their authors fought fascism; indeed, many of them had been fighting it for a decade before the war began. None of them felt that war was good; all of them felt that this particular war was necessary. And they tried to convey this combination of ideas in their novels by using the physical struggle metaphorically, as sign and symbol of the ideological conflict.

Christian Diestl in *The Young Lions* is shot; Colonel Pettinger in *The Crusaders* is entombed alive; the petty Italian official in Alfred Hayes's *All Thy Conquests* is stoned, then drowned. These physical victories stand symbolically for victory over the brutality, amorality, stupidity, self-seeking materialism, and end-means rationalism of the Italian and German brands of fascism.

But these writers and the others considered here are not satisfied with naive poetic justice. That is the principal difference between the truly ideological novel and the sentimentally propagandistic. The serious novelists are concerned with the premises upon which their convictions rest— with the dilemmas and paradoxes which often pervert or upset the nice conclusion.

They attack anyone who fails to support the crusade against fascism honestly and unselfishly—and that is very unlike the World War I novelists who accused those who supported their war either of ignorance or war-mongering for profit. They attack fascism wherever it appears, or anything that resembles it or threatens to develop into it. Thus they are frequently as savage in their criticism of Americans as were the World War I writers. *The Gallery* contains speech after articulate speech of acid attack upon American rationalistic materialism and the American inability to feel any emotion strongly. Alan Newcombe, one of the sacrificed in *The Big War*, is estranged from his father, who sees the war in terms of personal economics. The black-marketing soldiers who stall an advance by selling General Farrish's gasoline in *The Crusaders;* the rank-happy Captain Motes in *The Gallery;* the amoral, ambitious, war correspondent, Wexel, in Ned Calmer's *The Strange Land*—all these illustrate the novelist's denunciation of a leaning by Americans toward an inimical ideology.

But brutality, end-means expediency, and particularly racism, as it occurred among Americans, were given special consideration. The armed services are, almost by definition, fascistic; and the irony of defeating an enemy by using its own most deplorable methods deeply impressed the novelists. What impressed them as even more ironic was the fascism that individual servicemen brought with them into the war against fascism. The anti-Semitism of the entire Company in *The Young Lions*, of Dondolo in *The Crusaders* and of Gallagher in *The Naked and the Dead*, illustrates the novelists' shocked awareness of the bitter joke. In the sadism of Croft (*The Naked and the Dead*), and of Dondolo; and in the conscious amorality of Colonel Willoughby in *The Crusaders*, this awareness goes still deeper. Of all of the villains in these books, Willoughby is perhaps the most offensive. His crime is purposeful, intentional, rational, he protects war criminals in order to re-establish an international steel cartel.

An equal danger lies in Farrish, the politically ambitious general whom Willoughby serves. His chauvinism, coupled with his ambition, blinds him to Willoughby's crime; his egotism, nurtured by a hero-worshiping American public, makes him potentially an easy man to control once he gains power. But the most dangerous villain of all, because he can think for himself and do his own controlling, is the openly fascistic General Cummings in *The Naked and the Dead*. His considered opinions on politics and government, liberalism and conservatism, the common man, and the use of power, might have come directly from Goebbels' notes. It is worth noting here that the ideological novelists who fought the war of the Pacific had to choose Americans as their villains. Japan was not an ideological enemy in the sense that Germany was. Thus, while Shaw had his Diestl, and Heym his Pettinger, as actual Nazis, Mailer had to make use of the American Sergeant Croft and General Cummings.

However, the ideological novelists don't stop at a simple portrayal of the irony. They search for a means to resolve the dilemma from which it stems.

Two of the most successful serious novels to come out of the war, James Gould Cozzens' *Guard of Honor* and Herman Wouk's *The Caine Mutiny*, resolve it in the direction of what Mailer, Heym and their fellows would term expedient fascism. The war must be won, these books seem to say, regardless of individual rights and dignities. Queeg may be a bad and ignorant man, anti-Negroism may be a deplorable tendency of Southerners, but the correction of these conditions must not obstruct the war effort. The villains are not the paranoic Captain Queeg nor the sophist Colonel Ross, but the intellectual ideologists, Lieutenant Keefer and Lieutenant Edsell.

Such a resolution is actually no resolution at all, since it depends for its effect upon an evasion of the issue. More satisfactory, though not completely so, is the consideration of the causes behind the growth of army fascism by Theodore White in his recently published *The Mountain Road*. White comes to the conclusion that Lord Acton was right—power does corrupt, especially when entrusted to inexperienced hands at moments of crisis. Queeg's are such hands, as are General Beal's; but while these men are defended by their creators, and thus remain dangerous ideologically, White places the words about power in Major Baldwin's mouth; and they are spoken, not to excuse his crime, but as a humble statement of what he has learned.

Awareness of responsibility and guilt is at the root of the novelists' most satisfactory resolution of the dilemma in which they found themselves as they sought to justify the war. Those who are guilty must have their noses rubbed in their guilt, and must be made to accept responsibility and pay the penalty. On the simplest level, this is exemplified by Colonel Pettinger and Sergeant Diestl. But on a level far more complex, largely because it constitutes constructive rather than destructive criticism, it is exemplified by Hearn, Whitacre, Yates, Newcombe—by all of the individual and collective heroes of the books discussed here.

Mailer, Shaw, Heym, Myrer send their heroes to war as anything but crusaders. They are indifferent to values. They don't go along with the pinkish socialism of the 1930s, but neither can they revert to the so-called integrity of free spirits of the 1920s. They don't want war and they can't not want war. They are individualists, but in the worst sense: they stand apart from an acceptance or even a realization of the responsibilities of individualism. At the outset, Hearn is a feather-head who, as General Cummings points out to him, can't even decide whether he is a liberal or a conservative; Yates is a mouse, uncertain of the validity of his own convictions; Whitacre and Newcombe are convinced only that convictions are nonsense.

But, through traumatic experiences with war and with fascism in enemy, comrade and ally—a memorable scene in both *The Young Lions* and *The Crusaders* is concerned with the racism of liberated concentration-camp prisoners—each man gradually comes to realize that indifference and timidity have made him guilty of and responsible for the fact of the war. Each man commits himself to the struggle; a struggle no longer simply with German or Japanese, but with a hated ideology under whatever guise.

Thus, they earn their individualism as they relinquish it. But this is only an apparent paradox. Their involvement in the war is made voluntarily, and they attack without respite all things, men and institutions which destroy individualism. It is at this point that these novels veer sharply from *The Caine Mutiny* and *Guard of Honor*. For while Wouk and

Cozzens espouse enforced involvement and the postponement of individualism, Heym, Mailer, Shaw, Myrer let their heroes choose freely to relinquish their individualism, seeing clearly that only through such a choice can individualism be retained and buttressed.

In the lives of most of these heroes, human love mixes with war and fascism to accelerate the wakening responsibility and consequent loss of indifference. Most war novels contain a good deal of loving, a great deal of sex. It is frequently the novelist's way of portraying the chaotic letting down of bars that accompanies war; it is as frequently his way of assuring a good sale. In the serious novel it is more than either of these. To love means to accept responsibility and implies an ability to hate; loving therefore is beyond the capacity of an indifferent man. The love affairs in these novels help to convert the heroes by giving them something to feel strongly about; it is then a simple matter to transfer the strength to other feelings.

Experience with war and fascism on the one hand and with love on the other has led the ideological World War II novelist to insist that a man's loss of indifference implies his acceptance of responsibility, and results in his engagement and involvement as an individual in a world he did make and is continuously making. Much the same experiences led the World War I novelists to very different conclusions, primarily because they believed that someone else had made their world. Instead of involvement, there was retreat; instead of anguish, there was anger. Frederic Henry and John Andrews, as individuals, reject responsibility and desert. Danny Kantaylis in *The Big War* and Pete Donatti in James Garrett's *And Save Them for Pallbearers*, as individuals, accept responsibility so wholeheartedly that they voluntarily return to action and are killed.

This strong feeling of responsibility, coupled with the conviction that the war was a sort of crusade against irresponsibility, explains the novelists' continuing fervent anti-fascism so long after V.E. Day (for many of the books were written a decade after the war). The war was successful in what it set out to do, but the struggle goes on. Materialism, racism, amorality, brutality—whether they abide in the ideologies of Hitler, McCarthy, or Faubus—must be destroyed as Nazism, their epitome, was destroyed by the war.

Various Angry and Beat generations—somewhat like the World War I novelists, except for the very important difference that they are not war novelists—keep insisting that the ideals are illusory and the struggle futile. Their questions embarrass; they may be right. But their "We gotta go, man, and keep on going" answer to the problems of the world is hardly as satisfactory as the World War I novelists' slashing iconoclasm, or as the World War II novelists' insistence that "We gotta stay, and stay, and stay. And become part of what we hate in order to be free of it." The Angry and the Beat will not accept this answer, for it turns their anger in upon themselves—where some of it at least very probably belongs.

THE NEGLECTED HENRY MILLER /
KENNETH REXROTH

Henry Miller is a really popular writer, a writer of, for, and by real people. In other countries he is read, not just by highbrows, or by the wider public that reads novels, but by the people who, in the United States, read comic books. In the United States he has been kept away from a popular public and his great novels have been banned. Only highbrows who could import them from France have read him.

I once crossed the Atlantic with a cabin mate, a French-African Negro, only partially literate, who was able to talk for hours on the comparative merits of "Black Spring" and the "Tropic of Cancer" and the "Tropic of Capricorn." When he found out I came from California and knew Miller, he started treating me as if I were an archangel newly descended, and never tired of questions about Le Beeg Sur and Les Camarades du M'sieu Millaire. Miners in the Pyrenees, gondoliers in Venice, and certainly every *poule* in Paris, when they hear you're from California, ask, first thing, "Do you know M'sieu Millaire?" This doesn't mean he isn't read by the intellectuals. In fact I should say he has become part of the standard repertory of reading matter everywhere but in England and in the United States. If you have read Balzac, or Baudelaire, or Goethe, you are also expected to have read Miller. He is certainly one of the most widely read American writers, along with Upton Sinclair, Jack London, Fenimore Cooper and Caldwell.

This is the way it should be. Nothing was sadder than the "proletarian novelist" of a few years back. Nobody read him but other Greenwich Village esthetes like himself. The people Henry Miller writes about read him. They read him because he gives them something they cannot find elsewhere in print. It may not be precisely the real world, but it is nearer to it than most other writing, and it is certainly nearer than most so-called realistic writing.

Once the written word was a privilege of priests and priestly scribes. Although thousands of years have passed, vestiges of that special privilege and caste artificiality still cling to it. Can you remember when you first started to read? Doubtless you thought that someday you would find in books the truth, the answer to the very puzzling life you were discovering around you. But you never did. The written word is a sieve. Only so much of reality gets through as fits the size and shape of the screen, and in some ways that is never enough. Partly this is due to the structure of language. With us this takes the form of Indo-European grammar crystallized in what we call Aristotelian logic. Most of the real difficulty of communication comes from social convention, from a vast conspiracy to agree to accept the world as something it isn't at all. Even the realist novels of a writer like Zola are not much closer to the real thing than the documents written in Egyptian hieroglyphics.

Literature is a social defense mechanism. Remember again when you were a child. You thought that some day you would grow up and find a world of real adults, the people who really made things run, and understood how and why things ran. Then, as the years went on, you learned, through more or less bitter experience, that there aren't and never have been any such people, anywhere. Life is just a mess, and nobody knows what makes it go. Or anyway nobody tells.

Henry Miller tells. Anderson told *about* the little boy and the Emperor's new clothes. Miller *is* the little boy. He tells about the Emperor, about the pimples on his behind, and the warts on his private parts, and the dirt between his toes. Great writers in the past have done this, and they are the real classics. But they have done it within the conventions of literature. They have used the forms of the Great Lie to expose the truth. Some of this literature is called comic, but in the last analysis it is all tragic, even Rabelais, because finally life itself is tragic. With very few exceptions, however, it is conventional. It disguises itself in the garments of harmless artistic literature. It sneaks in and betrays the complacent and deluded. A great work of art is a kind of Trojan Horse. There are those who believe that this is all there is to the art of poetry—sugarcoating the pills of prussic acid with which the poet doses the enemy.

It is hard to tell sometimes when Miller is being ironic and when he is being naive. He is the master of a deadpan style, just as he has a public personality that alternates between quiet gentleness, "like a dentist," he describes it, and a sort of deadpan buffoonery. This has led some critics to consider him a "modern primitive" like Rousseau.

Miller is a very unliterary writer. He writes as if he had just invented the alphabet. When he writes about a book, he writes as if he were the first and only man who had ever read it—and furthermore as if it wasn't a book but a piece of living meat whacked off Balzac or Rimbaud or whoever.

Miller has preserved an innocence of the practice of Literature almost unique. Likewise he has preserved an innocence of heart. But he is not unsophisticated. In the first place, he writes a muscular, active prose which is always under control. True, he often rambles and gets windy, but only because he likes to ramble and hear his head roar. When he wants to tell you something straight from the shoulder, he makes you reel.

Now the writer most like Miller in some ways, is the eighteenth-century *naif*, Restif de la Bretonne. If you want the common man of the eighteenth century, with his heart laid bare, you will find him in Restif. But you will also find thousands of pages of sheer boredom, and hundreds of pages of quite looney and obviously invented pornography. Miller too is liable at times to go off the deep end about the lost continent of Mu or astrology or the "occult," but it is for a different reason. If the whole shebang is a lie anyway, certainly the amusing lies, the lies of the charlatans who have never been able to get the guillotine in their hands, are better than the official lie, the deadly one.

In all literature there aren't many people like Miller. The only ones I can think of are Petronius, Casanova, and Restif. Their books give an overwhelming feeling of being true, completely uncooked. They are all intensely masculine writers. They all are great comic writers. They all convey, powerfully, a sense of the utter tragedy of life. I can think of no more chilling passages in literature than the tolling of the bell from the very beginning of Casanova's "Memoirs," the comments and asides of the aged man, writing of his splendid youth, an old, sick, friendless pauper, in a draughty castle in the backwoods of Bohemia. And last, and most important, they were all what the English call spivs. Courtier of Nero or Parisian typesetter, they were absolutely uninvolved. They just didn't give a damn whether school kept or not.

Miller has often been compared with Celine, but I don't think the comparison is apposite. Celine is a man with a thesis. Furthermore, he is a litterateur. In "Journey to the End of the Night" he set out to write the epic of a Robinson Crusoe of the modern soul, the utterly alienated man. He did it, very successfully. Celine and his friends stumble through the fog, over the muddy ruts with the body of Robinson in a denouement as monumental as the "Nibelungenlied." But it is all a work of art. I have been in the neighborhoods Celine described. They simply aren't that awful. I am sure on internal evidence of the story itself, that his family wasn't that bad. Celine makes a sociological judgment on Robinson. Miller *is* Robinson, and on the whole, he finds it a bearable role, even enjoyable in its way.

Henry Miller is often spoken of as a religious writer. To some this just seems silly, because Miller is not especially profound. People expect religion to come to them served in miracle, mystery, and authority, as Dostoevsky said. Blake dressed his message up in sonorous and mysterious language, but the message itself is simple enough. D. H. Lawrence likewise. You could write it all on a postage stamp. "*Mene, mene, tekel, upharsin.* Your official reality is a lie. We must love one another or die." I suppose any writer who transcends conventional literature is religious in so far as he does transcend it. That is why you can never actually base an educational system on the Hundred Best Books. A hundred of the truest insights into life as it is would destroy any educational system, and society along with it.

Certainly Miller is almost completely untouched by what is called religion in England and America and Northern Europe. He is completely pagan. This is why his book on Greece, "The Colossus of Maroussi," is a book of self-discovery as well as a very true interpretation of Greece. It is thoroughly classic. Although he never mentions Homer and dismisses the Parthenon, he did discover the life of Greece, the common, real life of the peasants and fishermen, going on, just as it has gone on, ever since the Doric invasions.

His absolute freedom from the Christian or Jewish anguish of conscience, the sense of guilt, implication, and compromise, makes Miller humane, but it effectively keeps him from being humanitarian. He might cry over a pet dog who had been run over, or even punch the guilty driver in the nose. He might have assassinated Hitler if he had the chance. He would never join the Society for the Prevention of Cruelty to Animals or the Friends' Service Committee. He is not involved in the guilt, and so in no way is he involved in the penitence. This comes out in everything he writes, and it offends lots of people. Others may go to bull fights and write novels preaching the brotherhood of man. Miller doesn't go to the bull fights in the first place. So, although he often raves, he never preaches. People have been taught to expect preaching, and of course they are offended if they don't find it.

Fifty per cent of the people in this country don't vote. They simply don't want to be implicated in organized society. With, in most cases, a kind of animal instinct, they know that they cannot do anything about it, that the participation offered them is really a hoax. It is for these people, the submerged 50 per cent, that Miller speaks. As the newspapers never tire of pointing out, this is a very American attitude. Miller says, "I am a patriot—of the Fourteenth Ward of Brooklyn, where I was raised." Life has never lost that simplicity and immediacy. Politics is the deal in the saloon back room. Law is the cop on the beat, shaking down whores and helping himself to apples. Religion is Father Maguire and Rabbi Goldstein, and their actual congregations. Civilization is the telegraph company.

So there isn't any social message in Miller, except an absolute one. When you get through reading James Farrell or Nelson Algren, you have a nasty suspicion that the message of the author is, "More playgrounds and properly guided social activities will reduce crime and vice." There is nothing especially frightful about Miller's Brooklyn; like Farrell's South Side, it is just life in the lower middle-class and upper working-class section of a big American city. It certainly isn't what queasy reviewers call "the slums." It's just the life the reviewers themselves led before they became reviewers. What outrages them is that Miller accepts it, just like the people who still live there. Accepting it—how he can write about it! He can bring back the whole prewar America, the bunny hug, tunes from "The Pink Lady," Battling Nelson, Dempsey the Nonpareil, Pop Anson and Pearl White, a little boy rushing the growler with a bucket of suds and a sack of six-inch pretzels in the smoky twilight of a Brooklyn Sunday evening.

I think that is what Miller found in Paris. Not the City of Art, Letters, and Fashion—but prewar-Brooklyn. It is certainly what I like best about Paris and it is what I get out of Miller's writing about Paris. He doesn't write about the Latin Quarter, but about the dim-lit streets and dusty squares which lie between the Latin Quarter and the Jardin des Plantes, where men sit drinking beer in their shirt sleeves in front of dirty little bars in the smoky Sunday twilight. But he writes very convincingly about that most Brooklyn-like of all the quarters of Paris, the district near the Military Academy, across the river from the Eiffel Tower, where the subway becomes an elevated, tall tenements mingle with small bankrupt factories, and people sit on the doorsteps fanning themselves in the Brooklyn-like summer heat, and sleep and couple on the summer roofs.

In the same way his intellectuals in Paris are assimilated to Brooklyn. They may talk about Nietzsche and Dostoevsky, but they talk like hall-room boys, rooming together, working at odd jobs, picking up girls in dance halls and parks. "Batching" is the word. Over the most impassioned arguments and the bawdiest conversations lingers an odor of unwashed socks. The light is the light of Welsbach mantels on detachable cuffs and unmade beds. Of course that is the way they really talked and still do, for that matter.

There is a rank old-fashioned masculinity about this world which shocks the tender-minded and deluded. It is far removed from the Momism of the contemporary young American male. This is why Miller is accused of writing about all women as though they were whores, never treating them as real persons, as equals. This is why he is said to lack any sense of familial love. On the whole, I think this is true. Most of the sexual encounters in the "Tropics" and "The Rosy Crucifixion" are comic accidents, as impersonal as a pratfall. The woman never emerges at all. He characteristically writes of his wives as bad boys talk of their school teachers. When he takes his sexual relations seriously, the woman becomes an erotic giantess, a perambulating orgy.

Although Miller writes a lot about his kinship with D. H. Lawrence, he has very little of Lawrence's abiding sense of the erotic couple, of man and woman as the two equal parts of a polarity which takes up all of life. This again is Brooklyn, pre-suffragette Brooklyn. And I must admit that it is true, at least for almost everybody. A real wedding of equals, a truly sacramental marriage in which every bit of both personalities, and all the world with them, is transmuted and glorified, may exist. In fact, some people may have a sort of talent for it, but it certainly isn't very common. I don't see why Miller should be blamed if he has never found it. Hardly anybody ever does, and those who do usually lose it in some sordid fashion. This, of course, is the point, the message if you want a message, of all his encounters in parks and telephone booths and brothels. Better this than the lie. Better the Flesh than the World and the Devil. And this is why these passages are not pornography, but comic like "King Lear" and tragic like "Don Quixote."

At least once, Miller makes up for this lack. The tale of the Cosmodemonic Telegraph Company is a perfect portrait of our insane and evil society. It says the same thing others have said, writing on primitive accumulation or on the condition of the working class, and it says it far more convincingly. This is human self-alienation at its uttermost, and not just theoretically, or even realistically. It is an orgy of human self-alienation, a cesspool of it, and Miller rubs your nose in it. Unless you are a prig and a rascal, when you get through, you know once and for all what is the matter.

Once Miller used to have pinned on his bedroom door a scrap of paper, written on it "*S'agapo*"—"I love you" in Greek. In "The Alcoholic Veteran" he says: "The human heart cannot be broken."

THE AGE OF WOUK / MAXWELL GEISMAR

Time Magazine featured "novelist Herman Wouk" on its September 5, 1955 cover. The book column carried a large and laudatory article on the author of "The Caine Mutiny" and the current best-seller, "Marjorie Morningstar." A week later *Life* magazine featured both Herman Wouk and Sloan Wilson, author of another best-seller, "The Man in the Gray Flannel Suit." The September 12 *Life* editorial was devoted to the subject of the American novel. Such cultural enthusiasm is unusual in the Luce publications, it is even somewhat alarming, as when a banker endows a college; so let us try to see what it means.

The *Time* article was an incredible affair even for a magazine whose policy has always been to denigrate serious books and to elevate the mediocre. Mr. Wouk's new novel was a mutiny against "three decades of U.S. fiction dominated by skeptical criticism, sexual emancipation, social protest, and psychoanalytic sermonizing." I am not sure what the last item means, but if *Time* was referring to the tradition of social protest in American fiction, it dates back at least to 1880, or about seven decades. It includes Walt Whitman, who was for sex, and William Dean Howells, who was against sex, and practically every major American novelist since then. If Mr. Wouk is really leading a mutiny against this tradition, he is going to have his hands full.

Yet there is a curious and vital connection between sexual inhibition and social conformity that the editors of *Time* have smelled out, and Mr. Wouk is a perfect example of their thesis. He becomes indeed in their glowing eulogy the House Author of the American Way at the middle of the twentieth century. First of all, he is rich; no more starving artists with ragged clothes and irresponsible thoughts. No more Emerson or Melville or even Hawthorne, who was fired from his customs-house post, and had subversive ideas about the Puritans. The modern American novelist can look the American industrialist straight in the eye; in fact, if he is like Wouk, he is an industry by himself. Even lesser authors like Hemingway and Faulkner have not done so badly in a financial way lately, though *Time* does not list the current value of their enterprises as it does for Mr. Wouk.

And he also, as we discover, has spiritual or hidden assets. He comes from Russian immigrant stock and is a devout Orthodox Jew "who has achieved worldly success in worldly wise Manhattan while adhering to dietary prohibitions and traditional rituals which many of his fellow Jews find embarrassing." *Time* is more at home in this murky element, which carries the latent threat under the guise of paternal blessing. As a descendant of the same tradition myself, and with great respect for its true achievements, I find this passage not only embarrassing but vulgar. After all, Moses did not offer his people the choice between eating the Golden Calf or worshipping it. And now the *Time* article comes to the point. Although Mr. Wouk is a highly sensitive member of a religious minority, "he is one of the few living U.S. writers who carries no chip on his shoulder and who gives the U.S. straight A's in his fictional report cards."

Thus the Luce organization has redefined the meaning of the Jewish tradition in the New World (to make money) and the meaning of American literature itself (to write good report cards). "The Caine Mutiny" did just this, we are told, by affirming Mr. Wouk's belief "in 1) decency—in language as well as deeds, 2) honor, 3) discipline, 4) authority, 5) hallowed institutions like the U.S. navy." Remember that I am quoting, and there is even more: "In 'Marjorie Morningstar,' Wouk will set more teeth on edge by advocating chastity before marriage, suggesting that real happiness for a woman is found in a home and children, cheering loud and long for the American middle classes, and blasting Bohemia and Bohemians. Wouk is a Sinclair Lewis in reverse." And indeed, then, he is, for even Lewis never quite reached this unhappy ebb in his later novels.

Yet Mr. Wouk too must have shuddered and recoiled a little when he read this blunt summary of his aims; and I am treating him here as a symbolic figure. As a human being, as fellow-artist, he is being victimized as much by *Time's* praise as other writers have been by *Time's* malice. For even the Luce editorialist must have had his tongue in cheek when penning this *gemütlich* version of God, fatherland, family, and our leaders right or wrong. What about other hallowed institutions like the United States army—or the marines? What a howl must have gone up in the publicity offices of the Pentagon! More seriously, I submit that most serious writers do have an inherent belief in decency and honor. But it is just this belief that so often has made them rebel against empty discipline and blind, dangerous, or evil authority. Even Thomas Mann's Felix Krull thought it was a great triumph when he cheated the Prussian army out of his rogue's body.

Incidentally, while "Marjorie Morningstar" does advocate an odd kind of semi-chastity, it also describes the most prolonged necking-bout in recent literary history. By the time of marriage there is probably no need for sexual activity. As for the American middle class which, for example, William Dean Howells believed to have been corrupted by the plutocratic spirit in the 1900's, and which *Time* is now inculcating with such alien ideas, I still think it has that last atavistic democratic trait—a sense of humor. At least the *Life* editorial on the American novel was on a higher plane, and took a more generalized line. It did quote the man behind "The Man in the Gray Flannel Suit." "The world's treated me awfully well," said Sloan Wilson, "and I guess it's crept into my work." Yes, that, and a brilliant advertising campaign that also pushed the book, and created what we may call a "well-packaged novel."

Shades of Henry James, and of Theodore Dreiser—both of whom the world treated rather badly. But *Life* is still not quite satisfied with either Wilson or Wouk or even Lionel Shapiro's "Sixth of June" which, though it revolves about a triangle, "is not resolved by adultery." This is only a beginning, apparently; what is the real trouble? "Ours is the most powerful nation in the world. It has had a decade of unparalleled prosperity. It has gone further than any other society toward creating a classless society." Yet after all this, says *Life,* our literature still sounds "as if it were written by an unemployed homosexual living in a packing-box shanty on the city dump." Our writers can't forget the depression, or they are "obscenity-obsessed," as in the recent parade of war novels, or they lack spiritual purpose—"the unquenchable reaching of man's soul for a truth higher than reality."

Logically, I don't know what can be made of this hodge-podge of half-truths. There is also the little matter of the atomic bomb; but when, asks *Life,* was life ever secure? "Atomic fear or not, the incredible accomplishments of our day are surely the raw stuff of saga." Yes, they are, and one would welcome a new generation of novelists who would look into such things as McCarthyism, or the white-collar equivalent of Nixonism, or the loyalty oaths and security dismissals, or the large-size looting of our natural resources, or the marriages of the corporations, and the rise of the stock market while small business and farming declines; or the hostility of Asia and the alienation of Europe while our public mind is both intimidated and dazzled by a series of shifting advertising slogans. "Who speaks for America today?" *Life* asks, and I am afraid that the United States of America speaks for itself.

Our writers do indeed lack a spiritual purpose, which in former generations was accompanied by a broad social base; and the present stress of our most gifted talents on private studies of pathology is also symptomatic of the larger, the national disease.

What is clear, however, is that both *Time* and *Life* are laying down a program for a new slap-happy optimism mingled with a proper respect for whatever exists and a species of domestic drama that will avoid all bad language and all serious human issues. We are back again to that "smiling side of life" which the Victorians believed to be the true American side, though we have been through a sewer of corruption since then, and are now sitting on top of a volcano. This new literature will be based on the principle of "Woukism." The object will be to persuade millions of people that they are completely different from all the other people whom they are exactly like. "Peace, Prosperity, and Propaganda" will be the grand theme of the new literature, and all deviants from the norm, whether biological or esthetic or ethnic, will be tolerated so long as they do what they are told.

In the Age of Wouk, the new writing will certainly have the impulse of revolt, but not the act; just as Marjorie Morgenstern—the "American Everygirl," as we are told—must first rebel against her environment in order properly to conform to it. There will be a little, or quite a lot of sex, so long as it is never fulfilled and has no meaning. There will be the usual periods of doubt, heart-searching, and despair in the lives of these new folk-figures of the American Way—in order to have a happy ending. Marjorie will always marry the man in the gray flannel suit in the typical configuration of the classless—and mindless—society. Well, what does it all really mean? I suspect that the final impact of the atomic age has had the effect of a lobotomy upon the national spirit. Don't look now, but we're all dead.

THE LOST DREAMS OF HOWARD FAST / STANLEY MEISLER

For many years Howard Fast the Communist obscured our view of Howard Fast the writer. Flaunting contempt at Congress, issuing tracts against "bourgeois, decadent" authors, rallying sympathy for the Soviet Union, he stood between us and his books and kept us from a special insight into the intellect of an American Communist. Fast, who has left the party, may have represented, in some ways, the essence of America's own brand of communism. The clues to understanding him as a Communist lie in understanding him as a writer.

Fast's novels had tremendous circulation in the Communist world after World War II and, in fact, enjoyed much popularity here until the press advertised his link with the Communist Party in the late 1940's. His Soviet popularity ended when he left the party in 1957. Although his resignation helped reopen doors to American publishers and movie producers, most of the fiction of his Communist period has remained unread here. We have slipped Fast into our stereotype of the ex-Communist and perfunctorily welcomed him as one more defector who finally has seen the light.

The stereotype of the ex-Communist intellectual was fixed in that notable book, *The God That Failed*, which in 1949 presented the impressions of six men who broke from the party after years of membership or association. Editor Richard Crossman described this pattern for the group: Disgusted with their own societies and seeking an antidote for fascism, they saw communism as a vision of the kingdom of God on earth. "Devotion to pure utopia, and revolt against a polluted society," wrote Arthur Koestler, one of the six, "are . . . the two poles which provide the tension of all militant creeds." When the utopian vision clashed with the reality of the Soviet Union, Koestler and the others left the party.

Fast, in recent attempts at self-analysis, tends to use the characteristics of the Crossman group in describing himself. "My own generation of youth, bitter, robbed of any other hope, accepted that canonization of the October Revolution and its aftermath, and many of us dedicated our lives to a struggle that used us up and left us, in our middle age, soulsick and angry with the shattering of the Soviet illusion," he wrote in a recent article in *Midstream*. Yet there are differences. No matter how robbed and bitter Fast's youth became during the depression, he never had the sense of a polluted society that Koestler had when he joined the party in the waning moments of the Weimar Republic. When life seemed most bitter, Fast remained on the periphery of the party. He became a member only after the democracies began to show their greatest strength as battlers against fascism.

Fast even differed from such American Communists as John Gates, the party leader who quit several months after Fast did. Gates, who led an unsuccessful revolt against the rest of the leadership, wanted the party to adapt itself to American traditions. Fast also wanted to base his communism on American traditions but his approach was different. Gates wanted the party to move closer to American life, because he considered that necessary if communism intended to grow in the United States. Fast, on the other hand, viewed communism as the natural development of American democracy and history. This naive, distorted political perception, this confusion of democracy with communism, is a trait of Fast that we can uncover in even the briefest survey of his fiction.

The vision of a utopian future guided Fast through fiction and communism. He expressed it early and completely. "It would be a people's government for the people," he wrote in *Citizen Tom Paine* (1943), "a government to see that no man starved and no man wanted, to see that hate and misery and crime disappeared through education and enlightment.... There would be an end of war, an end of kings and despots. Christ would come to earth in the simple goodness of all men...."

Fast never has been clear about how to attain this utopia. At first, he assumed that the example of early America would lead the world there, and he set out to glorify the American Revolution in a series of novels. Misunderstanding much of its character, he viewed the Revolution solely as the beginning of a world struggle for liberty. Later, dissatisfied with the state of political freedom in twentieth-century America, he also grew dissatisfied with his interpretation of her early history. He started to look elsewhere for examples to inspire more struggles for liberty.

Significantly, he never used the Soviet Union as an example. He turned instead to the slaves of Rome and the ancient Jews. But his description of their struggles for freedom did not clear up his vagueness about how to achieve his goal. Through suffering and struggle, he said, freedom can be won, at least for awhile. He never was more concrete than that. Even since his break with communism, Fast has kept his utopian goal and his confusion about how to get there.

Fast's early books about the American Revolution reveal his dream of America: a land of freedom, fighting slavery throughout the world. In essence, his description begins as a simple ode to freedom, with no complications, no questions asked. A Jewish soldier, talking to his comrades at Valley Forge in *Conceived In Liberty* (1939), comes closest to defining Fast's early view of what America could be: "... the land for the dream of God in man."

By choice of hero, Fast amplified the universal aspects of the American Revolution in *Citizen Tom Paine*. The emphasis in this book lies almost wholly on the world significance of the colonies' struggle. Mankind, according to Fast, received two things from the Revolution: an example and a promise. The example was the "awkward, stumbling, self-conscious first citizen army the world had ever known." The promise was, as Paine tells the Philadelphia militia, "We are the beginning, and we are making a new world."

When we consider that Fast joined the Communist Party in 1943, the same year *Citizen Tom Paine* was published, the difference between a Communist like Arthur Koestler and one like Fast becomes apparent. Koestler, after rebelling against a polluted society, sought a utopia. Fast reversed the emphasis and sought the utopia first. While his society may have dissatisfied him, he did not view it as polluted and, in fact, found the vision of his utopia in the folklore of the society itself. The Communist Party became, for Fast, an American way of achieving an American end.

Not until he joined the party did Fast seriously start to criticize America. His first attempts to describe pollution in American society came with *Freedom Road* (1944) and *The American* (1946).

Although *Freedom Road* ends with a tribute to the unconquerable memory of Gideon Jackson, a former slave who becomes a congressman and then dies at the hand of the Klan, it is Fast's most despairing book. The Klan wipes out all, nothing remains of the democratic achievement of a few white and Negro farmers working and learning together in Reconstruction. The destruction was so great, Fast claimed, that "powerful forces" have kept the history of such successful experiments from the American people. His picture of Reconstruction was as all black as his picture of the Revolution had been all white.

The American, a biographical novel about John Peter Altgeld, reveals a more subtle and significant disillusion with American society. Altgeld, the governor of Illinois who pardoned the Haymarket martyrs in 1893, fights corruption and plutocracy in American politics with complete faith in the system that bred these evils. "He was not a Debs, a Parsons," Fast told us. "He was a democratic politician, and, as some said, the best America had ever produced." Altgeld refuses to look outside the system for weapons but uses his political power and own money in the battle, only to lose because his opponents have more of both. Fast, now become certain that they always would have more of both, felt that Altgeld failed because the possibility for decency in American democracy had ended. Altgeld refuses the plea of Eugene V. Debs to look toward socialism and so, in Fast's view, rejects the only true weapon.

This failure signaled the cracking of Fast's first dream. Somehow he had equated a Communist utopia with his vision of America, but now he decided American society, past as well as present, was too polluted to sustain it. The industrialization of the nineteenth century, with the accompanying concentration of power and wealth, had stopped the movement of America toward Fast's utopia. He no longer felt that American democracy and communism had the same goal.

In the years between *The American* and Khrushchev's speech on Stalin in 1956, Fast followed two paths. He wrote a series of novels carping at contemporary life in the United States, and he wrote two novels exploring ancient battles for freedom in Rome and Israel. *Clarkton* (1947), *Silas Timberman* (1954) and *The Story of Lola Gregg* (1956) read like Communist analogues to the cheap bestseller or the roaring Western. They are characterized mainly by a ludicrous struggle between the bad guys (either strikebreakers or FBI agents) and the good guys (either Communists or fellow travelers) and by a complete lack of understanding of the American judicial system. These novels were weak as political statements because Fast had no clear notion of what his Communist utopia should be or how it should be attained. He did not look toward the Soviet Union as an example nor, any longer, toward the goals of early America, but contented himself with trying to pick faults in the society around him. *The Passion of Sacco and Vanzetti* (1953), a departure from Fast's main paths during this period, expressed his Communist dream most clearly, and it is a very vague expression.

In this novel, perhaps Fast's finest during the boycott years, a professor, who has worked in defense of Sacco and Vanzetti, and a Communist discuss the meaning of the execution. "For you, when Sacco and Vanzetti die," the Communist tells the professor, "there will die with them all hopes and dreams of justice and reason." Fast explained that the professor will weep but the Communist will join the dry-eyed. The dry-eyed "pledged to themselves a long memory and an absolute identification. They made notations in their own hearts and they drew up a balance sheet that extended as far back as the memory of mankind and the first whiplash on the first bent back. These dry-eyed ones said to themselves, 'There is a better way than weeping and a better way than tears.'" This discussion is our only clue to the role of communism in bringing about Fast's fuzzy dream of utopia.

The novels of ancient history tell us even less about communism, although we can find unsubtle allusions, like, "Slaves of the world, we will cry out, 'Rise up and cast off your chains!'" in *Spartacus* (1951). This novel and

My Glorious Brothers (1948) follow in many ways the thinking of the earlier novels about the American Revolution. Instead of having 1775 open a great battle for world freedom, Fast now assigns this role to the unsuccessful slave revolt against ancient Rome and the Jewish uprising led by the Maccabees against Greek tyrants. These struggles, however, seem to be more important as precursors than as first steps. They change the world little, but give Fast an opportunity to pay tribute to what he considered the first outbursts against tyranny.

Although Fast did not leave the party until after Khrushchev's 1956 speech, a reading of the later novels makes it clear that that event was more a catalyst than a cause. The aimless generalizations in the novels of the late 1940's and the early 1950's indicate that communism without any special American character could not hold him. We can assume that Fast, never close to the leadership of the party, represented some attitudes of the emotional, intellectual, non-professional, rank-and-file member. From examination of Fast's work, we can fit together a picture of this kind of American Communist.

Such members saw communism as firmly rooted in American traditions of freedom and, more important, could not believe in communism if convinced that it did not have these roots. For many, doubts about the absence of these roots came early. Fast, for example, had difficulties in the early fifties because his fervor for communism was destroying his fervor for America. And the more communism separated him from American traditions, the more Fast became separated from communism. His later novels, carping about modern America and extolling ancient struggles, gave Fast only a sense of aimlessness. He could not borrow fervor from foreign sources.

It would be hazardous to generalize from Fast about the difference between the American Communist Party and other Communist parties in the world. The strong nationalistic feeling that pervaded the party in the United States is certainly not unique. Moscow has its differences with Poland, Yugoslavia, China and, of course, Hungary, and the French and Italian parties are thoroughly involved in the political life and traditions of their countries. But, insofar as Fast's attitudes are typical, we may note at least this difference: other Communists attempt to improve their nations by applying what they consider an international or even a foreign technique; many American Communists, perhaps we should say many of those who have since left the party, attempted to improve their nation by guiding it up what they considered a natural next step for American democracy. American Communists, deluded into thinking of themselves as super patriots, may have been less conscious of the international aspects of communism than Communists elsewhere. At least, Fast was less so.

Since his break with the party, Fast has published a book about his Communist experiences and a novel. *The Naked God,* his confession, is extremely disappointing, failing to explain adequately either his reasons for remaining in the party so long or the inner turmoil that led to his disillusion. Much of the book sounds like the musings of a patient as he wanders over his confused past for an analyst. Perhaps the book came too soon after the event. *Moses, Prince of Egypt* (1958), has some characteristics of his other explorations into ancient struggles for freedom, although, since it treats of the young Moses, there is no struggle, but only the knowledge that it will come.

This novel is perhaps evidence that Fast, the ex-Communist, will continue to study freedom, again seeing it as no more than an exciting, bitter struggle containing the seeds of some vague, utopian peace. It may also be evidence that Fast is fashioning a new dream in which the Jewish people lead the world, as he once thought America and communism did. His recent articles discussing himself as a Jew and the echoes of *My Glorious Brothers* add to the evidence.

But, whether or not he rushes on a new path to utopia, his older writings must not be ignored. They document a unique political record, a depressing American waste. They describe a man who distorted his vision of America to fit a vision of communism, and then lost both.

SALVO FOR WILLIAM CARLOS WILLIAMS / M. L. ROSENTHAL

so much depends
upon

a red wheel
barrow

glazed with rain
water

beside the white
chickens.

—"The Red Wheelbarrow"*

M. L. ROSENTHAL

This year [1958] William Carlos Williams becomes seventy-five. The event will be heralded by the appearance of *Paterson V*, from which we are privileged to publish, on the following pages, a few sections in advance. We seize the occasion to make this issue a small Williams-*fiesta*. Nothing very formal, but we are happy to have a poet of his kind writing in the United States today.

Perhaps any sort of literary occasion plays this poet false. Writing about Williams, one always wants to do things *his* way, with that same deceptive ordinariness, those wildly unaffected exclamations—

> The trees—being trees
> thrash and scream
> guffaw and curse—
> wholly abandoned
> damning the race of men—
>
> Christ, the bastards
> haven't even sense enough
> to stay out of the rain—
>
> Wha ha ha ha
> Wheeeeee. . . .

Williams' own talk, like his writing, is natural and simple, almost diffident though always frank.** But it gets where it wants to get; it moves without transition into profundities whenever he so intends. One suddenly grows aware of something precise emerging from the casual exchange, discovering itself, it may be, through a metaphor of green plants in running water or through some sharp, cold projection of thought thrusting above the kindly amenities. In his poetry there is a *mystique* of the physical, but here too one must qualify; austerity is behind it—the quiet irony and self-discipline of the sensitive medical man, reinforced by the artist-moralist's preoccupations. Even the Williams residence partakes of this austerity. The compact, old-fashioned doctor's-house is set right in the midst of Rutherford, with the "downtown" stores almost across the street and the traffic all around and the shabby crisscross of New Jersey's railroads and

---

* Copyright © 1938, 1951, by William Carlos Williams. Reprinted by permission of New Directions.

** For many engaging examples of the poet's conversation, see his *I Want to Write a Poem*, reported and edited by Edith Heal (Beacon Press, 1958.)—a scholarly bibliography combined with extended comments by the poet on each of his books.

highways not far off. It has a right relation to everything that holds clear of pretentiousness, whether out of choice or out of necessity.

So it's not quite "good old Bill" or "good old Doc." Apart from his magnificent ear, there is essential to this poet's achievement not only his generosity of spirit but a faith so intense and stern it all but becomes despair. It is a faith in the meaning of experienced reality and in the power of art to reveal it and, as he says, "to right all wrongs." "The Red Wheelbarrow," quoted at the head of these remarks, expresses this faith, quietly but with absolute authority. In each little stanza the opening line, with its two stressed syllables, prepares for a flight of thought and imagination, while the second weighs the tiny unit down with a turn of idiom or the name of a familiar concrete object. The poem's design is a striving for value, for significant realization, against the resistant drag of the merely habitual. Everything "depends" on the way we see color, shape, relationships; the scope of our understanding of life depends on it, the freedom of our consciousness, the way we transcend limitations and communicate with one another as human beings.

Williams' remarkable alertness to the subtler life of the senses—how it feels to be a growing thing of any kind, or to come into birth; how the freshness of the morning or the feel of a particular moment in a particular season impresses itself upon us; what impact the people glimpsed or encountered in a myriad transitory situations make upon us at the moment of the event—gives him a keener and more adventurous insight into the aesthetic potentialities of that life. The general population's insensitivity to those potentialities is one of his concerns. He links this problem to another: the absence of a "language" that will enable Americans to cultivate, direct and shape their crude and, at present, suicidal energies. "The pure products of America," he has written, "go crazy." They have lost contact with European tradition, and left to themselves they run to emptiness and depravity. His *In the American Grain* is an attempt to sum up the materials of an informing American myth; it is one of the truly germinative American prose-works of this century, a perfect complement to his fiction with its close-ups of the splintering violences and innumerable undeveloped sources of strength in American culture. The waste of possibility—it is in dealing with this crucial theme in poems like "To Elsie" and "The Raper from Passenack" that Williams comes closest to despair.

His greatest effort to deal with it is in the *Paterson* sequence. In this long poem he chose to base his structure on the movement of the river he has elsewhere called the "filthy Passaic." He sought an *open* structure like that of Pound's *Cantos*. "I decided there would be four books following the course of the river whose life seemed more and more to resemble my own . . . : above the Falls, the catastrophe of the Falls itself, . . . below the Falls and the entrance at the end to the great sea." At the beginning the city of Paterson (an epitome of the American scene, with the poet—sometimes called "Dr. Paterson"—its unrecognized prophet) is seen as a sleeping stone-giant. The people, automatons whom he *might* give more vital existence to, walk "unroused" and "incommunicado." They do not know the organic relatedness that gives unconscious meaning to every moment in the lives of primitive peoples. Grossness, destructiveness, dare-deviltry and divorce—and the constant dullness and blocking-off of self-discovery and communication—are the outward signs of our condition. Everywhere the sexual life is thwarted and distorted; we are the victims of a sexual confusion inseparable from our cultural confusions—Williams shares this theme with Lawrence, but gives it a peculiarly American emphasis. The first four books of *Paterson*, completed in 1951, were intended to be the whole work. They constitute a devastating comment on every phase of our life, though a comment relieved by momentary oases of perceived or envisioned beauty, and they "end" modestly and familiarly, as they began, in the midst of things, in the midst of predicament.

Now, in his fifth book of *Paterson*, Dr. Williams reopens the issues. Or rather, he refocuses them. The transforming and saving power of the aesthetic imagination is played like a brilliant light over old archetypal motifs and symbols—sexuality versus chaste love, reality versus the ideal, the Virgin and the Whore, the hunted-down Unicorn pictured, in a famous tapestry now at The Cloisters in New York, amid a setting both natural and courtly. Such themes and images do the refocusing, placing the poet's perspectives in sharper relation to the bedeviled perspectives of the culture at large.

The four passages from *Paterson V* presented in this issue can each be viewed as a self-contained poem. I see no diminution of the characteristic skill and excitement of their author's work in them, but rather a mellowing without loss of energy—*Paterson's* "roar of the present" removed just enough to give the poem another, a much needed dimension. The section we have titled "A Woman" shows how wonderfully human and personal is Williams' conception of the sexual confusion and the need for communication, and what a mysterious gift he has for making poetry out of almost purely private feeling. "The Satyrs" is one of his most concentrated poetic statements of what has been the main subject of the present essay—his view of the artist's relation to a world of distorted possibility, suffering and brutality, but at the same time one of heroism and love! In "A Brueghel Nativity" he shows, as he has before, the kinship of spirit he feels with the elder Brueghel. And in "The Measure" (these titles are all ours) he presents one of his most moving assertions of the function of art, "the measured dance," in the ordering of the poet's own life now, at the age of seventy-four.

A WOMAN

There is a woman in our town
walks rapidly, flat bellied

in worn slacks upon the street
where I saw her.
                Neither short
nor tall, nor old nor young
her
      face would attract no

adolescent. Grey eyes looked
straight before her.
                Her
                    hair

was gathered simply behind the
ears under a shapeless hat.

Her
    hips were narrow, her
                    legs
thin and straight. She stopped

me in my tracks—until I saw
her
     disappear in the crowd.

An inconspicuous decoration
made of sombre cloth, meant
I think to be a flower, was
pinned flat to her
              right
breast—any woman might have
done the same to
say she was a woman and warn
us of her mood. Otherwise

                she was dressed in male attire,
                as much as to say to hell

with you. Her
                expression was
serious, her
          feet were small.
And she was gone!

. if ever I see you again
as I have sought you
daily without success

I'll speak to you, alas
too late! ask,
What are you doing on the

streets of Paterson? a
thousand questions:
Are you married? Have you any
children? And, most important,
your NAME! which
of course she may not

give me—though
I cannot conceive it
in such a lonely and

intelligent woman

. have you read anything that I have written?

It is all for you

        or the birds . . . .

THE SATYRS

                        . . or the Satyrs, a
pre-tragic play,
      a satyric play!
                All plays
were satyric when they were most devout.
      Ribald as a Satyr!
Satyrs dance!
          all the deformities take wing
                Centaurs

leading to the rout of the vocables
             in the writings
of Gertrude
              Stein—but
                         you cannot be
an artist
        by mere ineptitude
The dream
         is in pursuit!
The neat figures of
          Paul Klee
                      fill the canvas
but that
        is not the work
                      of a child   .
the cure began, perhaps,
          with the abstraction
                      of Arabic art
Dürer
      with his *Melancholy*
                  was ware of it—
the shattered masonry. Leonardo
       saw it,
                the obsession,
and ridiculed it
       in *La Gioconda*.
                Bosch's
congeries of tortured souls and devils
         who prey on them
                          fish
swallowing
          their own entrails
Freud
      Picasso
                    Juan Gris.
a letter from a friend
         saying:
                   For the last
three nights
           I have slept like a baby
                           without
liquor or dope of any sort!
         we know

                                that a stasis
from a chrysalis
            has stretched its wings   .
                        like a bull
or a Minotaur
        or Beethoven
                        in the scherzo
from the 5th Symphony
            stomped
                        his heavy feet
I saw love
        mounted naked on a horse
                    on a swan
the tail of a fish
        the blood thirsty conger eel
                    and laughed
recalling the Jew
        in the pit
                among his fellows
when the indifferent chap
        with the machine gun
                was spraying the heap
he had not yet been hit
        but smiled
comforting his companions
            comforting
                        his companions
Dreams possess me
            and the dance
                        of my thoughts
involving animals
        the blameless beasts

A BRUEGHEL NATIVITY

Peter Brueghel, the elder, painted
a Nativity, painted a Baby
new born!
among the words.
                Armed men.
savagely armed men
                armed with pikes,
halberds and swords

whispering men with averted faces,
get to the heart
               of the matter
as they talked to the pot bellied
greybeard (center)
the butt of their comments,
looking askance, showing their
amazement at the scene,
features like the more stupid
German soldiers of the late
war

—but the Baby (as from an
illustrated catalogue
in colors) lies naked on his Mother's
knees

—it is a scene, authentic
enough, to be witnessed frequently
among the poor (I salute
the man Brueghel who painted
what he saw—
               many times no doubt
among his own kids but not of course
in this setting

The crowned and mitred heads
of the three men, one of them black,
who had come, obviously from afar
(highwaymen?)
by the rich robes
they had on—offered
to propitiate their gods

Their hands were loaded with gifts
—they had eyes for visions
in those days—and saw,
saw with their proper eyes,
these things
to the envy of the vulgar soldiery

He painted
the bustle of the scene,

the unkempt straggling
hair of the old man in the
middle, his sagging lips
—incredulous
that there was so much fuss
about such a simple thing as a baby
born to an old man
out of a girl and a pretty girl
at that

But the gifts! (works of art,
where could they have picked
them up or more properly
have stolen them?)
—how else to honor
an old man or a woman?

—the soldiers' ragged clothes,
mouths open,
their knees and feet
broken from thirty years of
war, hard campaigns, their mouths
watering for the feast which
had been provided

Peter Brueghel the artist saw it
from the two sides: the
imagination must be served—
and he served
                dispassionately.

THE MEASURE

—learning with age to sleep my life away:
saying   .
       The measure intervenes, to measure is all we know,
              a choice among the measures . .
                    the measured dance

    "unless the scent of a rose
            startle us anew"

Equally laughable
is to assume to know nothing, a

>   chess game
> massively, "materially," compounded!
>
>   Yo ho! ta ho!
>
> We know nothing and can know nothing
>   but
>   the dance, to dance to a measure,
>   contrapuntally,
>   Satyrically, the tragic foot.

J. D. SALINGER: THE MIRROR OF CRISIS / DAVID L. STEVENSON

It is a curiosity of our age of criticism that J. D. Salinger, one of the most gifted of the young writers to emerge in America since World War II, is rarely acknowledged by the official guardians of our literary virtue in the quarterlies. He was extravagantly praised by the nation's book reviewers for his best-selling novel of 1951, *The Catcher in the Rye*. His short stories turn up regularly in Martha Foley's and in Paul Engle's yearly audits of the "best" American fiction. His work has become standard reading in Freshman English. One hears his name occasionally above the noise of a cocktail party when a new story appears, in the last few years usually in *The New Yorker*. But he has remained outside the interest of our seriously dedicated critics.

Perhaps the most obvious reason for this neglect is the fact that, as a writer, he exists almost wholly beyond the fixed orbit of their attention. He has never been an artist in residence at a summer session. He has published no critical treatise in a literary quarterly on the mythic symbolism in Faulkner, no "thoughts" on the conversion of Edith Sitwell or on Wimsatt's theory of the intentional fallacy. He is not a proper man of letters who occasionally publishes a short story or a novel; he is that rare thing among contemporary writers who take their craft seriously, a complete professional.

Because of this diffidence to things dedicatedly literary, Salinger is usually identified by book reviewers, and properly, as a *New Yorker*

Above selections are from *Paterson V*, copyright © 1958 by W. C. Williams. Reprinted by permission of New Directions.

writer, implying thereby both city wit and surface brilliance in his use of prose and stylized irony of situation in his use of plot. Such an identification suggests that his published work is meant to satisfy the reading tastes of a fairly heterogeneous audience, composed more of the highly literate men and women of the upper middle-class than of the "avant garde" or of the peer group of the quarterlies. Such an identification means also that any attempt to define the nature of his excellence as a writer and the serious but elusive sense of commitment in his work must take into account his use of the design and structure of the *New Yorker* story itself.

Salinger is surely one of the most skillful practitioners of the *New Yorker* short story or sketch. And, invidious critics aside, his sketches show it to be, at its best, one of the truly distinctive and definable fictional types of mid-century American letters. This kind of story contains no more than two or three characters, seen always at a moment of crisis in one of their lives. The concentration is on the crisis: the relationships which have led to it are indistinct, only suggested by the tone of the dialogue, by characters' momentary actions and gestures. The Salinger-*New Yorker* story is always a kind of closet scene between Hamlet and his mother with the rest of the play left out. It accomplishes its shock of surprise, and it evokes our emotions, by a frugal underplaying of plot and event, by its very minimizing of narrative. The reader is usually not projected into the problems of its characters because he is not given enough of the fabric of their lives to make such projection possible.

What a Salinger story *does* involve the reader in is something quite different. It is his awareness that the crisis of the sketch is a generic one of our time and place. The crisis of the usual *New Yorker* story may be fairly casual, and we have come to expect a Salinger story to be more stern in its implications because its roots are stronger and probe more deeply. But its crisis runs true to form. Salinger does not take you out of yourself into a living, substantial world of fiction. He throws you back into your own problems, or into an awareness of them in your contemporaries. His characters do not exist in a rich narrative, in a detailed setting, so that they become wholly separable, fictional beings. Rather they give us a feeling of our own sensitivity to compensate for their lack of created density.

One can best illustrate this quality of a Salinger story by comparing his *New Yorker* sketch "Pretty Mouth and Green My Eyes" with Hemingway's "The Short Happy Life of Francis Macomber." The two stories offer the same basic character relationships: passively suffering husband, aggressively lustful wife, and casual, opportunistic lover. In Hemingway's version, however, the characters are embedded in a full, complex plot in which motive and event are made inexorably overt. The tensions of the characters are in open balance for the reader, and the husband's declared failure of nerve is what provokes his wife's ruthless retaliation in taking a lover. The Macombers exist in the round as "created" individuals in a self-contained narrative which could be translated into Mandarin and remain comprehensible.

Part of the virtue of "Pretty Mouth and Green My Eyes," on the other hand, is that it is not a self-contained narrative. We know of the characters only that they are apartment dwellers in New York. They exist as voices on a telephone to illustrate the desperate irony of a husband calling his wife's latest lover, after a party the three of them have attended, at the moment when the lover is in bed with the wife. The tearing crisis of the story is the husband's slow realization, as he complains in hideously maudlin, drunken terms of his wife's infidelities, that he has put his own self-respect beyond the point of salvage. Salinger's characters, here, come alive *New Yorker* fashion through the skillful verisimilitude of their conversation. But, like E. B. White's famous figure in "The Door" (also untranslatable into Mandarin), they have social rather than narrative roots. They are important to us in direct proportion to our recognition of them as generic sketches of our urban, childless, apartmented men and women, alienated by the hectic nature of their lives from all quiet interflow of love and affection.

One significant element in the structure of a Salinger story, then, and a source of his power over us, is that his characters come alive in our recognition of them. In complementary fashion, an equally significant element is the effect on us of the special kind of crisis he asks us to identify. As in "Pretty Mouth and Green My Eyes," it is a crisis in a character's life that results from an erosion of personality peculiar to upper middle-class, mid-century America. It is related to our sense of the heightened vulnerability of men and women to emotional disaster.

I am not prepared to argue that the Salinger species of crisis is unique, and that other ages did not feel themselves alienated from inner security and outward affect. *Hamlet* alone would suffice. I should only assert that in our time and place the individual estranged from his fellows seems peculiarly understandable and therefore touching to us. If one needs outside documentation, I cite the fact that no age but our own has found a partial picture of itself in such a sociological study of estrangement as

David Riesman's *The Lonely Crowd*. It is not that we, as a generation, are defeated, or without will. Perhaps it is merely that our religion, our family ties, our cultural traditions now give us a lighter armor than our predecessors wore.

At any rate, Salinger's fiction convicts us, as readers, of being deeply aware of a haunting inconclusiveness in our own, and in contemporary, emotional relationships—members all of the lonely crowd. His characters exist outside the charmed circle of the well-adjusted, and their thin cries for love and understanding go unheard. They are men, women and adolescents, not trapped by outside fate, but by their own frightened, and sometimes tragic-comic, awareness of the uncrossable gulf between their need for love and the futility of trying to achieve it on any foreseeable terms.

Salinger's short stories are all variations on the theme of emotional estrangement. In "Down at the Dinghy," a small boy runs away when he overhears his father referred to as a "kike." In "Uncle Wiggily in Connecticut," two women, unsuccessful adventurers in love, let a Connecticut afternoon drift away on highballs and reminiscences, while the timid child of one of them retreats farther and farther into compensatory fantasy as the two women get progressively more sodden. In "A Perfect Day for Banana Fish," a young soldier released from an army hospital confronts his wife's complicated indifference during their first reunion. When he is forced to weigh a small child's warm, intuitive sympathy against his wife's society prettiness, he shoots himself. The actions of the characters in all these stories could seem arbitrary, judged by the sketchiness of Salinger's narrative. In fact, however, the actions seem real and shocking because they are the kind of thing we can anticipate from the needs and stresses we share at least in part with the characters.

Salinger's most ambitious presentation of aspects of contemporary alienation, and his most successful capture of an American audience, is in his novel *The Catcher in the Rye*. It is the brief chronicle of Holden Caulfield, a sixteen-year-old boy who escapes to New York after flunking out of his third prep school. The novel is written as the boy's comment, half-humorous, half-agonizing, concerning his attempt to recapture his identity and his hopes for belonging by playing a man-about-town for a lost, partially tragic, certainly frenetic weekend. *The Catcher in the Rye* is a full-length novel, and yet gives much the effect of his shorter pieces. Its dimensional depth is extrinsic to the narrative, and is measured by the reader's response to the dialogue, and the background of city America. It is supplied by one's recognition that Holden Caulfield, sensitive, perceptive, is too aware of the discrepancies between the surface intentions and the submerged motives of himself and of his acquaintances to feel at ease in any world. Through him, Salinger has evoked the reader's consciousness of indefinable rejections and rebellions that are part of the malaise of our times.

As we have come to expect from Salinger's other work, the main devices of characterization in *The Catcher in the Rye* are an apparently effortless verisimilitude of dialogue and an unerring sense of the appropriate in details of gesture, of bodily movement. There is a further fictional device, used elsewhere in his short stories, but of paramount importance in his novel in creating a hold on the reader. It is his use of almost Chaplin-like incidents and dialogue, half-amusing, half-desperate, to keep his story always hovering in ambivalence between comedy and tragedy. Whenever a character approaches hopelessness in a Salinger sketch, he is getting there by the route of the comic. It is usually both the character's way of holding on for a moment longer (as when the husband in "A Perfect Day for Banana Fish" goes out of his way to insult a proper dowager just before he kills himself) and, at its sharpest, a way of dramatic irony, a way of heightening the intensity of a character's predicament (as when Holden attempts to be bored with sex to get rid of a prostitute). But no single scene from his novel completely demonstrates this peculiar strain of comedy in Salinger: it pervades, seeps into, almost every incident.

When one is reading Salinger, one accepts his carefully placed "New Yorkerish" style and tone, and surrenders one's mind almost completely. It is only when you put the story aside and turn to other contemporary writers and to other fictional methods and techniques that you begin to wonder whether the immediacy and vividness of Salinger might be limited in power. Nowhere in Salinger do we find ourselves plunged into the emotional coiling and recoiling provoked by passages from Styron's novel, *Lie Down in Darkness*. Nowhere in Salinger is a character moved against the murky intensity-in-depth of a Nelson Algren Chicago scene, in *The Man with the Golden Arm*. Nowhere is a character revealed by the great clots of heterogeneous detail yoked together in single crowded sentences, as by Saul Bellow in *The Adventures of Augie March*.

But despite the temptations of comparison there remains one's conviction that Salinger is deeply and seriously committed in his fiction. Further, a little research into the Salinger canon reveals that two of his major creations, Holden Caulfield and Seymour Glass, the young husband of "A Perfect Day for Banana Fish," have deep roots in Salinger's own imagination. His novel, in its way, is as much a final version of "work in progress" as are the novels of his more literary contemporaries, pulled together from fragmentary excursions as short stories in *Partisan Review*, in *Hudson Review*, in *New World Writing*. Only with Salinger, the professional, early sketches of Holden Caulfield occur in a series of stories published in *The Saturday Evening Post*, *Collier's*, and in *The New Yorker*, in the years 1944–1946. And Seymour Glass turns out to have rich inter-connections in Salinger's mind with the uncle of the runaway boy of "Down at the Dinghy," with the older brother of the heroine in a sketch "Franny" (*New Yorker*, January 29, 1955), and with the bridegroom in a novelette *Raise High the Roofbeam, Carpenters* (*New Yorker*, November 19, 1955).

This extrinsic information helps verify one's feeling that there is actually more weight to his explorations of human alienation than his bright dialogue and his frugal use of background and event might suggest. Moreover, Salinger's non-literary status leaves him, as a serious writer, almost unique as a wholly free agent, unhampered by the commitments of his more dedicated contemporaries to one or another school of critics. One might guess that this is Salinger's most precious asset. Rather than wishing quarterly significance or "greatness" on him, we can be content to take him for what he is: a beautifully deft, professional performer who gives us a chance to catch quick, half-amused, half-frightened glimpses of ourselves and our contemporaries, as he confronts us with his brilliant mirror images.

POPULAR CULTURE

SOPHISTICATION IN AMERICA / DAVID CORT

Sophistication is one of the most embarrassing words in the language because one can hardly tell whether it is being used in a complimentary or derogatory sense. It may refer to a person with a lack of taboos, an experience of wines and women, mere unshockability, a fatigue of life, an affected manner, three university degrees, or true wisdom, whatever that is. Originally, according to Merriam-Webster, it meant altered or adulterated.

Nevertheless, when I speak of sophisticated magazines, everyone knows I don't mean *McCall's* or the *Reader's Digest*. Indeed the sophisticated magazines are for the people who are presumably tired of these others.

The incredible news is that sophistication, or a reasonable facsimile, has quietly become the most profitable line, dollar for dollar, in the magazine business. The highest rates for an advertising page per thousand of circulation have long been charged by the sophisticated magazines (and five business magazines). The 1956 figures (in dollars), omitting the business magazines, are: *Town and Country*, 22.16; *The Bride's Magazine*, 18.58; *Gourmet*, 9.96; *Harper's Bazaar*, 9.19; *Vogue*, 9.12; *Saturday Review*, 7.27; *Esquire*, 7.20; *Theatre Arts*, 7.10; and *The New Yorker*, 6.62. In the first six months of 1956 nearly all these showed good gains in circulation, while some of the mass magazines were floundering. Furthermore, they were selling lots of advertising.

A grateful nod is indicated toward our first sophisticated magazine, *Vanity Fair*, and its creator, Frank Crowninshield, the last great American gentleman. *Vanity Fair* reflected the real sophistications of moribund Vienna and the Parisian painters, as well as the manners of the World War I-decimated English upper class. With the Depression, it came under the influence of lady assistants headed by Clare Boothe, and it expired in February, 1936, after the advertisers discovered it was also read by ladies instead of just gentlemen. In the last issue the night-life column was headed "The doe at eve" and the sex was a picture of Josephine Baker.

The loss was not considered serious at first because, besides the Depression, there was also *The New Yorker,* whose 1933 circulation of 114,000 has moved today to 415,000. The magazine has given much pleasure and instruction and is still regarded as the arbiter of big-city sophistication. Yet today most sophisticated people who see it at all, often look only at the cover and the cartoons. Its curious prestige has escaped serious examination, perhaps because the jokes are surprising and the formula is at once disarming and iron-bound.

The New Yorker has in fact a peculiarly fixed attitude, which comes in several sections. The early hands were debonair; Phil Wylie, Herman Mankiewicz, Peter Arno, Lois Long. But their boss, the late Harold Ross, met their high spirits with the manner of an unreconstructed hick or bashful farm-hand at a barn dance. He doggedly stuck to this wooden pose in New York, perhaps to emphasize his differences from Crowninshield and Woollcott. The effect on a new arrival from *Fortune, Newsweek,* the *New York Times, Partisan Review,* etc., was inevitably as if the newcomer had been plunged into a fit of the sulks. A pretense of defeatism and callousness soon enclosed him. He looked hangdog. He learned better than ever, ever to be the life of the party. I have sat at lunches with four of them where nobody spoke for five minutes. In this form of yoga, each tries to be more of an outsider than all the others. The winner is the real insider.

This is *la haute manière;* defeatism and callousness are the culture in the laboratory bottle. The people there are no longer to blame for it; the culture has a rampant life of its own.

The defeatism and callousness—or call them impotence and cruelty—are most easily read in the cartoons. (Incidentally, a great virtue is that the magazine can be read in one minute—just the cartoons; five minutes—cartoons and Talk of the Town; fifteen minutes—add the play reviews; several hours—throw in the rest.) Others may not see these qualities in the jokes I will give, but I am more often saddened than exhilarated by *New Yorker* jokes unless they are Arno's.

Thus in a barroom fight: "Go pick on someone your own size. I'm wearing elevator shoes." Or a sign-painter indoors finishes an "Exit" sign that happens to be pointing toward the window, puts on his hat and walks through the window. Or a wife snarls at her sick, bedded husband: "You called, master?" Or a suburbanite, glancing at a melting snowman on his lawn, notices a human hand emerging. Or a cruise tourist worried about the pay-later plan joins the native boys to dive for pennies thrown by the other tourists. Or a broadcaster, just fired by his sponsor, tells the TV audience "... typical of the Strobolene approach.... And heaven knows what harm their cheap lubricant does to your car." Or an executive says to a man peeking over the edge of the desk, "Bascomb, why don't you come back when you have more courage?" Or a sultan, surveying an empty harem, says, "One day they all up and left me. The whole kit and caboodle."

Most comedy anywhere is based on the fat man falling down, but *The New Yorker* makes him unnaturally impotent first and then trips him up when he feels perfectly safe or superbly angry or sedately amorous or already flat on his face. The comedy is more or less existentialist: defeat is the only destiny; man is a cockroach with false teeth and a truss. The fiendishness is repeated in some of the stories and gets a college try from Wolcott Gibb's play reviews which suffer from a do-it-yourself understatement and owe the word "captious" a long rest in Nassau.

The fiendishness is offset by the very gentle Talk of the Town and a run of stories that can only be identified with the *Reader's Digest's* unsophisticated fixture, The Most Unforgettable Character I've Met. These are usually a memoir of an elderly relative of the writer, or the writer herself in a more youthful phase in Beirut, Old Cracow, Philadelphia or the Bronx. This stuff seems to demand total recall, but is inexhaustible.

Talk of the Town brings up E. B. White and James Thurber, *The New Yorker's* two greatest practitioners. Between them they made the magazine what Ross really wanted: a therapy for neurotics who make up most of its circulation. White gave them his limpid sanity and his love of New York. Thurber gave them detailed proof of terrible feelings and fantasies, beside which their own paled into laughter. The secret of *The New Yorker* is that Ross had recognized his friends as neurotics and himself as their physician. The boorish manner was meant to have a bracing effect.

But the analyst died, and the 415,000 patients were left staring at naked defeat, impotence and cruelty. Now look at the current jokes again. Their common trait is that one cannot imagine any possible sequel for the character *as given*. They present neurotic, or insoluble, situations; something has been added, or left out, to take them out of real life. Anybody can find one woman to replace another, but how can the sultan find even one, not to speak of twenty, if twenty rejected him? How can the man who could only peep over the edge of the boss's desk carry on any sort of business relationship?

To re-define sophistication, a healthy ego thinks he is superior to other people because his bits of experience and knowledge are the key bits. But *New Yorker* characters believe that their data is worthless. Thus, after *The New Yorker* has told its readers how to judge wines, it will run a cartoon of a suburban lady offering a wine with the tag derogation, "Its pretentiousness may amuse you." This brutality is fine in the hands of a good psychiatrist, but. . . . The audience is regarded as literally on the couch.

Several *New Yorker* campaigns have been fought against other people's "captive audiences," yet it treats its own as utterly captive. It will devote to a single piece a half, two-thirds or all of one issue. In that of December 1, 1956, fully half the editorial words were given to a story and a memoir, both very good once you got into them: one cruel and defeatist, the other hopeful. Over 200 pages of the issue were editorial and advertising mixed, doing a selling job. The editorial heartland of the issue—i.e., editorial text without advertising—was only nineteen pages long. By contrast, *Town and Country* runs a solid block of forty-five to sixty editorial pages, *Vogue* the same or more.

Sophistication really breaks loose in *New Yorker* advertising. "Onward and Upward with the Lower Montgomery Olive or Onion Society" —a vermouth. A picture sequence is captioned: "This is a Dry Martini Olive—going down the Throat of—a Man who is Celebrating—the new Shave Lotion—that's dry as a Martini—and Just as Bracing!" "It's not as if we were going to call the law on you if you want to drink akvavit and tonic. . . . We're grateful if you buy a bottle. Buy two and use them for bookends"—akvavit. "If you like your ostentation undiluted . . ."—a tape recorder. "The Lord St. Audries writes . . ."—a cummerbund. Much of the writing, it may be noted, is defeatist—in the advertising yet! The futility of it all is developed by the existentialist poses of the models, part Dali, part ballet, part burlesqued Victorian portraiture. Women crouch under tables, men look up the barrels of rifles, everybody stares blankly. Often, on the wall behind the dry martinis, is a gun collection—a dangerous combination for neurotics.

What has been described here is *The New Yorker's* inner dynamic, the culture in the laboratory bottle. It is all denied by the occasional highly intelligent writer, like Liebling, who ignores all the little psychiatric games and acts himself.

A juvenile sophisticated magazine coming up fast behind *The New Yorker* is a comic book called *MAD* which carries this fashionable mode of impotence and cruelty to a conclusion. Once children start reading it, they throw away all other comics, for *MAD* is an all-out satire on all other comics, printed and human. The draughtsmanship is extraordinarily good. In one issue a bludgeon job is done on Elvis Presley, Gunsmoke (my favorite radio program), Hollywood, mice, traffic police, bowling, Moby Dick, pulp magazines and Disney. The effect is indescribable and to me distasteful—*The New Yorker* essence is too concentrated. The whole idea is implicit in an advice department item. The problem is that the man loves to stuff birds, but also loves his wife who hates his stuffed birds. The advice, illustrated in awful detail: stuff your wife. The cover shows a gap-toothed boy, *MAD's* candidate for President; the back cover shows him, logically, from the rear, looking out at an audience of celebrities. He has big ears. *MAD's* circulation is reported at about 500,000.

Women's magazines (overlooking *Bride's Magazine*, in deference to the unsophisticated groom) are not sophisticated at all in their readers' frantic desire to be told what will make them beautiful and chic. Yet *Vogue* and *Harper's Bazaar*, as well as *Glamour* and *Mademoiselle*, regularly publish very superior material as well as the prize short stories of the year.

The models must be described. A little while ago they were all gaunt, blaze-mouthed, narrow-headed girls with aimed nostrils. But *Mademoiselle's* models, presumably college girls, showed their teeth, as if while beauty kept its mouth shut, eager intelligence kept it slightly open. Lately more and more of the models are showing their teeth, and a successful search is on for the Garbo type, which is slightly more brachycephalic.

The writing, too—"strange and wonderful," "flattering as mascara," "raffish jewelry," "demurely delicious," "precise elegance"—has lately undergone a change. It suffered from the need to get into a high key too quickly, assuming a reader so hysterical that such word combinations sent her instantly into a swoon of precious delight. Lately the sophisticated women's magazines have lowered their key close to plain talk. They can be read with great profit by a curious man. *Vogue* in its Spotlight and People Are Talking About tells you what, if you are already sophisticated, you are already talking about. This is really a kindly service.

Asking forgiveness, I must note that one associate of Frank Crowninshield is still at *Vogue*, having bowed under the tidal waves of exquisite new words, having seen them all pass, from Robert Benchley to Clare Boothe, and still kept her poise and continued to live in Brooklyn. I believe that the Crowninshield values are still high style in this field. Crowninshield either meant exactly what he said or very clearly didn't mean what he said.

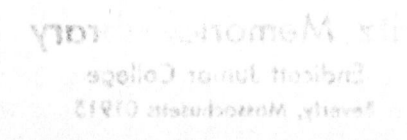

In approaching the sophisticated men's magazines, I have to transit by way of the quarterly, *Gentry*, which gives out no circulation figures but is probably under 100,000. It is a male attempt to replace the late *Flair* in the same—or modified—lavish portfolio style of fold-out art, paste-ups, curiosa and almost anything one wouldn't normally run across. The first effect is of a convulsion of sophistication like a catalepsy. For example, there are Matisse cutout pictures of his old age, a handbill by Topolski and a booklet of Fredenthal's sketches of Toscanini from a radio station soundbooth. But there is also a lot of solid stuff: Ring Lardner, Thomas Eakins, Kipling, Somerset Maugham on Henry James and the last photographs of the defunct Weehawken Ferry. The editors seem to know that if you're looking for oddities, reality is the best place to look. *Gentry* is in constant danger of leaving the planet but never quite does it. After it has worn out its conversation-piece welcome, there is something more, I am glad to report. It costs two dollars a copy.

Esquire is too well known to need description. Rejecting *The New Yorker's* impotence while keeping the cruelty (it officially hates women), it is doing very well at 778,000 circulation. Its format is essentially that of the old *Vanity Fair*, vulgarized by locker-room jokes, naked women and a somewhat uncrystallized editorial policy.

The recent phenomenon of the sophistication business is *Playboy*, which has moved in a year from 393,000 circulation to a claimed million, and is still moving. Starting bawdily and naively, it has grown progressively subtler, having lately taken on A. C. Spectorsky, author of *The Exurbanites* and demonstrably one of the most sophisticated editors in the United States. A lot of young men, mostly college boys and G.I.s, were obviously just waiting for it.

The clue to its appeal, really very sophisticated, is to be read in the monthly foldout naked girl. Instead of being an unattainable and in that sense undesirable mannequin, as in *Esquire*, she is the girl next door or at the next desk with her clothes off and looking very well, thank you. One month the naked girl was the lady author of a story in the magazine.

As a male writer, I must protest unfair competition, but as an editor I must applaud a brand-new invention in eroticism which grew out of the free-wheeling, ebullient attitude of the editors. Essentially, *Playboy's* subject is mating. But it likes to have fun with it, as in a touching love story of a pair of whales. It has its sights firmly fixed not on the outdoor man, but on a strictly indoor man (if not an indoor whale). Ruggedness is to be directed where it will do the most good to perpetuate the race. Sophistication here is primarily sexual, yet this is a subject on which, unlike the subjects of *Vogue* and *Harper's Bazaar*, nobody can really instruct anybody else. It is a treacherous subject, and I get the feeling that *Playboy* is trying to switch its readers to some firmer ground.

In this superficial survey I have omitted such specialized productions as *The Bride's Magazine, Gourmet, The Saturday Review, House and Garden, Theatre Arts* and the admirably produced travel specialist, *Holiday*, which does mankind the favor of disseminating Perelman and Bemelmans. The place to end is with the sophisticated and most indifferent magazine of them all, *Town and Country* (circulation: 1933, 16,000; 1956, 72,000). This and *The New Yorker* are the only general sophisticated magazines of today that existed in 1933.

Town and Country exudes such a tone of upper-class that for a moment I was credulous when I read of a man who had been given for Christmas a diamond-set alpenstock when his wife could have had for less money what he really wanted: the Philadelphia Athletics. My credulity was not shameful because the issue of January, 1957, describes Venice, where the Communist poor really love the rich, and where, in society, one never introduces two people until one has privately asked them whether they want to be introduced. Nobody there reads the newspapers and the only title of consequence is not Prince but *Nobil Homo* or *Nobil Donna*, the old Venetian titles. One should really dress (black tie) to read this. True, we also have to inspect Miami, Palm Beach and Fort Lauderdale, but this magazine sells about 45 per cent of its pages to advertisers (more than *McCall's*) at a far higher rate per thousand of circulation.

The really interesting question is how many more or less sophisticated people, or aspirants, there are today in the United States. Adding the circulations of the magazines noted here, and excluding *MAD* as well as the other equally sophisticated magazines not reviewed, the total is over four million. The exclusions must certainly more than equal the duplications. Using the formula invented by Time Inc., one must multiply that figure by five (for readers of a single copy) to arrive at more than twenty million Americans who at least aspire to be sophisticated. I find this a formidable, instructive and hopeful fact for America, even knowing that deadly serious people will reproach me for my frivolity.

If the vogue of sophistication is indeed on the rise, one can say it had to come: the mass life was too boring to last. But in the sophistications briefly examined here, one finds a repeated flaw. Each has a fixed attitude, a formula, a style from which nothing in the magazine can vary. As

Malcolm Muggeridge wrote in *Time and Tide:* "I, or any other practicing journalist, can tell at a glance whether an article is suitable for this or that magazine." On such a system, sophistication will become as boring as mass conformism, in fact only a narrower sort of conformism. *The New Yorker* gives us an example, to everyone's great regret.

A fixed attitude exposed to life does not know how to survive. What all the sophisticated magazines need is something unexpected, something not in the prospectus.

THE AMERICAN THEATRE:

SHOW BUSINESS IS ALL BUSINESS /

RICHARD HAMMER

On the face of it, it would almost seem that the Broadway theatre has never been in better health, economically at least. With the number of new plays arriving each year pretty well stabilized over the past decade at about seventy (compared with 260 thirty years ago), and with the number of theatres holding at thirty-two (against eighty only twenty years ago), box office receipts and audiences have been mounting. During the 1958–1959 season, in fact, 11,720,000 theatregoers paid more than $40,150,000 to see seventy-one Broadway dramas, comedies and musicals—an audience increase of 863,000 and a box office boost of $3,000,000 over the 1957–1958 season. What's more, for the first time in the history of the theatre, last year saw weeks in which more than $1,000,000 passed into the till—and not one such week, but eight.

This is the outward face of prosperity; behind it lies the inner face of trouble. For, despite the record audiences and gross, the season as a whole ended up $500,000 in the red. And, as usual, five out of every six shows were financial flops (the percentage of artistic failures was even higher). Costs of everything continued, and still continue, to mount. To bring a straight drama to a Broadway house now involes an outlay of $100,000 or more (three times as much as twenty years ago, twice as much as ten years ago), while the cost of producing a musical may run to the astronomical total of $350,000 to $400,000. Merely to keep pace with operating expenses, without doing anything at all toward paying off the original investment, a straight play must gross $20,000 or more every week at the box office.

This means, in terms of audiences, 60 per cent to 70 per cent of capacity at every performance, with the entire orchestra floor sold. The needs of a musical are even greater. Little wonder, then, that only smash hits last for more than a few weeks and that few producers take a chance on anything new or with a potentially limited audience.

In some cases, certainly, there are legitimate reasons for increased costs: the salaries of supporting and minor actors have at last reached a livable level, as have those of backstage personnel. The costs of materials—scenery, lighting, costumes, advertising and the like—have gone up not only in the theatre, but all over. But where some cost rises have been inevitable, and even desirable, others are in a different category. Theatre owners, with several plays competing for each of their houses, now demand a larger share of the receipts, higher guarantees against losses, and sometimes even reductions in their share of such expenses as stagehands, advertising and the like. The stagehands' unions, watching the decline in the number of playhouses and the resultant contraction in available jobs, have demanded, and gotten, regulations establishing a minimum number of jobs for each theatre and carefully limiting the functions of each worker. And because these are strictly minimum regulations, a show which has a higher budget or a larger cast is required to hire more stagehands—even if the additional men have nothing to do but sit backstage and play poker.

Designers, lighting men, costumers and other technically creative people, working toward what they call "perfection," demand the best possible materials, regardless of budgets. The experience of one producer in this respect is particularly illuminating. Just starting work on a new play, he had spent the summer watching a Connecticut neighbor build a new home at a cost of $25,000. At the theatre, that fall, his set designer asked for $40,000 to put up an impressionistic frame house on the stage. "Would it be cheaper," the producer finally asked in desperation, "if we installed real plumbing?"

As long as everyone else is getting theirs, the stars and the playwrights are not to be denied. Top stars can now command a base salary of $2,000 or more a week against a percentage of the gross. In some cases, this brings their weekly income to $7,000 or more—a high price to pay for talent on any terms. And the authors, long the forsaken men, have at last come into their own, largely through the intervention of their agents. Not only do authors draw their legitimately handsome royalties, but they now have gained a veto right over stars, cast, directors and other aspects of the production. While not too important to the authors themselves, this power gives the big agents a hold which is clearly apparent.

The man on the spot, then, is the man trying to put on the show: the producer. While meeting the demands of stars, the theatre owner and the unions, he must also try to protect his investment and that of his angels (still relatively easy to find). The easiest way for him to meet these financial pressures is to increase the price of tickets and deal with people who will buy them in huge lots. Thus, musicals this season will have a top of $9.90, while seats for straight plays will cost up to $7.50. At these rates, almost everyone except the expense-account boys and the theatre parties is priced right out of the audience.

That ubiquitous institution, the theatre party, has come to the rescue of many a producer in the last couple of years. With its aid, he can come into New York with an advance sale of $500,000 to $1,000,000 or more, knowing that he's going to run for a good, long time and very probably turn a profit—or, at least, break even.

Arrangements for the theatre parties—there are thousands every year and the number is growing—are handled by any one of twelve different theatre-party agents, who get 6½ per cent of the price of each ticket. In some ways, these parties make it easier for a producer; in others, more difficult. If the producer has something the agents think will sell, then he's all set; they will work to get as many organizations as possible interested, and sell as many tickets as they can. But if the agents think the producer has a lemon, or a show which won't interest their clients, they will sit on their hands. (The tickets they handle, of course, go to organizations which in turn sell them at high premiums, which are tax deductible. Thus, the audiences brought in by the agents don't generally go to the theatre because it is the theatre: they go because the $25 or $50 they pay over the ticket price make it a tax-deductible evening.)

The power of the party agents is obvious. With their control over vast audiences, they can break or make a show by their recommendation or lack of it. Only recently theatres were forced to call off a plan to experiment with an early, 7:30 P.M., curtain on Wednesday nights because agents had already booked 120-odd parties for these midweek nights.

Under all of these pressures—mounting costs which mean higher ticket prices which mean reliance on theatre parties and expense-account crowds —the New York theatre, at least on Broadway (and increasingly off-Broadway, too), is losing its real audience. A love for the theatre is something that is built early in life and lasts a lifetime. But today, the newly-married young people, the kids out of college, just cannot afford to go. This potential audience doesn't exist any more; and the steady, every-week theatregoer has become a thing of the past.

With producers reluctant to take a chance on anything but pure entertainment, the vitality that was once New York theatre is gone. The effect is sometimes as baleful upon the critics as upon the theatre. Nowadays when an occasional producer does show a spark of vitality by putting on something even a little off-beat, critics are inclined to praise him. In their desperate attempt to save the theatre for the theatre, the critics, too, along with everyone else, seem to have lost their critical judgment. Seriousness alone is not enough for a play; there must be artistic merit as well. The theatre isn't going to be saved by praising its every valiant failure.

What becomes obvious about the Broadway theatrical scene is that art and economics have become one and indissoluble. In order to try to make money, the producers produce only what they think the majority want. Even the serious drama is generally only pseudo-serious, but since it is "different," it is greeted with praise, may make some money (which Shakespeare rarely does), and presents a general impression that things are returning to greatness. But the impression is only fleeting. The total impression of the theatre in the United States today is of gloss and polish and technical finesse; of an art form without art; of a vital aspect if life without vitality.

HUGGER MUGGER IN THE 57TH STREET ART GALLERIES / WALTER GOODMAN

One morning in the summer of 1954, Emanuel J. Rousuck, vice president of the Wildenstein Galleries—one of the largest international art dealers in the world—received a visit from an old friend, John G. Broady. Now, one might have expected that the entry of Mr. Broady, a private detective who was soon to be proclaimed the nation's foremost wiretapper, into the rarefied atmosphere of Wildenstein's richly appointed East 64th Street salons would have caused at least a small explosion. But the Messrs. Broady and Rousuck had apparently long since achieved a chemical compatibility. In the course of their eight- or nine-year acquaintance, private detective Broady had performed numerous services for Mr. Rousuck. As the latter himself recalls: ". . . from time to time he checked on various people for me, got information for me. When I wanted to get the pedigree of a man or something, he would find out as to what he was and so forth."

On this particular morning, Broady made a point of going to the men's room after the amenities of greeting had been completed—leaving his briefcase behind on a chair in Mr. Rousuck's office. When he returned, he strode to the briefcase, snapped open the lock, accomplished some rapid technical maneuvers and played off for the man of art a tape recording of every word that had been uttered in the office during their brief separation. At the conclusion of this dramatic offering, Mr. Rousuck recalls, his friend advised him that "it was a very good thing to get information from time to time . . . and it was perfectly legal."

Mr. Rousuck accepted this statement at face value, but he let the opportunity pass anyway. Some weeks later, however, after Broady had repeatedly reminded him of the resource which was, so to speak, going untapped, the art dealer admitted to the private detective a large curiosity about the operations of an eminently successful rival named Rudolph Heinemann. "Do you think you could get me the information as to what has been going on?" he inquired.

Broady did indeed think so. As a matter of fact he had been tuning in on Mr. Heinemann's phone calls for the preceding eight months from his wiretapping headquarters at 360 East 55th Street. Mr. Heinemann, whose residence at the Ritz Towers put him within the compass of Broadys' extensive East Side operation, is a prominent art expert and dealer who works closely with the Knoedler Galleries, Wildenstein's arch competitor. With a host of important and intimate contacts in art centers around the world, Heinemann is able to lay his hands on valuable pictures for Knoedler to dispose of at a substantial turnover. As the *nouveau riches* in New York these days far outnumber the *vieux riches* in Europe, a seller's market exists here for objets d'art. The problem is getting the merchandise. The man who can track down and obtain the most desired paintings is an important man. That Mr. Rousuck should have taken so personal an interest in Mr. Heinemann's telephone conversations was a tribute to the latter's connections.

Once each week after the agreement had been made, a man named Louis Arion—another friend of Mr. Rousuck—delivered to the Wildenstein vice-president a record wrapped in a brown paper package, for which Mr. Rousuck paid "$125 or $150; I don't recall exactly." The art dealer took the disc home with him and played it on a phonograph purchased especially for these weekly occasions. He listened in on conversations in English, French and German. He heard Mr. Heinemann discourse with

Gelbert Kahn, a well-known patron of the arts. He intercepted many of Heinemann's conversations with the Knoedler Galleries, as well as with his stock broker and ticket agent. Once Rousuck called Heinemann himself just for the satisfaction of hearing his own voice on the next weekly record.

This Heinemann-to-Broady-to-Rousuck arrangement lasted until February of last year when the 55th Street wiretap den was raided and Broady and his associates were put under arrest. Mr. Rousuck told the foregoing story at the trial in November, which resulted in the sentencing of his old friend to two to four years in prison. The Wildenstein Galleries announced after this testimony: "Mr. Rousuck has tendered his resignation."

The resignation was still hanging fire four months later when M. Knoedler and Company brought a $500,000 suit against Wildenstein and Company, Georges and Daniel Wildenstein and Mr. Rousuck himself for damages resulting from the wiretap. Although Broady's associates have testified that they had listened in on Knoedler's three lines from February through October of 1954, Mr. Rousuck has declined to accept the credit for authorizing this particular effort. Knoedler nevertheless seemed to take Rousuck's guilt for granted and explained in March why the resultant pain to an art dealer was worth a half million dollars:

> The nature of plaintiff's business requires that it keep confidential a large volume of information, including, but not limited to, the names of its customers and potential customers, the sources of works of art, the prices quoted for works of art and the identity of works which are or may be offered for sale. Important portions of its business are necessarily transacted over the telephone.

The counsel for Wildenstein countered with more vigor than clarity:

> It would appear that Knoedler has instituted this action for selfish business reasons, hoping thus to obtain unfair competitive advantage. The Wildenstein Galleries, established over eighty years ago, have a reputation which is unequalled in this field. The Wildenstein Galleries welcome this opportunity to prove, in open court, that Knoedler and certain persons associated with them, have deliberately perverted the testimony in the recent Broady trial.

Just what return did Rousuck get for his $2,000? Well, once he found out that Heinemann was cancelling theater tickets to a Broadway show and another time he discovered that somebody was giving a dinner party for an acquaintance from Baltimore. The most relevant piece of news he came upon was that the Heinemann-Knoedler team had sold Van Eyck's "Rothschild" Madonna to the Frick Museum for $750,000—the highest price paid for a painting since Andrew Mellon's purchases from the USSR two decades ago. When the sale was closed, all parties were pledged to secrecy for six months. Within days, the deal was the talk of 57th Street. The Knoedler forces charge the leak to Rousuck.

Perhaps the most provocative aspect of the whole affair is the state of mind revealed by the Knoedler complaint against Wildenstein. It alleges:

> . . . Defendants obtained much information which, in the interests of plaintiff as well as its clients, was of a confidential character, and defendants used such confidential information to compete unfairly with plaintiff. The possession and use by defendants of such confidential information caused plaintiff serious injury in its business, goodwill and reputation, in that defendants utilized such information to compete with plaintiff for the acquisition and disposition of works of art, and in that doubts were created among plaintiff's clients as to the reliance which could be placed upon plaintiff to maintain the confidential character of information acquired from such clients.

Shades of Sherlock Holmes! No matter that all Mr. Rousuck got for his $2,000 was early news of his rival's triumphs and a great deal of embarrassment. No matter that the $500,000 suit will probably be settled with a quiet handshake. On 57th Street there is more at issue than the matter of keeping secret the immense profit that a middleman runs up on the sale of a single item in a world of ethereal values, where buyers and sellers conspire to perpetrate an outrageous parody of a supply and demand curve.

The significance of the Wildenstein-Knoedler row lies in another realm. It helps to preserve the art world's illusions about itself in an age of disillusionment. By rating its secrets at $500,000, Knoedler's has helped to reassure the fellow denizens of its odd world that they exist apart from the main stream—that they, at least, still cherish Intrigue, Mystery, Romance and other obsolete virtues.

Our art dealers, breathing the air of more regal centuries in their everyday labors, absorbing it from their deep carpets, their red velvet walls, their heavy gold-threaded chairs, as well as from the pictures themselves, have apparently been infected with certain tingling court convictions. It is not unfitting that Mr. Rousuck of Wildenstein, a firm that specializes in eighteen-century French works, should have turned to a wiretapper for an assist. Would Talleyrand have done otherwise? Broady is the contemporary version of that minor, yet indispensable, character in dozens of old melodramas—the shady noble who actually purloins the damning letter, who overhears and relays the crucial conversation. When it comes to paintings, all conversations are clearly of this character.

The world at large tends to view the small art-dealing fraternity as rather a precious phenomenon. And so it is. But it takes imagination to exploit the imaginative creations of others into a flourishing trade. Art dealers are not mere commissionaires; they are adventurers on the high seas of luxury and prestige where other adventurers, learning of the treasures in the hold, the millionaire in the cabin, may swoop down and take all before home port is reached.

Behind the decorous facade of New York's art galleries runs a network of dark and curious alleys. And through these alleys night after night pad nameless men dressed in black, their shapeless hats pulled low over their eyes, their shoulders hunched, the odor of the snooper's world around them. Who is that particularly nasty looking fellow skulking at this very moment in the shadows between those decaying buildings? Why, he's a Wildenstein agent (or is it a Knoedler agent?) on his way to a rendezvous with the wastrel scion of a grand old Viennese family which has had a priceless Rembrandt in its possession for six generations. Three hours of debauchery in a Grinzing saloon and the boy will have sold his birthright for a mess of Rhine wine. In the distance, the Orient Express shrieks terribly into the night.

NEWSSTAND STRIP-TEASE / MILTON MOSKOWITZ

New magazines are being launched today at a feverish pace. Publishing houses in New York, Chicago and Los Angeles are disgorging them at the rate of one every two weeks, burying newsstands under a sea of pictures and literature whose common denominator is sex—generally in full-color slick-paper. Not that the dealers are complaining; far from being Puritans, they let their cash registers be their guides. These new magazines sell on exposure. Many carry a 50-cent price-tag (which means 10 cents to the dealer). There are no cut-rate home subscriptions to compete with the street sale. *Ergo*, these new contributions to our cultural life are getting prime positions at the point of sale.

Taking a census of the new magazines is not easy. Some are published at rather infrequent intervals. Others publish one or two issues and then fall by the wayside—and some of these are later revived, perhaps under a new title. Issue dates mean little. A magazine coming out in July is likely to be designated the "October" issue. This helps to give it a long life on the newsstand.

Here are some of the magazines which have been introduced in this country recently: *Revealed, Duke, Night World, High, Ho, After Hours, 21, Fling, Monsieur, Hollywood Confidential, TV Scandals, Behind the Scenes, Suppressed, Personal Psychology, Mr., Celebrities, Answer, Plowboy, Trump, Scamp, Rave, Sensational Exposes, Duel, Impact, Challenge for Men, True Men's Stories, Uncensored Confessions, Hunting Adventures, Casanova, Inside, Frauds, Inside Story, Cabaret, The Lowdown, Escapade, Exposed, Gay Blade, Good Humor, On the QT, Bachelor, Expose Detective, Adam, Rogue, Nugget, Tip-Off, Caper, Dude, Gent, Jem, Uncensored, Top Secret, Rage, Man's Illustrated, Men's Digest, Satan, Tiger, Relax, Ogle, Sh-H-H-H, Pleasure, Rugged, Hush-Hush, Battle Attack, Real Action, She, Hue, Bare, Pose, Pin-Up, Spick, Swagger, Span, Male Point, Tomcat, Dazzle, TNT, Humbug.*

And this imposing list is by no means all-inclusive. Has there ever been another three-year period in which seventy-five consumer magazines were born? The new publications can be divided broadly into three main groupings:

1. *The Playkids.* These are off-shoots of *Playboy,* one of the most successful new magazines of the post-war period (circulation, 900,000; 1956 gross, $3,500,000) and the first mass-circulation magazine to come out of Chicago since *Esquire* (now removed to New York). In this group are *Cabaret, Caper, Gent, Nugget, Dude, Satan* and *Jem,* among others— all glossy 50-cent vehicles for what is euphemistically called "urban male entertainment." Their staple ingredient is pictures of models in states of undress. Cheek-by-jowl with the pictures is racy fiction, often culled from gay old dogs such as Boccaccio and Flaubert or from magazine pieces done twenty years ago by name writers such as Irwin Shaw and Jean-Paul Sartre. However, this type of material tends to decline as the magazine becomes more successful. *Playboy,* for one, uses very few reprints today and, as a matter of fact, has published some notable original fiction in recent numbers (see Henry Slesar's "Victory Parade" in the April, 1957 issue). In their more pompous moments (when they are being interviewed by the *Wall Street Journal,* for example), the publishers lay claim to a sophistication that they allege is lacking in the older, well-established magazines. This may be nothing more than a pose, but it would not be

untruthful to say that the Playkids have in common an attitude best described as *off-beat irreverence*, a quality not easy to come by in the age of the packaged soul. John H. Holmes, who puts out *Gent* and *Dude*, told the *Wall Street Journal:* "These aren't family magazines. But everyone knows life doesn't go on as portrayed in the *Saturday Evening Post.*"

2. *The Peeping-Toms*. These are offshoots of *Confidential*, another success story of the post-war era (circulation, above 3,000,000). In this group are *Suppressed, Hush-Hush, Behind the Scenes, The Lowdown* and *On the QT*, among others—all smirking, 25-cent journals devoted to the reporting of the bedroom escapades of your favorite movie star. Some sample story titles: "The Night George Sanders Struck Out," "When Lana Turner Shared A Lover with Ava Gardner," "Why Ethel Barrymore Goes for Winston Churchill," "Eartha Kitt and All Her White Boy Friends." Actually, with the exception of *Confidential*, these *exposé*-sheets rarely deal with original material. Their stories are rehashes of old newspaper accounts of divorce actions and police cases. The publishing formula is simple: A movie star is stopped for speeding; you line up some suggestive photographs of the star (these are readily available from studio publicity offices); you get a sharp rewrite man at the *Daily News* to go through the morgue file on the star and relate all of the Page 4 stories involving him (or her) over the past ten years; you write a jazzy, orgy-promising headline; and *presto*, you have an *exposé*.

3. *The He-Man Adventures*. These are offshoots of Jack London by way of *True-Argosy* and the old pulps. In this group—the weakest of the three—are *Rugged, Real Action, Duel, True Men's Stories* and *Man's Illustrated*, among others—25-cent packages of blood-and-thunder. Some sample story titles: "China's Cutthroat Queen," "Jungle on Fifth Avenue," "The Man-Killing Monster of Honduras." Sex is usually sublimated here, although occasionally there is a juicy piece about a jungle goddess.

What's behind this spate of new magazines? Is the American male, after all these years, beginning to discover sex? Is the office girl weary of puffs for movie stars and hungry for the view from the bedroom? Are readers becoming more sophisticated? Do they want debunking instead of uplifting?

These are questions to raise if you take these magazines seriously. Many people don't. One publisher who will have no truck with any of these magazines told me: "Sex has always sold and always will. These magazines won't last. As soon as they become halfway successful, they start dropping some of the blatant sex, trying to tone up the book to attract advertisers. And what happens? As the sex disappears, so does the circulation. It's only the sex that is selling."

An editor of one of the Peeping-Toms offered me another theory. "We're the muckrakers of our times," he said. "People are tired of the pap and phoniness they are fed in many magazines, papers and television. They want to see public figures exposed. Sure, I know we're not doing anything socially constructive as the old muckrakers did. But times are good. This is the form of protest literature in prosperity." (Shades of Lincoln Steffens!)

In the publishing industry, these magazines are being watched (even as they are scorned). It is interesting to note that this torrent of new magazines occurs at a time when the major publishing houses have seemingly run out of ideas for new periodicals. In the past ten years the multi-magazine publishers have been more engaged in folding properties than starting new ones. It should not be forgotten, however, that our leading consumer magazines have not stood still. Look at some 1939 issues of the *Saturday Evening Post, Look, Life* or *McCall's* and compare them with current issues. You will see quite a difference, the change being in the direction of greater sophistication.

Magazines, they say, mirror the times. If so, what portion of our times is illuminated or reflected by the Playkids, Peeping-Toms and He-Man Adventures? They will, no doubt, provide future historians with interesting food for thought.

THE USES OF RELIGION / ROBERT HATCH

The author of this singular book* is a Presbyterian clergyman who found himself less than content with his spiritual calling by reason of earlier training as a chemist. Dr. Loehr had discovered in the laboratory the satisfactions of controlled experiments and verified data; he could find no similar objective tests for success in the world of faith, so he set about devising them.

Dr. Loehr's technique is to pray at plants, and he has a number of followers who assist him in this devotional horticulture. (He also distributes a kit containing all the materials necessary for home prayer enthusiasts.)

---

* The Power of Prayer on Plants, by Franklin Loehr. Doubleday & Co. 1959. 144 pp. $3.50.

Sometimes he prays *for* the plants, sometimes *against* them; being a well-trained and scrupulous scientist, he always prepares one pan of seeds which is ignored and serves as control. Dr. Loehr offers a section of photographs in his book, and you should see the dandy results he gets. Aldous Huxley is quoted as saying that this documentary evidence is "incredible," and it takes something pretty surprising to draw that judgment from the most credulous of Huxleys.

What puzzles me, though, is why the ceremony with corn and wheat seeds is called prayer. I have always understood that prayer was a communication addressed to God; Dr. Loehr and his friends are communicating with vegetables—"meeting them," he says, "on their own level and in terms of their own being"—and though this is certainly a remarkable feat, it is not essentially a religious one. Cinderella's godmother had a pleasing way with pumpkins, but no one has implied that she was a particularly devout old lady.

The fact is that Dr. Loehr, for all his scientific cackle and unctuous sermonizing, is an old-fashioned magician. He does not petition God for aid, he commands nature to forsake its ways and follow him. He can, he says, direct "several brief 'bursts' of negation" at a healthy young shoot, and the plant will forthwith wither and die. May the saints preserve us in our hour of peril—the man's a warlock!

All this, I make bold to say, is nonsense; but it is not in itself a very wicked sort of nonsense, nor sufficiently novel to occasion comment (at the age of ten I used to "will" people to scratch their heads, and surprisingly often they did). It becomes wicked, however, when Dr. Loehr suggests, as he does repeatedly in his book, that the same kind of "negative prayer" he uses to inhibit plant growth will, pretty soon now, be used to cure cancer. And it becomes noteworthy when to it you add all the other irrational exploits we have been invited to admire in recent years. There was the late Kenneth Roberts, dowsing for water over a map of distant Bermuda; there is Dr. Rhine down at Duke, flipping his cards, bandying words like "psychokinesis" and sending "trained investigators" all over the lot to look into poltergeists; there was that woman down in Texas who was inhabited by her Irish grandmother, and only a few nights ago I watched Oral Roberts effecting miraculous cures of cataract, goiter and mental disease on television. Quacks, mediums, gypsy fortune tellers we have always had, but these new prophets of irreason work close to the sources of influence. Dr. Loehr is given serious heed by Huxley; also by the F.B.I. and Richard Nixon, who think that his well-directed bursts of prayer might very well discourage crime and cause communism to wither at the root. He conducts large classes under the auspices of churches whose names at least do not carry a hint of madness and he teaches at prosperous "psychological" institutes. His book is not published by something called the True Light Press, but by Doubleday, a hardheaded corporation that knows there is a market for this sort of thing and is not embarrassed to sponsor it.

There is, in short, far too much irrationality abroad in the land and it is time to cry halt. The cause of this renaissance of magic is not obscure: men are overwhelmed and terrified by the consequences of the search for knowledge, and in mood to heed the easy solutions of the necromancers. But this of all times is the one in which we can least afford to take leave of our wits. I do not know whether or not reason is the gift of God, but it is assuredly the only gift that will save us. Praying at plants is asking for obliteration.

AMERICAN COLLEGE LIFE: MY CRUSADE AGAINST FRATERNITIES / WADE THOMPSON

> "Frat" is a contraction that is no longer in good usage. It is correct only in connection with Greek-letter high school and non-collegiate societies and then only as an expression of contempt.—*From the Pledge Manual of a great national fraternity.*

To anyone who has better things to do than to poke his nose into the idiocies of educational institutions, this account of fraternities and their frailties may seem like a sour fantasy—something spun out of the morbid brain of a disgruntled college professor who has nothing better to do than to play with words and distort facts. I can only promise the unbeliever that I record every word with gruesome sobriety, with malice toward none and strict justice and charity toward all. Motivated solely by a sense of wonderment at human behavior, I bring to the task a ponderous, porous and pedantic mind, through which I have squashed all facts, statistics and quotations in the best scholarly manner. (To preserve objectivity and strict impartiality, the terms "frat" and "fraternity" are herein used indiscriminately, with no pejorative connotations put upon either word.)

I was drawn abruptly to my scholarly duty toward fraternities the other day when I accidentally stumbled over an issue of the *National Interfraternity Conference Yearbook*—in this case, a record of the forty-eighth annual meeting of all social fraternities. This particular meeting was exceptional in that it was blessed by a wild kick-off from Dr. Ralph W. Sockman, a noted New York pastor. Dr. Sockman obviously knows his way around a pulpit, and I'll bet he has scared the living hell out of more people than Norman Vincent Peale can ever boast of. His address to the forty-eighth National Interfraternity Conference proved to be a real masterpiece, a positive symphony of high sentiment. Starting with a tender, pleasant pianissimo, he gradually and gracefully introduced a few contrapuntal themes, smoothly crescendoed to a grand climax, and ended with a smashing major key resolution. I have time to replay only a few climactic bars of Dr. Sockman's composition:

> America is showing something superior to the Kremlin at the moment. . . .
> We are the style-setters morally for the world. That is not boasting. It is just humble recognition. We are.
> These great college fraternities—sixty-one of them in this group—are style-setters under God for the world at large. . . .

Now men of the cloth are of huge heart and prodigious faith, but sometimes their very goodness disqualifies them to speak on certain subjects which they clearly wot not of. It behooves men of crasser and meaner composition to straighten them out occasionally, lest they inadvertently turn their ministerial cannon in defense of some other worthless cause. It is in this spirit that I point out to Dr. Sockman that a frat boy wouldn't know what a moral style-setter was if one came up and goosed him. "These great college fraternities," as Dr. Sockman calls them, are the silliest, stupidest institutions invented since the intussusception of the chastity belt. They have no more moral "style" than a collection of Mafia gangsters, D.A.R. girls, Army generals or ladies of joy.

When a young man is chosen to enter a frat, he is known as a frat-pledge, and he must pass through a period of pledgeship—roughly corresponding to an apprenticeship period for knights or bricklayers. As a frat-pledge, he is expected to undergo certain trials and to learn certain lessons, for which purpose he is given a *Pledge Manual*. The lessons he learns are three in number: (1) *Sentiment*—or how to love his brother; (2) *Smoothness*—or how to conduct himself; and (3) *Ritual*—or how to perpetuate the old frat.

So far as Sentiment is concerned, I cannot do better than to quote from a *Pledge Manual* of one of our most famous fraternities. (There is no point in getting this stuff second-hand.) On page 76 appear detailed instructions on how a frat-boy feels toward his brother:

> I love you not only for what you are, but for what I am when I am with you.
> I love you not only for what you have made of yourself, but for what you are making of me.
> I love you because you have done more than my creed could have done to make me good, and more than any fate could have done to make me happy.

I interrupt this tender lyric to assure the reader, who may have become confused at this point, that this is brother-to-brother sentiment, and not advice on how to seduce a maid or woo a wife. I go on, and now the rhetoric really begins to steam:

> I love you for the part of me that you bring out. (*Part not specified.*)
> I love you for putting your hand into my heaped-up heart and passing over all the foolish and frivolous and weak things that you can't help dimly seeing there, and for drawing out into the light all the beautiful, radiant belongings that no one else had looked far enough to find.

I turn off the steam here to assure the reader that I am not treacherously divulging sweet sentimentalities in contempt of an understandable request for privacy. On page 94 we learn that the frat-boy is urged to let his "Mom" and "Dad" read his manual, so that they too can appreciate the nobility of feeling and smashing tenderness of regard which frat-boys harbor toward each other. If Mom and Dad can stand this, so can we.

One more taste of the joy-juice:

> I love you because you are helping me to make of the lumber of my life not a tavern, but a temple, and of the words of my every day not a reproach, but a song.
> I love you for closing your ears to the discords in me, and for adding to the music in me by worshipful listening.

Boy, oh boy! That is sentiment like mother used to bake. Actually there is more, but the rest of it is, I'm afraid, just a pinch too much even for Dad or Mom.

After the frat-pledge has been dunked sufficiently in this vat of Sentiment, he must steel himself—it takes courage to join this outfit—to endure a lesson in Smoothness. Smoothness is a quality so devoutly to be desired that no fewer than forty-six brilliant metaphors are expertly mixed, amid incantations and mutterings, to insure its miraculous conception.

As the heavens are high above the earth, so is God above His subjects, and so am I far above any feeling of contempt for a frat-pledge who volunteers to be smoothed up. Like a rough and uncouth diamond, the brave boy must be chipped and sanded and polished before he can submit to be worn on his lady's finger. Fully 47 per cent of the *Pledge Manual* is devoted to a detailed description of the process. Time is limited, however, so I shall deal in the next paragraph with only one of the milder forms of smoothing—the Dinner.

The unassailable Saint George himself, during the great dragon-carnage of 744 A.D., could not have felt more trepidation at the prospect of battle than the modern frat-pledge must feel as he scrubs his face and lips in preparation for Dinner at the Frat House. The manual warns him that "the dining table is the Waterloo for those *who don't know*"—a terrifying proposition surely and one not calculated to allay the tensions and fears of the frat-pledge. Like a knight-fledgling in King Arthur's Court, he is instructed with hair-raising minuteness on the strategy of the diurnal battle of Waterloo: "The spoon must be held somewhat the same as a pencil, but at a different angle, of course, the handle passing between the first two fingers, and the thum [sic] resting on the upper side." And even if he gets his thum-*sic* firmly on the upper side, he now has the grim task of transporting the victuals while at the same time engaging in Conversation. ("Conversation at the table should be in a moderate tone and should be confined to agreeable and reasonably refined subjects. . . . Discussion of women should not be indulged in at the table.") But even if he leaves out women, he must know that many a mess has been made between the platter and the palate, and that one drop of a pea could mean the loss of the entire battle.

But let us suppose he wins the battle; he now has to learn his Ritual, most of which is so fantastic that it would put to shame the master of ceremonies of a Polynesian fertility rite. I personally was once privileged to witness a full-scale, nationally organized, recondite and highly esoteric ceremony—done up with full scenery, costumes, tears, nobility and appropriate moanings—so I know whereof I speak. I shall spare the reader any details: suffice it to say that the whole thing was excruciating; every last word, every last gesture, was drawn out, tortured and buried publicly to the unutterable misery of everyone present, so there is no point in trying to reproduce the affair on paper. Besides, all present had been enjoined to keep it secret (I can easily see why). It went on for two hours and fourteen ghastly minutes.

Beware of an organization that has to douse itself constantly in ritual and high nobility. Any enterprise worth its weight in salt can be shot heavenward with just a couple of ripping prayers and a handshake or two. It's the lame-brain outfits that traffic in high mumbo-jumbo and creep through their existence with the vitality of a snail: the D.A.R., the American Legion, the Society for the Admiration of Charlie Wilson. All such collections of dolts require enough ceremony to bore the archangels—as well as the cherubims, seraphims and ordinary angels—and enough nobility to bore Ralph W. Sockman himself.

Why do fraternities exist? Their demerits are so numerous, their shortcomings so short: they codify snobbery, they pervert values, they corrupt decent instincts. They eat on exclusiveness, they thrive on intolerance, they presume to stratify peoples and beliefs, they gorge on stupidity and inanity, and they disgorge heartache and viciousness. What amazing secret do they possess?

One popular myth has it that they have some remote relation to scholarship—that they actually promote it. This is so foolish as scarcely to warrant comment. Even deans and frat-boys know better. Any frat that can keep its scholastic average even close to the average of non-frat students for as long as six months is so rare that it can confidently expect to be pelted with plaques and trophies, and people will stand around and marvel at it.

No, the answer lies elsewhere, and if I may be pardoned for momentarily departing from stringent objectivity, I offer my own speculations.

A true education is a harrowing experience. A student who wants to be educated must be courageous indeed. He must expect all his comforts and illusions and complacencies to be ruthlessly ripped away. He must drink the cup of humility to its last lees and dregs. He must have the courage of a man about to sit in an electric chair; he must be prepared to watch his toenails curl and his flesh sizzle. In one sense, this is a lonely ordeal. Not that he can't communicate his experience—he can, of course—but he can't delegate it. He must feel it himself. The experience is intensely personal and individual, charged with pain and thrills, with glory and terror.

Not many people can stand this experience. Even fewer, I'm sure, want it. But the danger that it will happen to a few students is always present, so long as there are good teachers and good books lurking about. Frats offer the student an easy protection against electrocution. There is safety in a group, particularly if the group is identified and surrounded by inanity. The group says, in effect, let us all stick together and nothing much will happen to any of us. And nothing very much does.

I know whereof I speak, for I myself have tasted the divine nectar of fraternal brotherhood. It happened at the University of Chicago, shortly after the last war. At that time the entire university was infested by intellectuals and would-be intellectuals—with the result that frats were finding it mighty rough weather indeed. Frat chapter after frat chapter was forced to fold its tent like the Arabs and as silently sneak away for lack of patrons. The few that did manage to survive did so primarily because they offered a place to live—and places to live were then hard to come by. The result was that these frats found themselves occupied by the most unlikely and unfraternal brothers in creation—most of whom, like myself, had just been released from the armed services, and had had their fill of stratified idiocy. I confess the impurity of our motives, but I will say we gave the old frats every chance to endure, if only they had been endurable. At least I can speak for the one I belonged to. We even went through the ritual as prescribd—a minor duplication of the ritual I described earlier—although I admit we speeded it up considerably. Indeed we got so good at ripping through it, that we reduced the time to two minutes and fourteen seconds, and I am convinced we could have cracked the two-minute barrier if only we could have gotten over that lumber-temple-tavern business without faltering.

Now it so happened that the headquarters of the national fraternity were in downtown Chicago, and the permanent cadre of the frat were mighty suspicious of us. Once we took in two Jewish boys, and they swooped down upon us and gave us a terrifying sermon on the dangers of "mongrelization." Then one day one of the national brothers spotted a couple of Negroes in the house—and that did it. Brotherhood had gone too far, and the whole intention of this great moral style-setter was being subverted. The chapter was abruptly and unceremoniously closed, the house sold and the heretics were perforce scattered far and wide.

I mention this incident for two reasons—one personal and the other philosophical-historical. Philosophically-historically, the incident simply hasn't been recognized—even Alfred McClung Lee in his *Fraternities*

Without Brotherhood* does not mention the matter—possibly he didn't even know about it.

Personally, I was not on the scene when the climactic bit of anti-mongrelization took place, but I submitted a letter of protest to the Awful Powers, and announced my resignation. This seemed to me the only fraternal thing to do. A couple of days later I received, to my utter astonishment, a reply from the national headquarters to the effect that my request to resign was completely out of order, and that I should consult Section 7 of Article XV of the fraternity constitution before writing any more letters of protest. I consulted the vital section, and literally rubbed my eyes to see that "no member can voluntarily sever his connection" with the organization. The whole force of the revelation hit me. *You can't get out!* Like joining a penitentiary—you stay in till they put you out.

For seven years now I have been enduring, waiting, suffering—but always hoping, hoping, hoping that my misconduct will be heinous enough to warrant expulsion. If this article serves to reduce my sentence by even one day, it will have been worth the writing—if not the reading.

WHO'S ON FIRST: THE GREAT AMERICAN SPORTS RITUAL / EDWARD L. ROUSSEAU

Except for reading about them, no waste of time is more complete than watching or listening to spectator sports. Now surely we are given time in order to waste some of it, and the most rigorous moralist would concede that if little good is accomplished by watching the World Series, absolutely no harm is done. The innocence of money-making hours, so praised by Dr. Johnson, is as nothing in comparison. Yet there is a seeming contradiction that Americans, who value above all else the state of being busy, should be inordinately given to the idleness of watching games.

A similarity between the United States and the Roman Empire on this point is obvious; it might seem that we too have reached the stage of decline marked by bread and circuses. But some qualifications are in order.

---

* Beacon Press, 1955.

American crowds, though more boisterous than the English, are (to say nothing of the ancient Romans) not so violent as those of some other modern nations. With us, broken beer bottles tossed at the bad guy or slack upholders of the good, are not the rule—unless, if we may believe reports, in Philadelphia. The violent antics of wrestling fans belong to another category than professional sports and are not, in any case, typical. Baseball players who seek summer in January on the Caribbean find, to their horror, fans who are serious to the point of violence. Modern Americans easily approve violence in principle as a solution of civic and international problems, but only in the abstract. The same voters who were vehemently for getting tough (in theory) with Communists, and even for a hypothetical atomic holocaust, were equally opposed to actual fighting in Korea or anywhere else. Despite the traditions of the frontier and the South, American crowds are surprisingly good-natured, and more so than usual when in a holiday mood. Anyone used to the ineffectual waspishness of academics is, perhaps, especially surprised.

If force and seriousness always went together, it might be argued that our sporting crowds are relatively detached in their attitude. A strange symbiosis of athletics and higher learning—more grotesque than the myth about rattlesnake and owl living with the gopher in his hole—is an American peculiarity, but not evidence in itself of any special value attached to watching games. That sports are a concomitant of academic life is *prima facie* evidence that they are counted among the childish things that a man must put away. That football should be cherished as a souvenir of youth rather than organic chemistry or economic analysis is surely understandable enough. It has even been argued that interest in spectator sports is diminishing since, as the do-it-yourself craze shows, activity is replacing passivity in American life. The popularity of TV would seem to refute this explanation.

In any case, whatever the future may bring, at present sports do act as a link between social classes, with a special reverse snob appeal to intellectuals. Baseball is a universal subject of conversation at once innocuous and more personal than the weather. The case of baseball is enough to refute any minimizing of the place of passive athleticism in American life. Contrary to legend, relatively few among the past generation or two have played much hardball in their own youth. Unlike basketball or football, the so-called national game does not have the nostalgic association with high school or college days glanced at above. Like any ritual which has not degenerated into a relic, it is a unifying factor in society, imitating real life and yet different from it. The comparison sometimes made with ballet is false. The center of interest both in sports and in American life is a compulsive concern with what the score is. You don't keep score at the Ballet Russe—one reason why the American male is not at home there, in spite of the appetizing scenery. The world of professional athletics is as remote from the everyday round of American life as any art form, but sport—while sufficiently exotic to serve as an escape—appeals to a motive that is immediately intelligible. One of the most frequent complaints by listeners to a sports broadcast is that the announcer doesn't tell what the score is. Without a knowledge of who is ahead and by how much, the game is meaningless, just as our existence would be.

Americans can enjoy games both as active and passive participants without gambling, but not without keeping score. The same instinct is catered to by an immense flow of seemingly meaningless statistics and records from radio and television sports announcers. One reason, of course, is that the announcer needs to keep his jaw wagging when nothing much is happening, or at least nothing that he understands. The slower pace of baseball compared with basketball or boxing shows a reason for a plethora of statistics, though even in the fastest-paced sports enough figures are given to satisfy—one would imagine—the most avid. The announcer's convenience cannot be the sole explanation; the figures must please the customers, or they would not be given.

We seem to have a manifestation of an interest in facts, however useless, and even in abstract schematizations of fact, providing that they explain nothing. In some cases an undeveloped interest in truth, even trivial truth, for its own sake may be the cause of the attention paid to meaningless figures. "All men desire to know," as Aristotle says. Another cause is more important in the case of batting averages, one that applies to the interest in spectator sports itself. Even the most stupid human mind, like an athlete's muscles, calls out for something with which to occupy itself. But even the most intelligent find constant mental effort painful, and the best men find a real commitment of self guided by intelligence difficult. The difference between superior and inferior human types in these respects is one of almost imperceptible differences in degree. Man's need to pass the time without working forms a substratum in passive human interest in the arts—especially literature and music. The strength of this appeal is shown by quite honest irritation at whatever demands attention or judgment. But the need to waste time can be gratified with much less danger of effort and commitment in spectator sports, even when seen darkly through tables of statistics.

Another level of appeal is the entertainment value of sports—an intense but not demanding engagement in a spectacle with the attraction of an exciting story. As the old saw goes, the game isn't over till the last out is made. Modern literary criticism, both of the Freudian kind and by proponents of the new criticism, has neglected a similar source of interest in literature. It is hardly necessary to say that I don't intend a justification of the prize ring or of the gladiatorial games, but it is important to understand that their appeal is not altogether due to sadism. To say that sports appeal as an exciting spectacle is, then, an important part of the truth but not the whole truth.

Let us consider again the case of the so-called national game, baseball. People may enjoy it, but enjoyment by itself isn't enough to support the industry. Over the country as a whole the fans don't get enough fun out of going to the ball game to pay the price of admission. The minor leagues are dying. It may be argued that the fans want the best and, since they can get the majors free over television—so far as any immediate price of admission is concerned—won't buy an inferior product. However, even if it were possible to expose all or most of the people in the country to genuine major-league ball and make them pay directly for it, the economic problems of the industry might not be solved permanently. The fans who are now in major-league cities can, even with a losing team, see the most skilled players in the world—baseball as entertainment at its best. Is this enough? Of course it isn't. They demand a winning team. Entertainment as such isn't valued by American sports audiences—or rather, the fun is spoiled unless another condition is fulfilled: the simple-minded morality play of the good guys versus the bad guys must be acted out before their eyes. The good guys must win, or in baseball finish first. A first-division finish isn't enough if it happens too often. There is something disquieting about the morality of the play. The only difference between good and bad is that good is my side, and to stay my side it has to prove its goodness by winning. Such a game is the great American ritual. Mr. Perini, the owner of the Milwaukee National League Baseball Club, had a point when he suggested that baseball be given a tax-exemption status similar to that of religion or education.

His proposal has, nevertheless, some peculiar ramifications. What Mr. Perini seems to have in mind is that he should still get his profits plus the present cut of the Internal Revenue Service. But what the logic of the situation calls for is that the government support the proven bad guys, the perennial losers. The customers will support the good guys readily enough. Nobody except the courts takes seriously the pious disclaimers that baseball is not a business. The facts are too plain, but it is certainly a strange business. The baseball owners don't seem to realize how strange, and they act like ordinary capitalists when such an attitude is inappropriate.

The New York Yankees, for example, seem unaware that their success creates a dilemma for themselves as well as for their competitors. They understand well enough that you've got to win to make money. But there is another aspect to the problem. However much collusion there may be among capitalistic competitors, and however much may be necessary except in the never-never land of an abstract *laissez-faire* economics, still, in other industries competitors are not necessary—only customers. The process of carrying monopoly to its logical extreme might destroy even the customers, but that is another story. General Motors could in theory take over Ford or vice versa. But in professional athletics the existence of the competitor is necessary. The Yankees have to have the other clubs in the league to beat, and the other clubs can't stay prosperous unless their customers identify them with the good guys who, by definition, can't be beat. Within the present framework of organized baseball, the situation could be eased somewhat if the rich clubs would permit an unrestricted draft of minor league players so that talent would be distributed more evenly, but those in power are all too human in their willingness to murder Santa Claus any old time for first grabs at his pack.

My concern with some of the economic problems of baseball as a business has been only to illustrate the importance of winning, an importance that makes spectator sports as entertainment depend on a ritual identification of spectators with the triumphant good. As has already been pointed out, the skills that make for success in games are not really those used in everyday life, but nevertheless Americans often call life itself a game. It is precisely what is taken most seriously in life that is most often so compared —the life-insurance or real-estate business; I have even heard an eminent Thomist metaphysician describe his own activities as "this game." He was not looking at himself through the skeptical eyes of a logical positivist, but assimilating his activities to real American life, talking as if he were one of the boys and as good as anyone else. What spectator sports have in common with the main current of American life—in spite of the obvious differences—is not fun or relaxation, though Americans are in fact quite serious about fun, but again emphasis on keeping score. Parenthetically, it must be remarked that people who place emphasis not only on proving themselves competitively, but also on counting and comparing their self-proof, give evidence that their society places a great psychic strain on the individual. It is a curious coincidence that our predecessors on this continent, the Indians, were great and compulsive score-keepers, counting coups in warfare on the plains and giving potlatches in the Pacific Northwest.

The position of sports as a ritual representation of life rather than a part of it renders intelligible the curious fact that just in the age when sincerity, making a good impression, and security (rather than risk-taking) are coming to predominate in real life, aggressiveness, toughness and the cult of hustling should prevail on the sports page. A businessman in any ordinary pursuit would not risk bad publicity by endangering the lives of others in order to make money. This observation may seem somewhat naive in view of the practices of the automobile industry, but it would be still more naive to regard poor car sales as a protest in favor of safety or even of common sense. Here we are confronted with sins of omission rather than commission and have no reason to doubt that if safety were at all popular, the automobile producers would sell it. In baseball, on the other hand, the practice of throwing at the batter's head is justified with the excuse that it's all part of the game and by the remark that nearly always the pitcher does not intend to maim or kill but simply to keep the batter from crowding the plate. With their usual ineptness, the powers that be in baseball have made the gesture of giving umpires authority to read minds and to fine pitchers and even managers if they persist in a malevolent mental attitude. The whole problem could be solved in a minute by ruling that any batter struck above the neck would score, with all runners in front of him, and the pitcher immediately be ejected and suspended for thirty days. There would be no possibility of abuse; some players may very occasionally abuse the present rule which gives one base to a batter hit anywhere, but nobody would deliberately stick his head in front of a ball. In justice, it must be observed that the owners have the reverse of a financial interest in having a very hard object thrown through the skulls of their valuable chattels. Nobody can accuse them of deep thinking, malevolent or otherwise. It is also true that bean-balling is almost certainly not so dangerous to life as putting a usually harmless dose of poison in a food portion, but no food producer could publicly argue that poisoning is part of the packing game. Aggression that would no longer be approved in real life is approved in its imitation on the playing field.

There is a case for allowing youth to play moderately dangerous games when properly supervised. Physical courage and indifference to pain are not the supreme virtues, but they are a much more valuable endowment for life than their contraries. This has nothing to do with spectator sports as a business, even when supported on the side by educational institutions. One wonders how long courses of studies would be tolerated in which a sizable proportion of the students got broken bones every year. There is one department of our universities in which this is taken for granted. Public opinion would not tolerate a business which had a similar employee-accident rate, especially if the employees were under age.

Even the semi-sophisticated have learned to smile at the educational values of sport. But one pre-educational value they do have even for the audience: in the game all that really counts is competence. The student who tries to bluff himself into a grade of A would not expect to make the football team by the same tactics. Everyone even slightly able to judge gives professional athletes—if not the adulation they have learned to expect—the respect due to any competent workman.

But here we find the source of a clash with one aspect of sport as a ritual. Leo Durocher said that nice guys finish last; they don't if they have ability. A team of Musials wouldn't finish behind a team of Durochers and Stankys. All the color, toughness and aggressiveness in the world wouldn't help. It is part of the ritual character of sports that qualities are emphasized—if not on the playing field, then on the sports page—that are dying out in real life. The cult of the tough guy which, with one side of his nature, the American is taught to value, is acted out ritually and read about in escape literature just when the opposing characteristics prevail in real life. The great era of spectator sports began when the old values of the self-made man had begun to decay. Practices no longer attained or even tolerated in real life are acted out on the stage of spectator sports, where the good guys who are not the nice guys always win.

Art imitates nature, just the same, and nature art. The attitudes of the spectator do affect American real life. Our salesmanship and production have, as Mr. Galbraith has pointed out, some of the unreal characteristics of a game. But they are the simply given aspects of life and cannot be questioned, any more than the convention of three outs in baseball, even if survival is at stake. Then, too, we are the good guys, and the good guys always win, by a natural law, without any effort—in the grandstand. If things don't seem to be going too well temporarily, we can always change the manager and have the front office spend more money. The future we might have made may be a spectacle we shall die watching. But to expect this may also be a naive expectation of a dramatic and definite conclusion, like that of a game.

THE HAPPINESS RAT RACE /
GEORGE P. ELLIOTT

The famous, inalienable error is proclaimed in the Declaration of Independence. Jefferson might have been expected to write, in the Lockean spirit of the age, "life, liberty, and property," but I suppose the hypocrisy of that was so crass that it too harshly echoed a black undertruth, "life, bondage, and being property." Something high-sounding and *sincere* was needed. It might have been tacked on as fourth, but slogans thrive on triads; so "property" made room for a more comfortable phrase. Even a slave pursues happiness if it salves you to think so, a nice shiny banjo-banging slave: "life, liberty, and the pursuit of happiness": much more comfortable.

There's so much unmanageable luck to happiness that it won't be held on to any longer than it wants. "Count no man happy," the chorus said of Oedipus, "till he be dead." Indeed, the moment you grasp happiness like a possession, it alters. "He," said Blake, "who binds to himself a joy/Does the winged life destroy,/But he who kisses the joy as it flies/Lives in eternity's sun rise." To Sophocles and Blake, the world is unreasonable, and the gods meddle in our affairs as it pleases them, not as it pleases us. And Aristotle—who was like our Founding Fathers in that if a god should speak through his lips, his ears would refuse to hear more than human words, and the universe was as reasonable as he could make it—all the same Aristotle defined happiness not as a thing to be sought directly but as the result of a life lived in accordance with virtue and blessed with good fortune.

If you live as you ought *and* if you're lucky, then the adjective "happy" may be applied to you. But our FF's turned it into a substance for us to chase like a bird. What to do with the bird of happiness once it's caught? Cage it ("A robin redbreast in a cage/Puts all heaven in a rage"). Eat it. If you're a scientist, dissect it. But catch it, catch it, that's the big idea.

One who thinks of happiness as a thing, can be and wants to be persuaded that there are things for sale to catch it with, prepackaged, worth the money: Listerine, Mum, Joy, a Cadillac, a wall-to-wall split-level ranch-style fully-mechanized $28,000 home, those who care know it costs a few cents more, don't let your loved one suffer from seepage, a gold-plated shower-nozzle for the man who has everything, My Sin, Miltown.

So, since more citizens of this country now have money to buy these snares with than ever before—whether in this or in any other country, this or any other age—it follows that a lot of us ought to be happy. From the point of view of most men, it may look that way; they usually do not have even enough to eat, nor do they know the statistics of our despair, our rates of suicide, divorce, alcoholism, juvenile delinquency, murder, mental illness. Certainly from the point of view of such people as the Russians, who want what we have only more, it must look that way. Amazing, half the world wants to be Los Angeles—the Hollywooded dream, that is, not the actual place in a smog.

Happiness is an official U.S. product all right. We used to promise it wholesale to the poor, the homeless, the huddled masses (*from the right countries,* that is—beware any symbol which is aesthetically as ugly as the Statue of Liberty). Nowadays we quota that promise rigorously, but we are generous with our know-how in devising happiness snares and cages. We export do-it-yourself kits or completely ready-made snares to any country (*any Russia-hating country*) that wants them.

We also have plenty of custom-made items for the domestic trade. The D.C. publicity department says Washington is a summer festival. As Herbert Gold reports, for the admen this is an age of happy problems. According to The Native Sons of the Golden West, God created California to be a paradise for the white man. In New York, the city-owned WNYC signs off every night with a perfect lie in amber: "Where eight million people live in peace and harmony." And if you'll just adulterate your joy with some business, the government will subsidize you in the name of Expense Account.

Well, one thing is certain: from Key West to Puget Sound, from Bar Harbor to Tijuana, up, down and sideways, we do have a lot of fun.

Have fun: possessiveness is part of the very idiom: fun is a bird you can have if you catch it. (But only a flicker of a bird—you mustn't squeeze him.)

Not that there's anything wrong with genuine fun. It's as natural and healthful as any other form of play. Four Nebraska farmers pitching horseshoes at a church social, their wives setting out the thermos of lemonade and charcoal-broiling the chicken, their children playing hide-and-go-seek among the cars. Ten or twelve Columbus high school friends in somebody's living room on a snowy Friday night drinking pop and listening to records, from time to time dancing, a few of them ducking into dark corners to kiss. In Indianapolis, kids playing in the water which the firemen let gush from hydrants on a hot day. Driving fast on a Maryland country road. Bridge and coffee in the front room; poker and beer in the kitchen. Fishing. Ball games. Fireworks on the Fourth in the Riverside city park. A block party in East St. Louis, a hundred kids dancing in the street to canned music. The movies.

But this is only a hit-or-miss beginning to a list so huge and various it addles the brains to think of it. And every item on the list is in fact a fun worth enjoying if you take it for what it is, fugitive and not very important. Only Puritans would object.

And there's a good share of the trouble: the Puritans did, and do, object. They do all they can to pollute the springs of fun.

Take liquor, which has come to have a lot to do with having fun. In Mississippi it cannot be bought legally (Oklahoma just went wet in 1959). In three-fourths of the rest of the states of the union, there are restrictions (local option, buyers' licenses, papers to sign) which make you resentful or uneasy every time you buy a bottle, or at least conscious that the law watches you do it. And the public gathering places for drinking! In I don't know how many states, nothing, or nothing more than beer, may be served on the premises. It's scarcely worth trying to get good wine with dinner in a restaurant outside the metropolises, nor in most of the restaurants in them. And what kind of joy is the ordinary cocktail lounge arranged to generate?—a long, straight bar facing bottles and a mirror; backless stools, murk; no games to play but pinball; noise from the TV or the juke-box; no dancing permitted; about the entrance as you turn to go in, an aura of discredit: a meager, thick joy.

"We may not be able," said the pale-eyed Calvinist, "to keep you from sinning, but we'll do what we can to keep you from enjoying it."

So, an act which can be, ought to be, often is pure fun—dancing, for example—may be turned into an occasion of uneasiness and strain simply by being looked at with Puritan eyes. And when the dancers themselves so look, then the trouble goes far deeper. They may quit dancing entirely, or, quite as bad, they may dance in flagrant defiance of conscience. In this latter case, much liquor may be needed to keep the psyche quiet. (In Washington, D.C., where psyches need quieting for all sorts of reasons, the consumption of alcohol is much higher than in any of the states: two and a half gallons of wine and over five gallons of hard liquor per capita per year.) Or, worst of all, fun may become a desperate need and a cause, as sex became in the Twenties and still is for many; too many.

Yet, *fun!* For any adolescent, a fun-house—a traveling carnival—

Coney Island—are callow symbols of the meretricious; and surely anyone who becomes addicted to fun is his own contemptible dupe?

There's more to it than that.

The economics of fun is quite impossible to come by, if only because fun is an impossible economic category. Even if you identify it as "the entertainment business," you're going to run into all sorts of trouble defining entertainment. At the end of last year, *Life*, that magazine of Luce religiosity, gave as its Christmas present to the world a double issue devoted to the business of entertainment in the United States. But I at least run into aesthetic trouble immediately when I find that "entertainment" includes, at one end of the spectrum, any opera staged at the Metropolitan and, at the other end, anything broadcast over TV.

Pardon me, but no high art should be reduced to "entertainment" even when, like *The Magic Flute*, it entertains, and *Otello*, which I like better than any other opera I know, is no fun at all. And pardon me again, but if watching *This Is Your Life* is entertainment, then so is cutting up Siamese kittens with a dull pair of scissors.

And then (to get away from indisputable taste) a great many things which originally were luxuries and fun now have developed in us a craving as great as a need, like rum to a drunkard.

Take automobiles. Nearly all the people in the world seem to get along without them. Even in the United States, a few people manage without them; some of the Amish south of Iowa City still go by horse and buggy, and they look good too. Usually when I drive some place, I could just as well have walked, or gone by public transportation, or stayed home. But it's fun to drive!

Yet, car ownership has, for a very great many people, come to have so much to do with status and confidence and security and convenience that it couldn't be excised from their lives without effecting a profound dislocation. Maybe this dislocation would be good; I don't know; but my point is that it puts cars quite out of the order of what is meant by fun. Furthermore, by now so many jobs depend on cars, either in producing and maintaining them or else in using them, that the industry has become an inextricable part of our national life as well as of our private lives. Or so we think, as we do not think about basketball, bingo, the funnies.

How is an economist to categorize cars? They're a luxury, they're fun, they're a drug, they're a necessity—all at once.

Still, so nearly as I can guess by poring over various tables of family and national expenditures and of national business statistics, we Americans apparently spend more per year on liquor than on medical care, the "entertainment business" is financially more important than mining, and most families lay out as much for cigarettes in the course of a year as for charity.

I submit: this is not only wrong of us, but down underneath the official gloss of *Life*-like lies, in which we live, we ourselves know it to be wrong. So why do we do it?

Here, on the troubled waters of *why*, an unspecialized citizen like me can float as free as any sociologist, economist, psychologist, anthropologist. My speculations are going to be unabashed.

It has something to do with Puritanism all right. (Nothing but Prohibition could have made bathtub gin taste good.) But there's a lot more to it than that.

I can't see that it has anything directly to do with the class struggle (in fact, I have trouble seeing the classes struggling any more, at least one against another as they used to do). Nor with the loss of religious faith or with the pains and disappointments which come with groping for that lost faith. These and others like them may be, and I think are, involved in our fun-desperation, but in remote, pervasive, indirect ways. It has a great deal to do with our wealth, for our wealth gives us leisure for which we do not have good enough uses (we speak of "killing" time) and more money to spend than training in how to spend it responsibly. And it has a very great deal to do with the joylessness and lack of engagement most people feel about their work, whether office or factory or field. But these things have been talked about much and well.

Here, I want to look at two enormous, efficient causes influencing each of us Americans and all collectively. They are so monstrous that every time I really regard them my ears ring and I run for the fun-juice.

The first of them is our warmaking. The traditional political and nationalist reasons for making war are still about as good as they ever were, though there are a lot of obscure and very important new reasons mixed in with the usual ones. But ordinary Americans no longer go to war primarily for these reasons. Young men allowed themselves to be drafted, trained and shipped to Korea to fight, but they did not allow it for political reasons primarily, not as a police action to contain communism. I'm not sure why they did it, and neither, I believe, are they; nor do they or the State really want to know, just so long as they keep doing what seems to be (and perhaps used to be) their duty. And no more than 15 to 25 per cent of the

American riflemen in World War II (this is on the authority of Brigadier General S. L. A. Marshall in *Men Against Fire*, Morrow, 1947) would actually fire their guns even when attacked and not all of these fired *at* anything. They allowed the State to draft them, but they had trouble shooting its enemies.

But worse than our reasons for going to war are our ways of waging it. (Not ours alone, but ours, but ours.) The ways themselves challenge and overshadow and finally obliterate the reasons. Nothing could justify such abominations: I believe that we all feel this obscurely and refuse, in any effectual way, to look at it. Our United States used the Bomb, nobody else; our government is the one chiefly responsible for spreading radioactive particles over the world. *We had not thought we were capable of such evil.*

And we don't know what to do about it.

The second of the overwhelming causes of our fun-desperation, as I conceive the matter, is the dreadful social injustice which we are guilty of and benefit from, especially we white Americans and most especially we whose Christian ancestors came from Northern Europe. We stole the nation in the first place without believing that might makes right; we ravished millions of Africans from their homes, their pasts, their languages, their ways, enslaved them, and left them one great passion, hating us (yet those who can, would become like us); the Americans from south of us and the Asians who have come to our country we have insulted and do insult; our nation helps the poor primarily when it thinks that action will hurt its enemies or help itself; the productive modes of our gaining our inconceivable wealth we ourselves think to be unscrupulous and unjust, and they are so lunatic that one of our reasons to give to the poor is that that action will make our nation richer; and for this same bad-dream reason, to make ourselves the better off, we destroy, prohibit, or hoard vast quantities of food, which food we know we should give to the hungry.

We don't like it. But we are so rich, so comfortable, so powerful. We don't like to think about it.

Circuses. Bread and circuses.

Let's have us a ball.

If we tickle each other expertly enough, maybe we can just quit thinking about the whole business.

I want to leave with you a couple of images of fancy fun, Times Square and call girls.

The good-time girls!—fun is their life, they're the Social Register of pleasure, they have beauty and money and no responsibilities, they really kick their heels up at the law. So far as I know, the best literary portrait of a call girl is Holly Golightly in Truman Capote's *Breakfast at Tiffany's* (Random House, 1958). He takes her pretty much at her own estimation —fun and charm and wild, gay living, with accesses of the acute anxiety to be got through, and a fairy-tale ending. The trouble with Holly is that only the best part of her is there. For Capote never shows her to us in her chromium habitat, where in fact ordinary citizens with the price can observe her any time they want—in those mortuaries of fun, night clubs. Capote never asks us to take her anxieties as anything more than conversation pieces. He does not mention her pimp. Maybe she doesn't have one, but most call girls do; they need someone whom they can despise more than they despise themselves.

One of the saddest books I ever read is *The Call Girl* by a psychoanalyst named H. Greenwald (Ballantine Books, 1958). The author has little regard for English prose and less for the arts of narrative, but he knows his people well and makes it possible for you to know them too, the daughters of joy. In this book the girls come a lot closer to breaking your heart than they would in a night club or a hotel bed. Here, you understand they have to have their fun with such ferocity because they are so full of anxiety and self-contempt and because they do not really enjoy what they do: they are frigid; their customers, solid citizens very likely with families, want their sex perverse most of the time; they must pseudo-love a man fast to allay their appalling dread that no one will ever really love them, and of course the life they lead pretty well insures that no one does. Most of them will end in drug addiction, streetwalking, alcoholism, or suicide, as they know. . . . It takes a gruesome lot of fun to get through "the life."

The highest concentration of fun, everybody says, is Times Square on New Year's Eve. So I went a couple of years ago to see what there was to see. And that's what everyone else was doing, seeing what there was to see. There was a battalion of police and a fair number of youths with noise-makers. But mostly there were thousands of us just milling around. A third or so lined the store-fronts four or five deep, another third ranged along the curb and out into the street, and the rest straggled densely along in the course between, largely in a counter-clockwise direction. Mostly, we shifted from one group to another without any particular reason, just to be doing something. Few made noise. We looked at one another with eyes blanked from too much liquor or from looking at too many other faces or from madness. We smiled a lot; it was New Year's Eve; we were making merry. At midnight everybody croaked, and because there were so many of us croaking we seemed to roar. We watched one another for reactions to react to.

Someone—I think it was St. Augustine—suggested an image of hell for the intellect: two mirrors facing each other in a gray void. We have improved on all that.

Some New Year's Eve, if you're in a deserted fun-town, say Atlantic City, watch the Times Square celebration over gray-glassed TV, in a motel room or any bar. Or, if you're at home, invite a couple of friends over to watch with you and have plenty of drinks; your own living room will do just fine for having that sort of a hell of a time; as you watch people in the void-box watching one another, you and your friends can watch each other too. Double-distilled fun. I've tried it.

To be sure, having the kind of fun you have to have doesn't hurt as much as finding out what's really wrong and doing something about it. But finally, rather than that grinning stupefaction, I'd prefer to hurt.

ISSUES OF THE DAY
SOCIAL, ECONOMIC, POLITICAL

THE RANGE
OF SOCIAL PROBLEMS

FOUR MYTHS CRIPPLE OUR SCHOOLS /
MYRON LIEBERMAN

The most important educational trend in the 1960's is likely to be the decline of local control of education. Such a development is long overdue. Public education in the United States has been strangled for more than a century by the myth that local control is a good thing. National survival now requires educational policies and programs which are not subject to local veto; conversely, local communities must be relegated to ceremonial rather than policy-making roles in public education. This means that in the long run we shall be forced also to abolish state control of education, since from a national standpoint state control is only an attenuated version of local control.

Our present system cannot be justified in the light of the mobile and interdependent nature of our society. A vast majority of our people eventually move away from the school district and state which carried the responsibility for their elementary and secondary education. In the year ending March, 1958, 30,800,000 Americans changed their residence. Approximately 11,000,000 moved from one county to another, of whom about half moved to a different state. Thus, on the average, every American moves to a different state two times during his life. Under these circumstances, it hardly makes sense to contend that the citizens of one state have no legitimate right to insist upon an adequate education for the children in other states.

Some idea of the bankruptcy of local control of education may be gotten from the statistics concerning Selective Service registrants rejected for failure to pass the mental tests. In 1956, the lowest rate of rejection on this score was Montana's 2.5 per cent; the highest rate was Mississippi's 44.9 per cent. In ten states, fewer than one out of every twenty registrants failed to pass the tests; in eleven states, one or more out of every four failed to pass.

These vast differences are not due solely to the differences in the school systems from state to state. A registrant educated in Montana might take his Selective Service tests in Mississippi, or vice versa. Moreover, the statistics include failures to pass the tests because of inherited mental deficiency, and for other causes over which the schools have no control. Nevertheless, the differences cannot be explained solely by non-educational causes. And because some states and communities provide a decent minimum education for only a small minority of their children, we must, in all states, draft persons who ought not to be in the armed services at all.

This is only a small part of the price we are paying for local control of education. The intellectual smog that has prevented us from realizing just how exorbitant is this price is being cleared away once and for all by such related events as the riots in Little Rock and the Russian conquests of space.

Much like racial segregation, local control of education is based upon myths whose sun has now set. Particular individuals may continue to accept them for a long time, but our society would be committing suicide by doing so. The most important of the myths are these:

1. *The myth that local control of education, with perhaps a few concessions made to state control, is one of the important institutional safeguards of educational freedom and of our free society.*

Our present system of local control is far more conducive to totalitarian education and to a totalitarian society than a national system of schools would be. I know that this statement is not acceptable to the overwhelming majority of the American people, including the teachers; but I am willing to stand upon it.

The assertion that our present system tends toward totalitarianism seems absurd on its face. A totalitarian system is one which develops a massive uniformity of outlook; it is based upon intellectual protectionism for points of view which cannot stand the test of free discussion. But we have a multitude of schools of all denominations or no denominations at all; among our teachers and students are adherents of every major political, economic and religious point of view. What could be farther from totalitarianism?

In most states, the purposes and the content of education are left to local school boards to determine. Undoubtedly, there are constitutional limits to the purposes for which communities may operate public schools. However, these limits have never been spelled out, and great latitude is left to communities. Under these circumstances the predominant groups in each community tend to set educational goals which accord with their particular religious, political, economic or social points of view. As a practical matter, therefore, our present system results in the same kind of intellectual protectionism that characterizes schools in totalitarian countries.

Even where a community accepts the most liberal educational purposes, its interpretation of what programs fulfill these purposes may have the same stultifying effect as outright adherence to a sectarian purpose. Every pressure group is for the general welfare, but each has its own version of what measures do in fact promote the general welfare. Similarly, every pressure group is for a liberal education, but each has a special version of what educational programs lead to this result.

What is crucial is that at the local level, it is relatively easy for a preponderant group to enforce a policy of intellectual protectionism for its sacred cows. Thus the white majorities in Southern communities exclude instruction that is critical of racial segregation. Communities in which fundamentalist sects predominate exclude school instruction in evolution. Some communities have prohibited the study of the U.N. or of UNESCO. Ours is a heterogeneous country, but in most communities the predominant racial, religious, economic or political groups are able to veto whatever in the school program displeases them.

Looking at our system as a whole, and noting the existence of public schools teaching diverse doctrines, one might infer that our schools are free. We do not readily recognize the totalitarianism implicit in local control simply because not all schools protect the same dogmas. Nonetheless, a diversity of schools based upon intellectual protectionism for different dogmas does not constitute a "democratic school system"—not, at least, if "democratic" refers to the education actually provided rather than to the legal structure which facilitates a variety of one-sided educational programs.

The diversity of our undemocratic schools is not the only factor which maintains the fiction that we have a democratic school system. The power structure of American society is such that no single group is able to enforce its dogmas on the population as a whole. No matter how successful a group may be in excluding certain facts and ideas from the public schools, the mass media—radio, TV, etc.—are almost certain to expose students to some of them. People look at this situation and say, "Our schools have kept us free." They should say. "Our freedoms have survived our schools."

2. *The myth that public education was not made a federal responsibility in the Constitution because the founding fathers feared the potentialities for dictatorship in a federal school system.*

Actually, education was not included as a federal function in the Constitution because the idea of free, public education had not even occurred to the founding fathers. At the time of the American Revolution, the concept of universal public education was receiving attention for the first time—and only from a few frontier thinkers. Thus, our present decentralized school system was not an inspired stroke of genius, but a historical accident.

Our schools have never been an important foundation of our free society. Our freedom is partly due to a separation of powers which enables us to transact public business reasonably well while simultaneously avoiding excessive subjection to government officials. Perhaps for this reason, we tend to regard the diffusion of power over our schools as an essential element of our free society. But adherence to a general principle that we must avoid excessive concentration of power does not automatically justify every separation or diffusion of it. Everything depends upon the circumstances—what powers are involved, who is to wield them, and so on. It is preposterous to think, merely because their political genius was expressed through a Constitution embodying a remarkably successful separation of powers, that the founding fathers would align themselves today with the supporters of local control of education.

People tend to regard public education as a legal concept and to neglect it as an educational concept; that is why they are seldom aware of its non-public aspects. The ideal of public education means more than having some government unit—local, state or federal—provide the funds. Public education has a referent in the quality of education as well as in its financial basis. The qualitative referent is an education in which the search for truth is carried on regardless of what empires topple, interests collapse or heads roll. Without this, public education is a delusion as dangerous as the notion that mere government ownership of the means of production will automatically result in their operation for public, rather than for private, interests. The socialization of a service at any level of government is no automatic guarantee that the service will be performed in the public interest.

Although the legal structure under which schools operate is only one factor which serves to shape their educational program, it is an extremely important factor. Because a national system of educational controls is more likely to broaden the purposes of education and to preserve the professional autonomy of teachers, it is much more likely to provide a truly liberal education than a multitude of totalitarian systems under local control. It is a striking fact that in England, which has a national system of education, teachers are opposed to local control precisely because they fear that such control would undermine their academic freedom. Meanwhile, teachers in the United States continue to act as if local control must be maintained inviolate lest academic freedom (which they do not possess) be imperiled.

3. *The myth that local control of education is a boon to educational research and experimentation.*

We have fifty state school systems, each free to try something different. Each state has delegated considerable power to local school boards, which multiplies the experimental possibilities. This is supposed to make for progress, since each school system is not only free to try something new, but also to benefit from the experience of others.

There is no doubt that some change for the better occurs this way. Nevertheless, the enormous decentralization cannot be justified on this ground. The different schools do not constitute experiments except in the loosest sense of the word. They do not operate under conditions carefully controlled for purposes of analysis and comparison; they just operate.

Much of the experience of different systems is valuable only on the premise that education should be a state or local responsibility. A school board may indeed be interested in how another community put over a school-bond campaign. However, if the funds came from the federal government, the experience of a particular school system in raising money would be academic.

The truth is that local control of education has obstructed rather than facilitated educational research. By and large, only large, urban systems allocate funds to research—and when they do so, the research is generally limited to problems of local concern. This is only natural. No one normally looks to a local farm community to finance a program of basic agricultural research; why should we expect local communities to support educational research in local schools from local funds? In agriculture, the federal government supports basic research because the futility of waiting for a small operator or a local community to do so is clearly evident. The same policy can and should be followed in education.

The U.S. Office of Education, a branch of the Department of Health,

Education, and Welfare, has conducted research on certain administrative problems for many years. Not until 1956, however, was it granted funds for research in the art and science of teaching. In that year, $3,000,000 was made available by Congress for grants in various fields of education. The National Defense Education Act, passed in August, 1958, included an appropriation of $18,000,000 over a four-year period for research on the educational use of radio, television and audio-visual aids. But as long as education remains primarily a state and local responsibility, educational research will never receive the support it ought to have.

Public education is a $16,000,000,000 enterprise. Enlightened practice in large-scale industry and government is to spend 3 to 6 per cent of the total budget for research. In education, this would call for an expenditure of from $480,000,000 to $960,000,000 annually. In fact, it is doubtful whether we are spending more than $25,000,000 a year from all sources on educational research.

Proposals for a twenty-fold increase will be dismissed as a pipe dream by most educators. Nevertheless, such an increase might still leave research expenditures at a conservative level even if we are now spending considerably more than $25,000,000 annually for the purpose. We are currently spending well over $300,000,000 annually for medical research, and a distinguished advisory committee of medical educators and research executives last year recommended that this amount be increased to $1 billion by 1970.

In this connection, one of the most persistent and most pathetic arguments against a national school system is that it would not permit experimentation. The broad assumption seems to be that centralized administration is necessarily non-experimental or that it necessarily insists upon uniformity down to every detail. Actually, several federal agencies subsidize programs of research which dwarf anything we have ever seen in education. The defense and agriculture departments illustrate the possibilities.

The present structure of American education, far from conducive to the support of research, is well designed to obstruct it. Consider, for instance, the scandalous lags which occur between the discovery and the application of knowledge in education. These lags are reflected in *what* is taught, as well as *how*. For example, one of the country's outstanding authorities on the teaching of mathematics recently pointed out that a seventeenth-century mathematician would feel perfectly at home teaching in an American high school. A similar comment has been made by an outstanding physicist about the physics curriculum in our secondary schools. Even in the area of methodology, there is overwhelming evidence that vast numbers of teachers adhere to methods and techniques which have long been discredited by reliable research.

4. *The myth that state governments and local school districts have the financial resources to support an adequate educational system.*

To grasp the fallacious nature of this proposition, first consider some of the practical problems involved in introducing basic educational changes which involve heavy expenditures. Let us assume a proposal that every student who has the ability to do college work be required to take two years of physics in high school. At this point, consider only the financial problems involved. If a school is to offer two years of physics instead of one or none, extensive remodeling will almost certainly be required, plus substantial expenditures for equipment and supplies. (Just how substantial is evident from a survey made in March, 1957, by the NEA's Research Division; more than half the schools responding to its inquiries did not even have direct current in their physics laboratories; the average total expenditure per pupil for supplies and consumable equipment in science classrooms was discovered to be exactly 57c.)

In this connection, it is interesting to note that the National Defense Education Act passed in August, 1958, provided an appropriation of $300,-000,000 over a four-year period for science equipment in high schools. But it should be obvious that this appropriation, welcome as it is, will only help to solve a small part of the problem. Before most high schools could offer two years of physics, local school boards would have to adopt salary schedules much more attractive than the prevailing ones. Even though physics is now offered for only one year in the overwhelming majority of schools where it is offered at all, there is already a large and growing shortage of physics teachers. It will be interesting to see how long it takes Congress to recognize the futility of waiting for local school boards to institute salary schedules which are high enough to attract reasonably competent science teachers.

The preceding comments by no means exhaust the financial problems involved. To secure more and better physics teachers in high schools, we must first secure more and better physics teachers in colleges and universities already confronted by serious shortages. Indeed, these institutions are not even producing enough high school physics teachers to offer one year of competent instruction for all students who should take the subject.

Under our present system of financing education, the states and local communities supply over 95 per cent of funds for public education. There are several reasons why this structure is not working and can never be made to work. In the first place, some states have four to five times as much taxable wealth, on the average, as other states. The differences between school districts are even greater; some school districts have several hundred times as much taxable wealth as others. Ability to support education has also been studied in terms of what educators call "personal income payments per pupil enrolled," that is, by taking the total income received by the residents of a state and dividing this figure by the number of pupils enrolled in its public schools. In 1956–57, this ratio worked out to $17,432 in Delaware and $3,754 in Mississippi. Needless to say, the variations between school districts were even greater.

For many years, authorities on school finance have pointed out that the poorest states and school districts usually devote a higher proportion of their resources to education than do the wealthier ones. Theoretically, one might argue that this is not too important because all states and school districts should be making a greater effort to support education. However, this argument overlooks many basic factors.

One such consideration is the competitive aspect of state and local taxation. In New York City, there is a concentration of high incomes unequaled anywhere in the country. Nearly 20 per cent of all internal revenue is collected in New York State. Thus it would appear that New York City, which is permitted to levy an income tax but does not, and New York State, which does levy an income tax, could easily have the very best schools in the nation. The difficulty is, however, that many high-income persons and corporations might move if tax rates were raised substantially. This is why it is often fallacious to criticize states and communities for not raising taxes; if they did so, they would lose people and businesses to areas less concerned about education. The need for, and justice of, federal taxation would thus remain even if there were substantial equality in wealth and revenues among all states and school districts. The fact that a federal tax cannot be evaded at the expense of children in a particular school district is one of the most compelling reasons why we must move toward an educational system financed by the federal government.

Still another factor makes it very unlikely that an adequate educational system could be financed without massive federal support. School districts have been forced to raise most of their funds (54 per cent in 1953–54) by means of the property tax, the levying of which—unlike most other taxes—must usually be submitted to popular vote. As is usual in this type of situation, the people who are badly hurt by a substantial tax increase are more effective politically than the diffuse majority which benefits. The result is that an increasing number of bond issues for school funds are being defeated in communities sympathetic to public education. Here is some indication of the rising, and often justified, tide of resentment against such discriminatory taxation.

The need for federal support of public education, if not for a federal system, is also related to the way in which the federal government supports non-educational activities. In the new highway program, for example, the federal government will spend $9 for every dollar appropriated by the state governments. Obviously, this will result in a bigger share of the state dollar being spent on highways. Will this be at the expense of education? The only way that education can compete for funds, *even at the state level*, is for the federal government to assume a much bigger share of the educational budget.

Local control over curricula will be a major casualty of the growing national stake in the quality of public education. Within the foreseeable future, communities will no longer decide what subjects are to be taught in the public schools—nor will local PTA's, citizens' committees, veterans' organizations and other pressure groups which currently influence the school boards. Eventually, authority over the curriculum will be lodged with national professional agencies.

Of course, even today authority in this regard does not rest solely with local boards. In some states, certain subjects are required by state law; in others, a state government may make its financial support to school districts contingent upon compliance with state regulations concerning the curriculum. Furthermore, in approving curricula, local boards must respect the policies of accrediting agencies in order to ensure that students will be given credit when they transfer to other schools or apply for admission to college. The colleges, through admission requirements, also exert heavy pressure on the public school curriculum. Nevertheless, granting the existence of these and other pressures, it is the school board—composed of non-professionals—which ordinarily has the final word on curricula.

The folly of handing this authority to non-professionals is illustrated by the manner in which foreign languages are handled as a school subject. Many school systems offer no foreign language at all. This is not as foolish as offering it for only one or two years, as is common practice. There is no real point to the study of a foreign language unless the students acquire the power to use it—and this, with a normal curriculum, cannot be done in less than three or four years.

Offhand, one might suppose that local school boards customarily follow the recommendations of their professional staffs on all professional matters. This supposition is misleading even when true. The advice proffered by professionals is heavily influenced by their need to cater to the board's prejudices. In many communities, the professional staff dares not recommend policies which are professionally sound simply because they are not politically expedient. This point is most clearly reflected in controversies over "subversive" instructional materials. It is or ought to be obvious that instructional materials are neither subversive or non-subversive in isolation; the Constitution can be utilized for subversive purposes, just as the *Daily Worker* could have been used to expose the nature of the Communist Party. However, very few public-school teachers or school administrators would have dared to order the *Daily Worker* for classroom use. The teachers are not going to take any chances with a school board which, if it is typical, divides instructional materials into such ridiculous categories as "subversive" or "patriotic. . . ."

Many prominent critics of public education believe that public-school personnel are responsible for introducing trivial subjects into the curriculum past the unsuspecting guard of school boards. No diagnosis could be more stupid. Subjects which have no real content or professional justification do not get included because school personnel *ignores* public opinion, but because it *follows* public opinion. The criticism that school administrators try to engineer public opinion to put over their own curriculum ideas is absurd; this is precisely what they ought to be doing, and are not.

The notion that public-school personnel should not make an important change in the curriculum without first securing community support has been propagated by schools of education, and especially their departments of educational administration. This counsel is typically labeled a "democratic philosophy" of education. Advocated, as it usually is, without any conception of professional autonomy, its effect has been to make insistence upon such autonomy appear undemocratic to the teachers themselves. Indeed, it has tended to eliminate the concept of professional autonomy from the consciousness of teachers. In effect, the schools of education tell teachers they are "professionals" while simultaneously undermining the autonomy which is an essential ingredient of professional status.

Today, advocates of professional autonomy in education are often regarded as "authoritarians" or as persons who have lost faith in the democratic process. The reason is not difficult to understand. The operative cliché here is that the public should determine *what* should be taught, and the teachers should determine *how* to teach whatever it is that the public wants taught. Like most educational clichés, this one has just enough plausibility to hide its absurdity.

The crux of the matter lies in the words "what" and "how." The public determines *what* should be taught in the sense that it sets the broad purposes of education. The fallacy lies in regarding the *what* as a list of subjects instead of a set of purposes. "Teachers should teach students to communicate effectively" is one thing; "teachers should teach penmanship one hour per day in the sixth grade" is something else again. The first statement is one of purpose which should be made by the public; the second is a statement of the means to be employed, and this should never be a matter of legislation or of decision by a non-professional agency. At any time, research may justify changes in the time devoted to a subject, or the grade levels at which it is taught. This is why it is foolish for a state legislature to prescribe the curriculum.

The other side of this coin is the confusion over the *how* in "how to teach." Once it is accepted that the public should determine *the broad purposes* of education, then it becomes clear that "how to teach" refers to subjects as well as teaching methods. When we say that a doctor knows how to cure, we do not mean to limit the *how* to a bedside manner. We mean it to include the substantive knowledge which the doctor applies to achieve a desired end.

The public expects the medical profession to prolong life and to reduce physical pain. No one in his right mind assumes that the public should decide what drugs should be used and that doctors should decide only how to apply them. Absurd as this would be, it is exactly analogous to the notion that the public should determine the subjects to be taught and that teachers should decide only how to teach them. "How to teach" should be interpreted to mean, "How to achieve the goals set for the profession by the public." It would then be clear that non-professional determination of the curriculum is a threat to, not a safeguard of, our democratic institutions. And it would also be clear that the decline of local control of education means more than a simple transfer of authority from communities to the states or to the federal government. It can, and indeed it must, mean a tremendous increase in the power of the teachers as an organized group. This is the key to a number of problems which will arise during the transition to a centralized educational system.

It is difficult to predict the form which centralization will take. It may take place even while a great deal of our present educational structure formally remains intact. To understand this, one must bear in mind that a *national* system of education is not necessarily the same thing as a *federal* system. Under a federal system, the schools are operated by the federal government. But education might continue to be the legal responsibility of state and local communities, yet become substantially similar all over the country as a result of non-governmental pressures. Under these circumstances, it would make sense to speak of an educational system that was national, but not federal.

The point can be illustrated by the situation in medicine. Legally, medical education and licensure are controlled by state medical boards. Actually, these state boards are so dominated by the American Medical Association that we have, in effect, a national system. A similar situation exists in other occupations which involve professional training and licensure.

In the next few decades, it is unlikely that we shall have a *federal* school system which covers the entire country. Such a development would occur only if the failure of states and communities to carry out their educational responsibilities were to be brought home dramatically to the American people by some such event as the abolition of public education in the Deep South. I am convinced, however, that we are about to move rapidly toward a *national* system. The idea that the present chaos in education is the price one has to pay for living in a democracy, or the even more nonsensical notion that this chaos is actually a pillar of our democracy, will linger on, but without any real force in our society.

Unquestionably, the most important barrier to a centralized educational system is the notion that it would provide an opportunity for a pressure group, say a political party, to seize control of the schools, and by introducing its point of view, maintain itself in power. Those who think this way usually point to Soviet Russia to illustrate the dangers. But one cannot assume that a centralized educational system *per se* is more likely to be totalitarian than our own. England, France and the Scandinavian countries all have national systems of education. In all of these systems, there is less political interference with teachers than there is in the United States. Put positively, there is more freedom to teach and to learn in all of these national school systems than there is in the overwhelming majority of public schools in the United States.

How would any particular group in this country—religious or economic—achieve such complete control of all schools as to produce a generation of unthinking disciples? To develop such a generation would require complete control of our mass media; this, in turn, would presuppose fairly complete control of the government. Any pressure group which could achieve such controls would have no need to control the schools. Indeed, it could safely permit schools to operate as they do now, preparing generations of civic illiterates who firmly believe they have fulfilled the highest obligations of citizenship when they have flipped a lever in a voting booth.

People are opposed to a centralized system of schools for many reasons, not all of them noble. Some of the opposition comes from private-school interests which would not share in the federal funds necessary to undergird such a system. In this connection, it requires little imagination to realize that the arguments which some private-school spokesmen make against federal aid to education, or to a federal school system, are ludicrous. Private educational institutions, whose *raison d'etre* is to keep the faithful from being exposed to heretical points of view, oppose federal aid on the grounds that it would mean mass conformity and indoctrination. But the free and independent mind which these institutions claim to nurture is what some of them fear above everything else.

Nonetheless, it must be conceded that many people have a gnawing fear of a centralized school system which is devoid of any selfish motivation. Their fear is for the integrity of the system, not for the fate of their particular views on political, economic, religious, racial or other controversial issues. Ironically, their doubts are often based upon experiences with local control; and every inanity committed by a local board reinforces, rather than weakens, their distrust of a federal system. For they argue that, under the present system, the worst blunders are confined to a limited area; what would happen, they ask, if a national school board or federal school administrator were to engage in the educational follies which characterize some local school boards?

The answer is that it would be a calamity—but that the more we centralize our school system (up to a point, of course), the less likely is it that such a calamity will occur. *The crucial point is that at the national level, no one group has the kind of power to interfere with the educational program that one sees every day under a system of local control.* The rabble rousers who can successfully frighten a large city school system like Los Angeles to drop an essay contest on the United Nations would find it much more difficult to undermine the curriculum in a federal school system. Even the more legitimate pressure groups, such as the

AFL-CIO and the NAM, would be unable to shape the educational program in a federal system to their own ends. Each would be watched and checked by all the others if it attempted any massive interference. Thus, since no non-professional group would have the power to dictate, and since classrooms would not be subject to local censorship, teachers would be free to discuss points of view which are now proscribed by local boards.

But the contention that no pressure group would be able to dominate a centralized educational system does not sound very persuasive. What assurance is there that the balance of power will not change suddenly so as to provide one of the groups, or a combination of them, with the opportunity it seeks to subvert the school program to its own ends?

If by "assurance" is meant an iron-clad guarantee, of course there is none. We are choosing between practical alternatives, not between mathematical solutions, one of which is the perfect answer. It is local control of education which provides the greater opportunity, on a *national* basis, for national pressure groups to dominate the educational program of the public schools. *Local* school boards are unable to withstand the pressures which can be generated by powerful national organizations. On the other hand, in a centralized system, teachers' organizations would probably play a much more important role in protecting the integrity of public education than they do at the present time. To grasp the significance of this possibility, it is necessary to consider briefly some fundamental changes which have taken place in American society during the past 150 years.

When our nation was founded, the American people were a much more homogeneous group, in terms of occupations, than they are today. In 1789, over 90 per cent of the people made their living directly or indirectly from farming. At that time, therefore, the problem of avoiding an excessive concentration of federal authority required a geographical, rather than an occupational, distribution of power. Today, the reverse is true. A cotton farmer in Mississippi has more interests in common with cotton farmers in neighboring states than he does with engineers, teachers or grocers in his own state. Thus he attempts to advance many of his major interests through his occupational group rather than through state or local communities. I do not wish to oversimplify this situation, but there is no doubt that the distribution of power among occupational groups has tended more and more to overshadow its distribution among geographical groups.

As occupational specialization increases, so does our interdependence; and as interdependence increases, the regulation of occupational affairs becomes more and more a federal instead of a state function. And as this happens, it becomes apparent that powerful occupational organizations are necessary to prevent an excessive concentration of federal power. Example: As an increasing portion of industry and commerce becomes interstate rather than intra-state, there is more and more regulation of industry and commerce at the federal level; but standing in the way of arbitrary federal action is the emergence of occupational autonomy and strong national organizations of employers and employees.

These considerations are appropriate to education, and especially so because education is or should be a profession. A profession is an occupation which requires some kind of expertness. It is in the public interest to accord the professional worker the autonomy to make the decisions which call upon this expertness. This is why it is undesirable to have non-professional control over the curriculum in any school system.

In asserting the need for professional controls in a centralized system, I do not mean to contend that *all* professional decisions, such as those relating to curricula, should be made at the national level. Some should be made at state or local levels; others should be regarded as the prerogative of the individual teacher. This is also true of educational decisions of a non-professional nature: some should be made at the national level, others at state or local levels, and still others should be made by parents or students.

Regardless of whether a decision is professional or non-professional, the extent of state, local, and/or individual option to make it must be decided in the first instance at a more inclusive level. This is only common sense. For obvious reasons, the American people as a whole have made national defense a federal concern. On the other hand, we provide individuals with many options concerning the ways in which they can fulfill their military obligations; they can, for instance, within the limits of national policy, choose their branch of service or enlist in the Regular Army. In education, there is an urgent need for a clear-cut, comprehensive national policy outlining the educational decisions to be made at the national, state, local and individual levels.

Our chief concern should be the way in which professional opinion is recognized and articulated in a centralized educational system. For example, the fact that some educational decisions may be made by federal officials is not important *per se*. What is important is who these officials are, how they are appointed, what specific decisions they have the power to make, to what extent their tenure is dependent upon satisfying professional opinion, and so on. Those who attempt to settle concrete questions of power and authority in education by generalized appeals to the virtues of a particular level of control can be ignored with great profit.

At present, there is confusion in every direction. The line between professional and non-professional decisions has all but disappeared, with non-professional agencies making an enormous number of professional decisions. In addition, local school boards currently have the power to make all sorts of non-professional decisions which should be made at state or national levels.

It must be clearly understood that both professionalization and centralization can be overdone. There is no calculus by which we can classify decisions; each must be evaluated on its own merits to determine whether it is professional in nature and at what level it should be made. We will never make educational sense until we stop using phrases like "local control of education" or "federal control of education" or "academic freedom" as substitutes for clear thinking about the decision-making structure of education. For example, there has always been *some* federal control over public education; like any activity of state or local government, it must be carried on within the limitations set by the Constitution. All the furor over racial integration in public education should not blind us to the fact that the Supreme Court has long been deciding such issues as whether or not children in public schools must salute the flag in school, or be released for religious instruction. And although some critics may have questioned the wisdom of the Court's decisions, no one has seriously questioned its Constitutional right, its duty even, to make them.

Because, under our present system, people are accustomed to having pressure groups of every kind shaping the school program, they presuppose that the same policy would prevail under a centralized system. Obviously, if the educational program in a centralized system were to be placed under Congressional control, or under the control of a politically dominated national school board, the ensuing political melee could be disastrous. But the way out is to realize that the problem is not which public—local, state or national—should shape the educational program, but how to make certain that the program is in the hands of the teachers, where it belongs. Once the American people understand the occupational dimension to the distribution of power in our educational system, they will have overcome the major psychological barrier to centralization.

It is not just a question of whether a more centralized system would be better *if* it were characterized by professional autonomy. The crux of the matter is that centralization itself will hasten the establishment of professional autonomy. It will dramatize the admittedly abysmal weaknesses of current teacher organizations and put in motion the forces eliminating the weaknesses. Centralization and professionalization are inevitable not in spite of what people think, but because enough people will eventually think long enough and hard enough about public education to realize that no other policy makes sense.

THE QUESTION OF FOOD: BRANNAN TO BENSON TO BRANNAN / REO M. CHRISTENSON

Although Ezra Taft Benson's political foes haven't been able to reverse the drift of his policies for five long years, the American farmer may be ready to do the job himself. A recent bulletin from the crop-reporting service indicates that the farmer, operating under conditions approaching those recommended by the Secretary, is girding himself to produce the most handsome surpluses yet. With the government's hoard already exceeding $9 billion, another record crop should just about set the stage for the derailing of Benson's program. It may also bring about the resurrection of the much abused but perennially intriguing Brannan Plan.

Brannan's program, badly mauled by its enemies and then kicked to death in 1949, has been twitching in its grave ever since. According to the politically sagacious columnist Joseph Alsop, a modified form is "almost certain to become the Democratic farm plank in 1960." Certain or not, a system of free market prices combined with direct payments to maintain a minimum income for family farmers stands an excellent chance of getting the kind of serious Congressional attention it has never really had.

Our mountainous pile of surplus commodities is only one factor paving the way for a radical shift in national farm policy. Another is the breath-taking and somewhat absurd $7 billion agricultural budget, which includes more than $1 billion annually just for managing the government-held surpluses. This budget is causing more head-shaking than almost any farm phenomenon since Henry Wallace's massacre of the poor little pigs in 1933.

Still another factor is the steep rise in our feed-grain supplies, which threatens a major decline in hog and—later—other livestock prices. Here is one of several developments which lead even the Department of Agriculture to predict a drop in farm income this year. Finally, the Democrats, well pleased with 1958 election returns in rural areas, are out to tighten their grip on the votes Benson has so obligingly tossed their way. Under these circumstances, it would be remarkable if the farm program were to escape the Congressional scalpel much longer.

Beyond the budget statistics and the policies is a growing awareness that Benson's analysis of the farm problem is both superficial and faulty. The Secretary has declared repeatedly that our price-support system is primarily responsible for surpluses. He insists it has artificially stimulated excess output, distorted the production pattern and kept land in cultivation that ought to be retired. Above all, he has preached with evangelical zeal that government controls and subsidies rob farmers of that independence and self-reliance which have been the glory of American agriculture. Get the government out of the farm sector—well, almost out—and the self-correcting forces of a free economy will bring blessed relief from the iniquities of the paternalistic state.

All this is hailed by practically all businessmen as the kind of turkey-talk which may be politically inexpedient, but which represents sane, sound, 100 per cent Americanism. But thoughtful students of agriculture are increasingly of the opinion that Benson has been ignoring or minimizing vital facts.

They argue that the primary blame for farm surpluses rests not on the system of price supports, but rather on science. Recent advances in technology have been more spectacular in agriculture than in almost any other phase of American industry. Improved machinery, insecticides, fertilizers, seeds, chemical weed-killers, the use of antibiotics in livestock feed, the spread of artificial insemination and other improved breeding practices—these and other technical developments primarily account for the amazing productivity of American agriculture. Technology explains why crop production in 1958, although it involved the fewest acres in forty years, exceeded previous records by about 11 per cent. Technology also principally accounts for the fact that annual farm output is increasing considerably faster than increases in demand.

As for the comfortable assumption that lower price supports will help persuade the backward, marginal farmer to seek greener pastures in the city, leaving the more efficient farmers to prosper despite lower price levels, reputable studies show that it is the presence of off-the-farm job opportunities, rather than low farm prices, which accelerates the exodus from the farm. For that mattter, it is argued plausibly that whenever less efficient farmers decide to leave the soil, their land is usually purchased by the more efficient, whose enlarged holdings and superior practices enable them to increase production. With the nation's agriculture already turning out 5 to 8 per cent more farm commodities than the market can absorb at reasonable price levels, this looks like something less than a sensible solution.

Benson's theory, it is conceded, might work if it were carried to its logical conclusion. Dr. Walter W. Wilcox of the Legislative Reference Service, Library of Congress, and one of the nation's foremost students of agriculture, has calculated that a completely free market would slash net farm income by from 25 to 40 per cent. This in turn might cut farm production by (1) touching off a wave of bankruptcies and farm foreclosures, and (2) putting most remaining farmers in such straitened economic circumstances that they could not obtain the credit they need, or buy new machinery, or otherwise take advantage of the latest technological advances.

No doubt there is a point at which agriculture becomes so financially depressed that output will fall. But is this really the way to solve the problem? Unhappily, a 25 to 40 per cent income cut would leave the average family-farmer sagging against the ropes, with only the biggest, most highly mechanized farmer able to carry on at reasonable income levels.

If farm income were already at satisfactory levels, a decline of 25 to 40 per cent might be looked upon with somewhat greater equanimity. But returns to farm labor and management in 1957 approximated only 69 cents an hour, compared to $2.07 an hour for workers in manufacturing concerns. And the average income of the 2.2 million most productive American farmers in 1956 was about $1,500 less than that of the average non-farm family. For the other 2.6 million farms, incomes from all sources fall far below urban levels (about 1.5 million net less than $1,500 a year). Under these conditions, a major reduction in farm income can be regarded only as a major disaster.

Congress has other alternatives, of course, than a refurbished Brannan Plan. Some economists insist that overproduction will be with us until Congress musters the courage to take some sixty to seventy million acres of land permanently out of production. Land retirement on this scale would admittedly be a costly operation, but spending billions to solve the surplus problem might be preferable to spending billions not solving it, proponents declare. Even Secretary Benson is reportedly preparing to recommend further enlargement of the land-retirement program. This could be done by expanding the "conservation reserve" residue of the "soil bank," which has already retired about twenty-three million acres of relatively poor and unproductive land.

But such a plan, applied on a sufficiently grand scale to eliminate surpluses, would create some serious problems of its own. As long as land retirement affects only the poorest land, it makes only a minor dent in the surplus stockpile. But when it begins to embrace more productive land, two things happen: (1) costs rise steeply and (2) small-town merchants in areas heavily affected by the program experience a local depression because purchases of machinery, feed, seeds, fertilizers, etc. fall off sharply. Solving the surplus problem by depressing the income of thousands of small businessmen is not an attractive solution, as Congress concluded when it killed the acreage-reserve program in 1958, largely because this unexpected side-effect emerged in so many Southern states.

A further complication lies in public resentment of programs which enable farmers to place their entire farms in a soil bank while they slip off to Florida and live off their federal rent checks. This goes against the grain of farmers and city folks alike and constitutes a formidable barrier to important extensions of the program. An alternative might be a federal *purchase* program, but this would involve a staggering initial investment.

Congress might also revive, in some form or other, the 1958 proposal of the National Conference of Commodity Organizations for dealing with the disturbing increase in feed-grain supplies. The NCCO suggested that farmers be paid from surplus grain stocks for retiring a substantial percentage of their acreage from feed-grain production. This would slacken current feed-grains output and reduce government holdings without obliging farmers who feed their grain on the farm to cut back livestock production. This program (which actually originated among career men in the Department of Agriculture) has considerable merit, and there is a good chance it will be given a trial one of these days.

It is probable, however, that none of these programs will satisfy Congress or the Democratic Presidential candidate in 1960. Indications are that Senate Democrats (led by Senators Hubert Humphrey and Herman Talmadge) will eventually rally behind a modified Brannan Plan which will guarantee farmers producing major commodities 90 or 100 per cent of parity-income protection on that portion of their output which is used for domestic consumption. To prevent large producers from gorging at public expense, a fairly low ceiling on total payments to any individual would be established.

For example, under the plan wheat producers would sell their wheat in the open market for whatever it would bring. But if only 70 per cent of the total national production is consumed domestically, the individual producer would get a federal check for the difference between the market price and a price equaling 90 or 100 per cent of parity on only 70 per cent of his wheat up to a maximum payment of $12,500 per farmer (this ceiling is some 50 per cent below the figure suggested by Brannan in 1949). Since farmers net from 35 to 40 per cent of their gross, the plan would provide income protection up to $4,000 to $5,000 per farmer, while leaving the big producer to shift for himself in a free market to whatever extent his annual sales exceeded $12,500.

The ceiling is an eminently sensible device. One of the glaring defects of the farm program to date has been its tendency to lavish federal aid on those who need it least, while providing precious little help for those who need it most. And while it is true that American farm income is generally inadequate, scores of thousands of farmers have been and are doing very well indeed. Some of them rake in scandalous sums from the federal government. Helping reasonably efficient family-farmers to obtain incomes comparable to those of manufacturing workers can be defended; using factory wage-earners' taxes to put many farmers on easy street cannot.

Of crucial importance, also, is the fact that a low ceiling would keep total farm-program costs at levels the taxpayer could afford to pay.

The purposes of the Democratic plan are fairly obvious. It would eliminate most of the present system of agricultural-production controls. It would halt most government purchases of surplus farm commodities. It would protect the family farm while preventing the biggest and wealthiest farmers from plundering the public treasury. It would put a stop to the nonsensical practice of using tax money to raise the price of food (which the price-support system does). It would reduce inflationary pressures. It would encourage a major shift toward livestock farming, thereby diminishing the huge stockpile of feed-grains and cutting the price of meat to the housewife without breaking the livestock farmer in the process.

And, of special interest to Messrs. Humphrey and Talmadge, it might go a long way toward cementing the Democratic Party's hold on the affections of the family farmer.

Would such a plan have a chance in Congress, considering the rude reception the Brannan Plan received in 1949? At the time it was proposed, the plan ignited the most intense hostility of the Farm Bureau, the Republican Party and virtually every conservative newspaper, magazine and organization in the country. CIO Political Action Committee support for it was effectively used by labor's enemies to prove the plan's sinister character. Every epithet in the arsenal of political abuse was hurled at Brannan (although it might be noted that Brannan often gave even better than he got). Southern Democrats finally broke ranks under the massive propaganda bombardment and joined the GOP in plumping for 90 per cent of parity-price supports as an alternative to a trial run for the plan.

Things are different today. For one thing, Brannan invited legitimate criticism by calling for farm-income protection tied to the inflated farm-income levels of World War II. This cost him the support of many responsible groups which found the plan attractive in other respects. Moreover, the Farm Bureau has less influence with Congress than it had in 1949, and it has lost a valuable ally in the National Grange. The ranks of the GOP have been heavily depleted in recent years and further thinning may lie ahead in 1960.

Finally, Southern legislators are much less likely to defect from a Brannan-type plan these days. For several years the South has been ready to accept a free-market, direct-payment plan for cotton, and only Benson's adamant opposition has prevented it from becoming enacted into law. Not only will Senator Talmadge (who has already introduced a Brannan-type bill) help hold the South in line, but Lyndon Johnson is known to be sympathetic to a farm program of this general character. Johnson presumably realizes that it can be helpful in preventing a party split in 1960, and he is anxious to latch on to any policy which can provide a bond between the Southern and Northern wings of the party.

No one can predict just what will happen in 1960, but something big is almost sure to shape up on the farm front. Whatever its anatomy, it can hardly fail to improve upon the crippled critter Benson rides today.

HOUSING: HOW TO BUILD A SLUM /
TIMOTHY J. COONEY

It might be felt that in the richest nation on earth—indeed, in one that has been accused of sacrificing the "truly important" for physical comfort and good health—the building of a slum would be a next-to-impossible task. Fortunately, however, in this welfare age the United States is still a land of opportunity. If you are willing to work and have a bit of that old American know-how, there are limitless horizons to be found in slum-building. In this brief article I would like to offer encouragement to those who are considering entering the field and outline certain steps that must be taken in the development of a first-class slum. For the purpose of illustration I shall refer to examples from New York City—my own city, where much fine work is being done.

Experts in the field recognize three opponents to successful slum development. They are: (1) old-fashioned, unimaginative landlords; (2) municipal ordinances and regulations; (3) the ghost of equal opportunity. Ironically, despite the fact that Opponent (3) is only a phantasma, it is potentially the most dangerous. Let us develop an imaginary slum and face each opponent as we come upon it.

The slum-builder must begin with a city with a tight housing market and a population of at least a hundred thousand. The bigger the city and the tighter the housing market, the better the chance of a good slum (but there is no reason to leave your own city simply because it doesn't have the population of a New York or Chicago—fine work has been done in smaller communities). The next job is to choose a particular area for slum development. Your goal should be to turn at least three-quarters of your city into a slum, but for several reasons it is necessary to begin with a particular area. Furthermore, it is important that this area be one of your city's most attractive, white, residential sections; if possible one that has qualities that make it "intrinsically desirable." For example, slum-builders in New York City showed amazing courage—matched only by their success—in attacking the famed Morningside Heights area. What was done to Morningside Heights—"intrinsically desirable" with its park, view of the Hudson River and Columbia University campus—is a credit to the profession. There is not only an increased sense of achievement in ruining a nice area, but, of practical importance, there is the psychologically devastating effect—if it could happen there, it could happen everywhere. The ruination of a nice area serves to break down the will to resist further slum development.

Having chosen a site, the next step is to choose a particular apartment building. At this point you probably will face your first opponent—the old-fashioned, unimaginative landlord. Basically, this type of landlord (happily fast disappearing) is an opponent to slum development because (1) he adheres to the "keeping up the property" fallacy; (2) he tends to be squeamish. The "keeping up the property" fallacy is that in apartment-house ownership, as in other forms of business, it is necessary to repair and maintain one's property, in order to assure profit. The fact is that if Opponents (2) and (3) can be licked and we can build our slum, there is *more* profit to be realized from a deteriorating apartment building than from one that is kept in repair. In the beginning, this fact, so contrary to common sense, can be grasped only by the imaginative landlord.

Yet even if the landlord can grasp "keeping up the property" as a fallacy, he may be troubled by a certain squeamishness. Neighbors have a way of making the landlord who is preparing his property for slum development uncomfortable. Consequently, you, the slum-developer, are most apt to find enlightenment among those landlords who do not live on or even near their property. The absentee landlord's appreciation of the added income that a slum property will bring is inviolable; it cannot be spoiled by the stares and old-fashioned ways of his neighbors. If you find a landlord who can comprehend the irrefutable logic of this, you may proceed; if such a landlord cannot be found, you may have to purchase and develop the first slum building yourself. In either case, all that is needed is one building to get the ball rolling.

The next step is to take apartments, as they become vacant, and divide them into many "apartments" of one room each. These new "apartments" must now be rented to members of minority groups (preferably Negroes) with families. The "apartments" must be rented to these people regardless of who else wants them or what others are willing to pay. The importance of renting to minority families cannot be overemphasized. As we shall see in a moment, they are the key to successful slum development and they reward the landlord with a "special bonus."

Once the building is 50 per cent rented, all services and maintenance must be stopped. Heat and hot water must be all but done away with. The savings to the landlord will be considerable. The effect on neighboring buildings will be immediate. The most old-fashioned landlord will begin to appreciate the fact, even if he doesn't like it, that there is much money to be made by stopping all repairs and services. The "keeping up the property" fallacy should begin to crumble.

At this point, however, two things will happen. Opponent (2) will appear, and those living in the building of the enlightened landlord will want to move out.

Opponent (2) will rear its bureaucratic head in the form of health, fire and building regulations; but its bark is worse than its bite. There are a number of factors working in favor of the landlord who will not be intimidated. Regulations do not enforce themselves; men enforce them—and men, as the New York example has shown, can be bought. If the inspectors become greedy, it may be cheaper for the landlord to pay the trivial fines that are imposed. Such is the extent of the "keeping up the property" fallacy that—with the one exception of arson—there are no substantive laws hampering the landlord who has conscientiously decided to let his property go to pot. However, at this point it may be advisable for you, as a public-spirited slum-builder, to go directly to the politician and soft-head types with the plea, "If every silly rule and regulation is enforced, where will these poor unfortunates live?" This argument is sure fire and does much to take the pressure off enlightened, though timid, landlords.

Naturally those living in the deteriorating buildings will want to move. Despite some helpful and popular stereotypes to the contrary, no one likes to live in a slum. Now however, our original planning will begin to pay off, provided we can lick our third and final opponent. In every American city there are exclusive, white, residential sections—even white, Protestant sections—maintained by statute, agreement or custom. The slum-developer must do all within his power to still the ghost of equal opportunity that threatens this American institution. The all-white sections are essential to successful slum development. They must be maintained (until we decide to turn *them* into slums). The reason is obvious. With a "whites only" barricade (or other slums) surrounding our developing slum, there will be no escape for our selected tenants. Their color and ancestry will trap them.

In a country where little children hear tell of the Declaration of Independence and the Bill of Rights, Opponent (3) will always be a threat. But this ghost—and surely it is no more than that—should be no match for a cunning, living body of bigotry. If we will sustain the bigotry, it will sustain our ghetto-slum. And with our ghetto-slum thriving, it will be time for the landlords to realize their "special bonus." *They may begin to raise their rents.* Impossible? Not at all. It is only in those naive books on how to manage a budget that families are advised to spend but a fifth of their income on rent. In 1957, Governor Harriman of New York made a tour of Harlem and discovered that Negroes, living in highly developed one- and two-room slum "apartments," were paying $20 to $25 a week per room. If they didn't like the price for what they were getting, they were free to drop dead. The ghetto is a seller's paradise.

What landlord can resist the lure of the slums once the facts are known? Contrary to current mouthings, there is much money to be made in bigotry.

The slum we have been considering is now, for all practical purposes, complete. It just requires aging. The ambitious slum-builder will move on to new areas and even new cities. The keys to successful slum development are a tight housing market, enlightened landlords, graft, avarice and, most important of all, plenty of Americans whom other Americans don't want to live next to. If we can just maintain an environment in which this happy combination can flourish there is no reason why, in time, every city in America can't have a substantial slum. The task is a challenge in such a wealthy country as ours, but it is a challenge that men are successfully meeting every day of the year.

LEADERLESS DECENCY: THE SOUTH STALLS ITS FUTURE / HARRY GOLDEN

The majority of "white" Southerners believe that racial segregation can no longer be maintained on a moral, religious or legal basis; the business community itself is becoming completely bored with the entire controversy, and the boredom may be related to the highly significant fact that the several state public relations commissions have stopped issuing reports of the influx of new industry into the South.

The tragedy of the moment is that this "majority" is silent, and in all fairness it must be said that it is silent for good and sufficient reason. The changing of a social order is not a simple matter, not even for the decent, warm-hearted people of the South. It requires Leadership, a leadership which unfortunately has not yet materialized. The politicians in the state capitals have a vested interest in this "silence." They have been riding the race issue for seventy-five years and they will not surrender it without a bitter struggle. If all the obstacles were to be removed from the Negro's path to the voting booth, the white man would also begin to vote, and there is no telling what could happen under those circumstances.

And the most amazing thing of all; that in this vacuum President Eisenhower has said, not once, but twice: *"Mere law will not solve this problem."* One hundred and eighty years ago another Presbyterian, the Reverend William Tennant of South Carolina, said it in another way. In those days the Presbyterians had to build their little church with an open fireplace. When the Anglican sheriff came along the worshipers could say that they were merely visiting a private dwelling. Reverend Tennant went to the South Carolina Constitutional Convention and demanded freedom of worship; complete separation of church and state; and he refused to be sweet-talked. He said, "The Law does not change as often as the hearts of men; put it into the Law; this is all I want."

With all due respect to the noise about "states' rights," the tremendously expanding middle-class of the South is the direct result of the "interference" of the Federal Government since March 4, 1932, and it is the President of the United States who has it in his power to establish the atmosphere, actually to set the pattern which would break the "silence." I'll give you an example of the extent of this "silence."

A week or so ago [August, 1958] I visited the home of Dorothy Counts, the 15-year-old Negro girl of Charlotte, North Carolina, who had been forced to leave the all-white school to which she had been assigned, due to an ordeal of uninterrupted harassment and violence. Her father, Reverend Herman L. Counts, on the faculty of Johnson C. Smith University, showed me the names of the people who had called him to express horror, chagrin and sympathy; and the list included some of the most influential citizens of North Carolina. Why didn't these people call the school board instead, or the principal of Dorothy's school, or why didn't they write a letter to the editor? The embattled editors of both the *Charlotte Observer* and the *Charlotte News* would have jumped for joy at the sight of such expressions from the "upper echelon." They might very well have settled the matter for at least one of the most progressive cities of the South; but as far as the public is concerned, "silence" prevails; this is the most important race relations story, as the South enters its fifth school year since the Supreme Court decision of May 17, 1954.

And because of "silence" the politicians with the vested interest and the bigots are allowed to confuse the problem further with a few more legends. The first of these is the myth that if the NAACP suddenly disappeared, everything would be right back where it was in the days when Sambo rolled in laughter under the old magnolia tree. Even the few outspoken liberals, when accused by Governor Faubus of being in the pay of the NAACP, defended themselves by saying that they hate the NAACP and the Ku Klux Klan with equal passion. And, of course, this renunciation of logic adds to the general stalemate. It is utter nonsense because the break-down of racial segregation is part of the greater story of the whole South and the overthrow of agriculture as the dominant way of life.

When the late James B. Duke, the tobacco king, built the first dam on the Catawba River to industrialize the South, he did more to end racial segregation than all the NAACP's put together. It is part of a development which wise Southerners saw long ago. I remember one afternoon when the late novelist James Street made a speech to a group of young Southern fiction writers. In answer to the inevitable question: "How can I get into the *Saturday Evening Post?*" the Mississippi-born Street replied: "First off, forget the 'Nigra' story you've been working on; the *Post* will not publish a story about Sambo with Dr. Ralph Bunche around." That was five years before the Supreme Court decision. There are sections of the South, for example, Montgomery and Birmingham, and certainly the cities of North Carolina's Piedmont, where the native Negro leadership is far ahead of the NAACP in its efforts to end segregation in the public facilities. Two years ago the governor of my state spoke at a convention of Negro school teachers. He hinted that many of them would probably lose their jobs if the public schools were desegregated. An hour later the teachers voted unanimously to support the desegregation of the public schools "with all deliberate speed."

And it is precisely the interpretation of this "with all deliberate speed" that poses a new problem in the way of compliance. Last year the school board of Charlotte assigned a "token" Negro child to each of five different public schools, and the fact that the board has decided against any additional assignments this year is not due entirely to the smashing victory of Governor Faubus of Arkansas. This "with all deliberate speed" will never work unless the individual school board announces a "blanket" decision to the effect that the schools of the city are hereby "desegregated" in accordance with the law. Even that will not take away from them the right, under various new state laws, to screen the applicants and make their assignments. And the tragedy of "token" assignments to a few selected schools is that it creates the atmosphere of "an experiment" instead of a basic law which accords twenty-six per cent of the South's population the right to enter the industrial age. Thus the mother of a child at the Fair Haven High School says, "We don't have any," which creates an entirely new problem for the mother of a child at the Central High School. Her protestation that "We only have *one*" is irrelevant. She fears the stratification of the "white" social classes at this new level. The struggle for status within the white population is keeping pace with the intense urbanization and the burgeoning of a new middle class from out of the farm houses and mountain cabins of the region.

These "token" assignments also set the stage for a bit of cruelty. In "screening" the twenty-two Negro students who had made applications for transfer to desegregated schools for the coming school year, the Mecklenburg County School Board (rural areas of Charlotte) asked each student: "Aren't you happy among your own people?" An adult can laugh off that old chestnut about "when did you stop beating your wife," but for a 15-year-old Negro child, caught up in a historical controversy and making his first foray into unsegregated society, it could be both bewildering and cruel. And the process is not without irony. When Dorothy Counts was so severely harassed on her first day in school, the principal suggested that she use the rear entrance, the "back door," and her father told him: "Why, that's the whole idea; the *front door* is the point of the whole matter."

I think it might be wise to break up this narrative with a light interlude. The other day the Fellowship of Reconciliation (my fellow pacifists), had written me to act as host for a day to their representative, the Methodist minister, Mr. Lawson. I had never met Mr. Lawson and when he called me late in the evening from the bus station, I told him that I had reserved a room for him at a downtown hotel, to have a good night's sleep, and come to my home for breakfast the next morning at eight o'clock. But at seven o'clock the hotel manager called: "Mr. Golden, what color is Reverend Lawson?" I told the hotel man that I had never met Mr. Lawson; "but how many colors are there; which color do you think he is?" The manager said that the consensus at the hotel was that Mr. Lawson was a Negro. But, of course, the fellow had already slept there and how could segregation be made retroactive? But a bit of kindness is never out of order. I told the manager that his overnight guest was from India; and I am glad to report that Mr. Lawson was very forgiving when I told him of the sigh of relief the hotel manager expressed at this reassurance.

But there's more trouble. The *Southern Advertising and Publishing*, a trade publication (Atlanta, Georgia) which serves the advertising agencies of the South, had itself a little editorial ("The South's Story Must Be Told,"—July 15, 1958):

> It is a notorious fact that every Jewish organization and every Jewish-controlled segment of the media of communication is siding with the NAACP in this vilification of the South.

... they [the Jews] have no business making common cause with the Negroes against the South.

When I read this editorial, I thought at once of Charles Bloch, the famous Jewish lawyer of Macon, Georgia. Mr. Bloch is the fellow who led the Georgia delegation out of the Democratic convention in 1948 as a protest against the "civil rights" plank and he was a stalwart of the Dixiecrat movement. Mr. Bloch is now the vice president of the Georgia States-Rights Society, and he has written a book (*States-Rights—The Law of the Land*, The Harrison Company, Atlanta) in which he says that we must construe the clause in the Declaration of Independence that "all men are created equal" in the light of the times when it was promulgated. "Since at that time Negroes were not 'men' but property, we are bound today to permit states to legislate about them as property." So help me, that's what Mr. Bloch says in his book; and a few miles away at Atlanta this *Southern Advertising and Publishing*, in its editorial about the "Jews making common cause against the South," does not even say "Except for Charles Bloch of Macon." As I told the few White Citizens Council Jews in Alabama: "Nothing helps, you may as well be humanitarians, nothing helps."

I think these sad tales are pertinent to the most tragic story of the South today. They underline the fact that this great civilization with its millions of kind people is wholly preoccupied with an unnecessary problem. The South has produced some of the most creative minds of the American civilization, but all creative intellectuality has come to a halt. They are not thinking about the basic strategy of the free world against totalitarian tyranny; they are worring about a 15-year-old Negro girl going to a public school. And the main point of the matter is not what this "resistance" is doing to the Negro children, but what it is doing to the white children. But that problem the segregationist refuses to acknowledge.

The real victims of Little Rock and Clinton and Dorothy Counts's high school in Charlotte are the small group of white students who sought to drive the Negroes from the schools. The record of the Negroes, what they did and their courage and good will, is already clear. But what has been little recognized is the fact that the segregationist students, the white students, really suffered and will continue to suffer all of their lives. And what a pity! They are the ones hurt by the willingness of school officials to let them run the school. Some of them in Little Rock and Clinton and Charlotte have always been problems. No school leader, academically, athletically or socially, was involved in any of these groups which resorted to abuse and violence against the Negro children. At least one of the white girls, now speaking throughout the South for the White Citizens Councils, lived a good part of the school year under a doctor's care and sedatives. These white students lost a school year—it would be an interesting study to find out how they fared for the year; how many passed. I was able to check up on only one of the white boys who had spit on Dorothy Counts and tripped her in the high school cafeteria, and he, himself, is out of school now—gone. For these few unfortunate white students the real issue is not "integration," but, "How can I escape my own problems?" The school authorities provided these students with a handy issue which kept them from ever having to face their real problems of the life ahead.

It is not on the basis of partisanship at all. I have a deep and sincere respect and affection for President Eisenhower and the tremendous burden he is carrying, but this matter is squarely up to him. He must provide the leadership, and it is well to note that the failure goes much deeper than the White House in setting the pattern. It involves the complete failure of the Federal Government's role in following up the order of the Supreme Court; the failure of non-discrimination in government employment and employment on government contracts as they apply particularly to the South. The Federal Government is the largest single source of potential jobs for Negroes, North and South, and now must assume the main responsibility for the "mass resistance" it has allowed to organize. The Southerners who eventually break the "silence" will one day look back upon it with great pride and honor as twenty-six per cent of the South's population takes its place with human dignity in the continued growth and accumulation of wealth and property of the great Southland.

YOUNG JIM CROW / C. VANN WOODWARD

"Oh, these grand, immutable, all-wise laws of natural forces," wrote Andrew Carnegie in 1886, "how perfectly they work if human legislators would only let them alone!"

For a long time this has been the classic appeal of those who want to be left alone by meddling lawmakers and courts. Defenders of segregation, like defenders of the status quo in other fields, have appealed to laissez-faire doctrine according to Herbert Spencer in their fight against innovation and reform. Leave everything to "natural forces," they argue, and all will be well.

Segregationists have supplemented the Spencerian argument with the doctrines of William Graham Sumner, the Yale sociologist, and his *Folkways*, published in 1907. It was Sumner's teaching that "state-ways cannot change folkways" and that "legislation cannot make mores." These folkways of Sumner bore a family resemblance to the natural forces of Spencer. They were the product of "natural" as against "artificial" causes and shared some of the irresistible nature of biological imperatives. Such imperatives, the nineteenth century had been taught to believe, were not to be regarded lightly. Good Darwinians held them to be the secret of survival and progress. Sumner described his folkways as "uniform, universal in the group, imperative and invariable." In addition they had the prestige of being very old, very durable, and of somewhat mysterious origin.

In their reliance upon the Spencerian and the Sumnerian imperatives, however, segregationists have involved themselves in some unacknowledged inconsistencies and contradictions. In the first place, in defiance of Spencer's principles, they have repeatedly resorted to legislation to interfere with and change the racial status quo. Indeed, they have cited Spencer and Sumner on the utter futility of legislation in support of an elaborate program of legislation to alter racial relations. In the second place, scarcely any of the adjectives that Sumner used to characterize his folkways can be accurately applied to the segregation code. Segregation practices have not only been changed but created by "stateways." They can be described neither as uniform nor as invariable, for they have varied widely both in place and time. There is nothing very mysterious about their origin. And, finally, they are not nearly so old as has been generally assumed.

Segregation is a relatively recent phase in the long history of the white man's ways of controlling the Negro and fixing his status, his "place." There have been other and harsher phases, including bondage and limited servitude. Slavery, peonage and abortive types of apprenticeship have had their day. Exploitation of the Negro by the white man goes back to the beginning of relations between the races, and so do race conflict, brutality and injustice, mitigated in some degree by various types of paternalism. Along with these practices there developed the old assumptions of Anglo-Saxon superiority and African inferiority, white supremacy and Negro subordination.

It is perfectly true, therefore, that some of the unhappy aspects of race relations in America have a remote origin and a long history. But this cannot be said of the segregation code of the present day. The physical separation of the races by law would have been inconvenient, not to say impracticable, under the slave system. The supervision, care, exploitation and policing of slaves on the plantation necessitated many close contacts and accustomed the races to a degree of intimacy that outlasted slavery itself.

It is a mistake to assume that segregation followed hard upon emancipation. The number of contacts between races diminished as the freedmen threw off old restraints. The withdrawal of the Negroes from the great Protestant churches and the establishment of independent organizations of their own were steps essential to their cultural freedom. The result was segregation in the religious community. The principle of separation of the races in public schools was entrenched during Reconstruction, and segregation in the military services, an old practice, was simply continued. Segregation in church, school and military was therefore a product of Reconstruction or earlier periods.

After Reconstruction was overthrown, the South retained such segregation practices as had already been established, but showed no immediate disposition to expand the code into other fields. Nearly a generation was to pass before segregation became the harsh, rigid and universal system that emerged in the twentieth century.

There were several reasons for this. In the first place, the Negroes had not yet crowded into the cities in large numbers and the racial tensions of urban industrial life had not yet taken the form of a powerful demand for Jim Crowism. Even when the demand did arise there were practical difficulties. It was expensive to provide separate facilities—however unequal—in trains, stations, streetcars and factories, in public buildings, parks, playgrounds and institutions. Taxpayers as well as private enterprise showed a natural resistance to the outlay involved. The Negroes themselves could offer some resistance, for until the end of the nineteenth century they continued to vote in large numbers in most of the Southern states.

More important still as a source of resistance to extreme racism was the conservative philosophy of the Southern rulers who took charge after the overthrow of Reconstruction and dominated the South for two decades. They professed an attitude of aristocratic paternalism toward the Negro. The conservative thought of himself as standing midway between the doctrinaire Northern Negrophile of the Left and the fanatical Southern Negrophobe of the Right, both of whom he pictured as enemies of the freedmen's true interests. He believed that the Negro belonged in a subordinate role, but denied that subordinates had to be ostracized; he thought that the Negro belonged to an inferior race, but denied that inferiors had to be segregated or publicly humiliated. Conservative politicians needed Negro votes to maintain their governments.

So long as the conservative truce prevailed and resistance continued in other quarters, Jim Crowism remained under control. Testimony of Northern reformers, foreign investigators, Southern writers and Negroes themselves agree that through the seventies and eighties and up into the nineties the Negro enjoyed a degree of freedom from segregation that he was not to enjoy in the twentieth-century South. This freedom lasted longer in the old seaboard South than in the western South. In 1885, a Negro newspaperman from Boston reported to his paper that he had traveled by train "through Delaware, Maryland, Virginia, the Carolinas, Georgia and into Florida, all the old slave States with enormous Negro populations" and that in all of them he found "a first-class ticket is good in a first-class coach." From Columbia, South Carolina, he wrote: "I feel about as safe here as in Providence, R. I. I can ride in first-class cars on the railroads and in the streets. I can go into saloons and get refreshments even as in New York. I can stop in and drink a glass of soda and be more politely served than in some parts of New England."

Conditions in Columbia were not the rule in the South, nor are they represented as typical. But the fact that they prevailed in South Carolina provides an instructive contrast with what was to come later. South Carolina was one of the last Southern states to capitulate to the movement for segregation laws. In 1897, the Charleston *News and Courier*, which calls itself the oldest paper in the South, voiced strong opposition to a proposed Jim Crow law for trains. "Our opinion is that we have no more need for a Jim Crow system this year than we had last year, and a great deal less than we had twenty and thirty years ago." Such a law was "unnecessary and uncalled for" and "a needless affront to our respectable and well-behaved colored people." The following year, 1898, the same paper ridiculed the proposal for a Jim Crow law for trains on the grounds that it would be just as logical to apply the same principle to streetcars, waiting rooms, passenger-boats, and all public accommodations, services and conveniences.

The segregation movement had already made some gains in the nineties, but the big turning point that marked the capitulation to extreme racism did not come till toward the end of the nineteenth century. The way was cleared for the extremists by a complex of events. A severe depression raised a demand for scapegoats and precipitated a political crisis. To divert the wrath of the Populist revolt, the conservatives abandoned their stand for moderation in race policy and lifted the cry of Negro domination and white supremacy. The Populists deserted their Negro allies, blamed them for the downfall of Populism and joined the white supremacy crusade. The Supreme Court of the United States removed the last constitutional obstacles to segregation in 1896 by the *Plessy vs. Ferguson* decision and endorsed the disfranchisement of the Negro in 1898 by the *Williams vs. Mississippi* decision. Within a decade the Negroes had been effectively and thoroughly deprived of the ballot throughout the Southern states.

In the meantime the country embarked in 1898 on imperialistic adventures that brought more than eight million people of color under American rule without their consent. These acquisitions and the problems of ruling them gave the North and West a new and much more sympathetic view of the aggressive race policy of the South. Imperialism did much to lower Northern resistance to Southern racism.

It was only after the turn of the century that the great proliferation of Jim Crow laws took place. Up to 1900 the only law of this type adopted by the majority of Southern states was that applying to railway trains. South Carolina did not adopt that until 1898, North Carolina until 1899 and Virginia until 1900. Only three states had required or authorized separate waiting rooms in railway stations before 1899, but in the next decade nearly all the remaining states of the South fell into line. Laws applying to new fields tended to spread in waves of popularity. Only Georgia had a segregation law applying to street cars before the end of the century. Then in quick succession North Carolina and Virginia adopted such a law in 1901, Louisiana in 1902, Arkansas, South Carolina and Tennessee in 1903, Mississippi and Maryland in 1904, Florida in 1905 and Oklahoma in 1907. Montgomery, Alabama, in 1906 earned the distinction of requiring the first completely separate Jim Crow streetcar.

The mushrooming growth of segregation laws during the first two decades of the present century piled up the huge bulk of existing legislation on the subject. Much of the code was contributed by city ordinances or local rules and customs enforced without the formality of laws. The little painted signs "White" or "Colored" appeared with increasing regularity over entrances and exits, toilets and drinking fountains, waiting rooms and ticket windows. The Jim Crow code was applied in sports and recreations, in public parks and cemeteries, in hospitals and prisons. Everywhere it appeared, the principle of segregation was defended as "inevitable" and as having the sanction of ancient and immemorial usage.

The fact is that many of those who are presently defending the Jim Crow laws as ancient and immemorial folkways are older than the laws they are defending.

NARCOTICS: CONGRESS ENCOURAGES THE TRAFFIC / ALFRED R. LINDESMITH

A year ago [1956] I warned in these columns that a Senate subcommittee chaired by Senator Price Daniel had recommended for passage a new antinarcotics bill which would set a new low in a field already characterized by ill-conceived legislation. Since that time the bill, known as the Narcotics Control Act of 1956, has become law. It increased the already severe mandatory penalties required by the Boggs law of 1951, and represents a further development of the punitive, prohibition type approach to the drug problem first established federally by the Harrison Act of 1914.

Both the 1951 and 1956 enactments, as well as the hearings and recommendations of the Congressional subcommittees which led to their passage, reflect conceptions of justice and penology which can only be adequately described as medieval and sadistic.

The 1956 act calls for the following penalties for illegal possession of drugs: (1) first offense, two to ten years' imprisonment and a fine not to exceed $20,000; (2) second offense, five to twenty years' imprisonment and a fine up to $20,000; (3) third or subsequent offense, ten to forty years' imprisonment plus a maximum fine of $20,000. For first and second *selling* offenses the penalties are the same as in (2) and (3); for the sale of heroin by a person over eighteen years of age to anyone under eighteen the penalty is the same as (3) with the additional provision that the death penalty may be applied at the discretion of a jury.

The minimum penalties for all offenses except (1) are mandatory; probation, suspension of sentence and parole are specifically forbidden. The elimination of parole means that persons convicted under the law will no longer be eligible for parole after serving a third of their time, but will have to serve at least two-thirds. The death penalty is primarily a gesture, since very few cases of the kind to which it might apply are ever tried before a jury and because juries are in any case reluctant to impose the extreme penalty.

One of the basic injustices of the narcotic laws in general, and of the recent laws in particular, is that the penalties fall mainly upon the victims of the traffic—the addicts—rather than upon the dope racketeers against whom they are designed. Assistant Attorney General Warren Olney III explained this to the Boggs subcommittee:

> Probably the most serious difficulty with the narcotic laws is the fact that they make no distinction between the violator who is a profiteering racketeer and the violator who in many respects is a victim of the drug itself, the addict. The same law is applicable to both and they are also subject to the same penalties. Unfortunately the addict and the petty pusher are much more easily apprehended than the major trafficker, who is the source of supply and is several echelons removed from the last seller who deals with the illicit consumer. The result is that the present rather severe penalties are more often applied to the relatively minor violator than to the "big shot" for whom they were designed.

The truth of this statement is borne out by the fact that even on the federal level, where there is a higher proportion of important peddling cases than in the state courts, over half of the defendants are addicts.

In Chicago, Senator Daniel and the state's attorney for Cook County, John Gutknecht, discussed the prevalence of Negro defendants among those charged with violation of narcotic laws. It was agreed that Negro peddlers operated mainly in the lower and middle branches of the illicit traffic and that they obtained their supplies ultimately from white gangsters who scarcely ever appear in the Chicago courts. Mr. Gutknecht said: "The white race is responsible for the distribution of narcotics in America, and let's not kid ourselves. The others are the victims." The discussion then turned to ways and means of providing more severe punishment for the "victims"!

There was agreement in the Congressional hearings concerning the difficulty in catching the "big shots." R. Tieken, United States Attorney for the Northern District of Illinois, testified:

> The narcotics importer and wholesaler are professionals. They have plenty of money, powerful allies and expert knowledge of how to evade the law and escape detection. They are not addicts and seldom handle drugs themselves. They have no bank accounts and deal only in cash. Their errands are run by others who transport the drugs and conduct the sales.
>
> To convict the big operator is a difficult task and we fully appreciate that we are nowhere near the big operator when we arrest the pusher who sells to the addict. Even when the pusher tells all he knows we only reach the dealer—merely one step up the ladder. The ladder may have several

steps before it reaches the big importer and the profits from importing and distributing narcotics are enormous.

The only measure suggested for getting at the "big shots" was legalized wire tapping; such a clause was deleted from the bill before passage.

Even assuming that the big traffickers could be caught, it is a further absurdity that the new narcotic laws do not necessarily increase the penalties against them. An illustration will clarify the point. In 1936, fifteen years before the Boggs Act, the Federal Bureau of Narcotics described in its annual report the breaking up of a dope ring which had operated in Texas, obtaining its supplies from a source in Chicago which in turn had gotten them from a higher source in New York. The six principals were convicted and received punishment as follows: L. Ginsberg, fifty years and a $10,000 fine; E. D. Smith, G. Payne and J. C. Allen, twenty years and a $2,000 fine each; J. Walker, seventeen years and $3,000; U. Eichenbaum, ten years and $2,000.

These persons were clearly not "big shots," but they were fairly important middle-echelon dealers. Offenders of this caliber are not very often caught and are therefore usually first offenders. Were they tried today under the 1956 law, the minimum mandatory penalty applicable to them would be five years—a much shorter sentence than they actually received. Of course, they could get more, but only at the discretion of the judge. Sentences tend to run longer now not because important operators are being caught more often, but because the law requires heavier penalties for minor offenders.

The Congressional subcommittees seemed to accept *in the abstract* the idea that drug users are diseased persons (the Supreme Court declared in 1924 in the Lindner case [268 U.S. 5] that "[addicts] are diseased and proper subjects for [medical] treatment"). But as a practical matter the "treatment" now accorded addicts consists of imprisonment and police harassment.

Besides being subject to punishment for possession and sale of drugs, and for crimes committed to raise money with which to purchase supplies, the drug user is subject to local police harassment merely for being, or having been, addicted. Illinois, for example, requires that addicts register as such; punishment is provided for those who fail to register or to carry identification cards. If the user has registered and possesses a card when he is picked up, he can be charged under a Chicago ordinance for "loitering." A state "needle" law provides penalties for the unauthorized possession of hypodermic needles or other paraphernalia of addiction. Police policy is simply to arrest and search any known addict and his companions on sight and to charge them in court with loitering if nothing more serious is turned up.

The local laws do not apply to non-addicted peddlers, who are thus in an advantageous position compared to the user. Moreover the peddler, generally represented by competent counsel, finds that illegal police practices often bring him acquittal and that he enjoys the full benefit of the presumption of innocence. To the addict, on the other hand, the presumption of innocence and other provisions of the Constitution are meaningless. For him the police state is already in being.

At the Chicago hearings of the Daniel subcommittee, it was testified that most of the drug users brought into the Chicago Narcotics Court were discharged as illegally arrested. Gutknecht commented:

> In view of my background as a law professor, I am very jealous of civil rights, civil rights of individuals. One of the things I determined when I got in there was that I was going to be particularly careful about that. I must say this to you, that where narcotic addicts are concerned, I haven't had many complaints, though I do know the police are a little prone to pick up these men. They [the police] have protection of an ordinance, and I must say the problem is so serious that even if we must admit some of their civil rights are being violated, you have to go along with a certain amount of that fringe violation, if you know what I mean.

The reaction of the members of the subcommittee was to complain that not enough of those illegally arrested were jailed and that, for those sent to prison, sentences were too short.

In the Chicago Narcotics Court and in other similar courts in our large cities, there is a long, shabby, pitiful parade of indigent drug users and petty offenders, mostly Negroes. These persons, except in the rare instances when they happen to be represented by lawyers, are hustled through the courts with such haste that a decent defense is precluded. The notion that punishing these victims will deter the lords of the dope traffic is as naive as supposing that the bootlegging enterprises of the late Al Capone could have been destroyed by arresting drunks on West Madison Street or Times Square.

Apart from the fact that jails and prisons are not currently supposed to be regarded as appropriate places for diseased persons, the incarceration of addicts is bad on other grounds as well. James V. Bennett, Director of the Federal Bureau of Prisons, criticized the 1951 act as follows: "I feel the law is a mistake. It is certainly a mistake so far as addicts are concerned. I feel that it has handicapped our efforts to salvage and rehabilitate them and has complicated our institutional problems." Association within a prison tends to spread addiction among criminals and criminality among addicts. The stigma of criminality and the influence of prison associations make the drug habit more difficult to break.

Even if it were possible to establish institutions in which all known addicts could be locked up for the rest of their lives, such a program would be futile. The big-shot dealers would still be at large, creating new generations of users. There is, in short, no substitute for punishment of the guilty. As long as addicts rather than peddlers bear the brunt of the penalties, the traffic is bound to continue.

There is an economic reason for the persistence of the illegal drug trade in the face of growing public indignation and increasing penalties. Police success in arresting drug distributors inevitably raises prices and increases profits; the illicit traffic thus depends in part upon the efforts made to suppress it. Reports on the operations of dope rings and on the value of seized drugs act as advertisements which lure new talent into the business. Since those who make the profits are non-addicts, and not the same persons as those who take the risks, punishment of the latter does not deter the former but only increases their profits.

A curious feature of our narcotics laws is that their enforcement is to a great extent actually placed in the hands of the drug addicts themselves, who act as police informers. One purpose of police harassment of addicts is the securing of information and the recruitment of informers. Addicts are used to "set up" the peddlers from whom they buy their supplies. The addict-informer does this by making a purchase with marked money. When the transaction is concluded, the police attempt to clinch the case by arresting the peddler and recovering the marked money from him. Without this kind of help the police would be relatively helpless.

Since the informer, or "stool pigeon," is ordinarily rewarded by being allowed to continue his addiction (as well as in other more direct ways which cannot be disclosed in court), it is easy to understand why, when the defendant-peddler is a non-addict who can afford a competent attorney, it is at this point that the case for the prosecution becomes vulnerable. Since the stool pigeon is himself often a criminal engaged in the same enterprises as the defendant, and since he is being paid by the police to give testimony which will convict a fellow criminal, his evidence often requires police corroboration.

Mandatory penalties assist the police to recruit informers. The discretion, which mandatory punishment removes from the court, is transferred to the police and the prosecution, who use it to bargain with the accused for guilty pleas and for information. Addicts who inform secure immunity from punishment, lighter punishment or release on probation.

The use of drug-using stool pigeons in the enforcement of the law is a complicated and unsavory matter which was not examined by the Congressional committees. It sometimes involves the police in violations of the narcotic laws and of other laws as well, and it leads to erratic enforcement because the penalties may be inflicted for failure to cooperate with the police rather than for the crime committed. The very abundance of informers among street-corner drug users has become a problem, with the police of one jurisdiction sometimes arresting informers working for another or with informers trying to make "buys" from each other.

The informer technique almost never leads to the top operators. Important dealers take extensive precautions against betrayal and often kill those who squeal. Moreover, there are few informers in the upper branches of the traffic, both because addicts are excluded and because the bigger dealers do business only with persons whom they have known for a long time and who have already proved their ability to resist police "interrogation." The consequence of all this is that the chief result of the addict's activities as a minor law-enforcement officer is to send his fellow addicts to jail.

The present punitive controls have been in effect since the Harrison Act of 1914. The injustice of punishing the victim of the traffic instead of the real culprits has been evident from the beginning to those familiar with the operation of the law, but it has not been evident to the public. The emergence of the traffic into a national scandal merely enabled the politicians to exploit the problem; they point in alarm, they denounce—and they demand heavier and still heavier penalties. That the penalties fall upon the victim rather than the culprit makes no difference; what politician bothers to rush to the defense of "dope fiends"?

The pressure exerted by an aroused public opinion upon essentially unjust, ineffective and unenforceable laws has resulted in a process of degenerative change. Laws have become unreasonably cruel and inflexible and are now, to a considerable extent, designed in the interest of police expediency rather than of justice. In this whole process, the forgotten man has been the addict. His degradation and hopelessness have been made more complete by denying him the benefits of care from the healing professions and by turning the unsolved medical problem of addiction over to the police.

TOO MANY SEX LAWS / KARL M. BOWMAN, M.D.

Ancient Hebrew law made sodomy a capital offense. The Mosaic law, according to Goldin, included only thirty-six capital crimes; half of them involved illegal sex relations. Three of these described unnatural sex relations: (1) between man and animal; (2) between woman and animal; and (3) between one man and another.

The Christian religion largely took over the Jewish laws concerning sexual behavior. Sodomy came to be the crime *peccatum illud horribile inter Christianos*—that abominable sin, not to be named among Christians. The medieval ecclesiastic courts made it a serious crime, even when committed in secret. According to early English authorities, the guilty person was to be burnt or to be buried alive. By the time of Richard I, it was the practice to hang a man or to drown a woman guilty of sodomy. With the separation of church and state, the law was changed several times; once the penalty was even decreased. But in 1562–63 the original law was made perpetual and was not touched again until 1861, when a Victorian statute reduced the penalty to life imprisonment. American colonial laws inherited the early English enactments or English common law.

We thus find that our laws regarding sexual behavior have been largely inherited from, and mainly based on, the ancient Jewish code of over two thousand years ago. It would seem time, therefore, to re-evaluate our thinking, as well as our laws. In this connection, some questions are in order. First, what is "normal" and what is "abnormal" sexual behavior? In Moslem countries, a man may legally have four wives at the same time; in the United States, he may have four or forty different wives, but only one at a time. In many countries, homosexual acts carried out in private by two willing adults are not crimes. In fact, in some European countries (for example, France under the Code Napoleon), any sexual act carried out by two consenting adults which does not result in physical harm and does not offend public decency is not considered a crime. In contrast, our laws in the United States are highly restrictive. A great many types of sexual behavior are regarded here not only as immoral, but as illegal and punishable by law. It is of interest to note that some of the most highly praised books on marriage-counseling advocate sexual practices (when desired by both partners) which are felonies in most American states.

In other words, we have a situation in which leaders in science, medicine and religion advise that married couples should, if they wish, commit felonies.

Scientific observations show that many of the higher mammals indulge in various sexual practices such as masturbation, fellatio, cunnilingus and sodomy. To many investigators of human behavior, it seems that man inherits from his mammalian ancestry some or all of these tendencies; indeed, we all have various antisocial and undesirable impulses, not only along sexual lines, but also toward murder, assault, theft, and so on. Many great writers have expressed this idea one way or another. Goethe once said that he felt he had within himself the capacity for committing every conceivable crime.

Society recognizes the universality of these undesirable impulses and passes laws against the carrying out of some of them. Religion labels some as sins. As for the sexual impulses, it has been said that biologically there is no such thing as sexual perversion, that all perversions are culturally determined. Likewise, the society in which one lives decides what sort of sexual behavior may be practiced and what type is forbidden by laws. The forbidden practices are commonly referred to as "perversions."

We are beginning to see a breakdown of the long-standing taboo on public discussion of sex, and at the present time there is a revival of interest in the problem of sex legislation. Many persons and groups desire to modify the laws in the direction of greater leniency; on the other hand, some groups seek to restrict sexual behavior even more. Where we have honest differences of opinion about the propriety of certain types of sexual behavior, it would seem that we ought to rely on education, family training and the influence of society generally (including religious organizations), as a means of dealing with the problem, rather than on the passage of new laws.

The clearest current example of an honest difference of opinion is with regard to birth control and the dissemination of knowledge about contraception. At the recent Lambeth Conference in England, it was agreed that sexual intercourse in marriage is a normal expression of love and affection and should be indulged in freely without necessarily leading to pregnancy. At the other extreme on the same subject are statutes, effective in two American states, which forbid a doctor to give advice regarding contraception to a married woman even if he thinks pregnancy might lead to her death. This is, perhaps, an extreme example of how the law may seek to intervene in sexual behavior, even that of married couples.

Numerous countries and several states of the United States have tried to modify certain sex laws, particularly those against homosexuality, with varied results. A few years ago, New York reduced ordinary homosexual acts from a felony to a misdemeanor. At the same time, California raised the penalty from a maximum of ten years to a maximum of twenty years, later fixing a minimum of one year and a maximum of life imprisonment for anyone "guilty of the infamous crime against nature, committed with mankind or with any animal." Again we see the two forces at work; one to decrease the penalties, one to increase them.

Perhaps it might be well to define homosexuality and homosexual acts. According to the dictionary, homosexuality is a sexual propensity for persons of one's own sex. The recent Wolfenden Report (British) of the Committee on Homosexual Offenses and Prostitution insists that the mere presence of such a propensity is not a homosexual offense and cannot be legally punished. Legally, no state in the United States specifies homosexuality or homosexual behavior as a crime by that name. But I would point out that the federal government has taken a somewhat different attitude; in the armed forces, not only homosexual acts but even homosexual tendencies may lead to an "undesirable," or "blue," discharge. Such a discharge bars the holder from all Veterans Administration benefits, including compensation or pension. It may also prevent him from getting a job.

A recent directive issued by one branch of the armed services stated that although homosexuals are security risks as well as moral risks, and their presence reflects unfavorably on the service, their cases must be disposed of justly. Two points must be decided in the individual case: Is the "homosexual" label justified, i.e., *is* the individual a homosexual, whether or not he has committed a perverse act? If so, what type of discharge is suitable?

In other words, we find that a psychiatric diagnosis of *latent* homosexuality may conceivably result in a type of "undesirable" discharge. Since, as I have pointed out, some degree of homosexual impulse is present in practically everyone, it would be fairly easy to label a large percentage of our population as latent homosexuals and then proceed to discriminate against them.

Homosexuals are often classified as latent or overt. It seems extremely far-fetched to speak of an individual as an "overt homosexual" who has had a few homosexual experiences in childhood or adolescence particularly if as an adult he is leading a completely heterosexual life. Yet it has been reported that individuals with this kind of history have been discharged from federal service.

The latent homosexual can be divided into two subgroups. The first consists of those who consciously desire homosexual relationships, but who carefully control these impulses in the same way that others control their heterosexual desires—for example, young women with normal heterosexual drives who nevertheless maintain their virginity. The second group consists of those who have no conscious interest in homosexual relations and even react with disgust to the idea. However, strong homosexual drives are present at the unconscious level, and their behavior is often motivated by these drives, which emerge in disguised fashion. It seems probable that the tremendous degree of emotion which the subject often arouses in some people is due largely to the stirring up of their own repressed or latent homosexual impulses.

It is clear, then, that the term "homosexuality" does not describe a simple homogeneous group, but includes several groups which differ from each other in many ways.

From a legal standpoint, I would agree with the Wolfenden Report, which argues that laws and regulations regarding sexual behavior should accept the fact that homosexuality *per se* is not an offense. I also feel that legal procedures should be invoked only against persons who have actually committed homosexual acts.

There is much controversy over what causes homosexuality, and I will not attempt to settle the matter here. I would point to a study by Kallman on identical twins which indicates homosexuality as an inherited tendency. Various endocrinological studies show, at least in some cases, definite physical causes. There are many psychological theories. Freud, for example, considered that homosexual impulses are part of the normal state in the evolution of the sexual instinct through which everyone passes. In a letter to an American mother who asked about treatment for her son, Freud wrote:

Dear Mrs. ....

I gather from your letter that your son is a homosexual. I am most impressed by the fact that you do not mention this term yourself in your information about him. May I question you, why you avoid it? Homosexuality is assuredly no advantage; but it is nothing to be ashamed of, no vice, no degradation, it cannot be classified as an illness; we consider it to be a variation of the sexual function produced by a certain arrest of sexual development. Many highly respectable individuals of ancient and modern times have been homosexuals, several of the greatest men among them. (Plato, Michelangelo, Leonardo da Vinci, etc.) It is a great injustice to persecute homosexuality as a crime, and a cruelty, too. If you do not believe me, read the books of Havelock Ellis. . . .

Sincerely yours with kind wishes

Freud

Under Freud's theory, everyone would be classified as having latent or repressed homosexual impulses. Other students of the subject emphasize the conditioning experience of early life, the relationship of the child to the parents, the way in which he may have been initiated into sexual practices, and many other factors. Homosexuality may arise from a multiplicity of causes rather than from a single cause. There is evidence, moreover, that certain aspects of our culture may tend to drive individuals away from heterosexuality and into homosexuality.

Society has the right to protect itself against behavior—including sexual behavior—which it feels is a crime against the "peace and dignity of the state." The question is: Where should we draw the line and when should the state pass laws regulating sexual behavior? Society should be and is most concerned about two things: sex crimes of violence and sex crimes against small children. I think there is universal agreement that laws with strong penalties should be kept for these two offenses. I do not believe that anyone advocates any diminution of severe penalties for these two crimes.

The most controversial point is the problem of overt homosexuality. Regarding this, a number of medical and legal societies and some religious organizations in Great Britain and the United States have advocated less repressive laws. The report of a council representing the Church of England, the British Government paper commonly known as the Wolfenden Report, and the recommendations of the British Medical Society all advocate that homosexual practices between two willing adults, carried out in private, should not be considered a criminal offense.

In our own country, the American Law Institute (in May, 1955) after considerable argument, voted 35 to 24 to recommend that sodomy between consenting adults "be removed from the list of crimes against the peace and dignity of the state." In the final debate, Judge John J. Parker opposed any change in present law on the ground that many things are "denounced by the Criminal Code in order that society may know that the state disapproves." But Judge Learned Hand, speaking for revision, stated that criminal law which is unenforced is worse than no law at all. He declared that, after previously voting the other way, he had decided that sodomy is "a matter of morals, a matter very largely of taste," and not something for which people should be put in prison. Many members of the medical profession share this attitude.

I would therefore advocate that we should probably follow the Code Napoleon not only in the matter of homosexual acts, but as to other sexual acts of a heterosexual nature. I do not believe that bestiality, for example, should carry a possible maximum penalty of life imprisonment, as provided by the California statute. I would also advocate that the state has no right and should not seek to regulate the sexual behavior of married couples. Sending a married couple to prison because they were accidentally seen to be carrying out a so-called "perverse act," and placing their children in foster homes, seems to me an unwarranted interference on the part of the state. Nor has the state any right, in my opinion, to interfere with the use of birth control by married couples, or with the practice of medicine by physicians. Is it reasonable for a state to forbid a doctor to advise a married woman about the practice of birth control when pregnancy might endanger her life? Here I would like to quote from the Lambeth Conference Report:

> Sexual intercourse is not by any means the only language of earthly love but it is, in its full and right use, the most intimate and the most revealing.... It is a giving and receiving in the unity of two free spirits which is itself good (within the marriage bond) and mediates good to those who share it. Therefore it is utterly wrong to urge that, unless children are specifically desired, sexual intercourse is of the nature of sin.

The report of a council of the Church of England, drawn up several years ago and not for general publication, recognized the fact that although homosexual acts are a sin in the eyes of the church, they are not necessarily crimes punishable by the state. In England, fornication and adultery are sins, but are not crimes, although they may well have much graver social consequences than homosexual practices. It is therefore unjust that consenting homosexual men can be sent to prison under a criminal law that ignores both heterosexual sins and female homosexual acts. The present law, instead of protecting the young and preserving public decency, offers a chance for blackmail and may indirectly cause suicides. It also helps the homosexual, by giving him a just grievance, to ignore the moral implications of his act. For these reasons the council urged an investigation into all possible revisions of the law.

We have in the United States a considerable number of persons who want to regulate by law the behavior and even the thinking of others. I agree with Thomas Jefferson: "That government is best which governs least." The idea that the state should increasingly regulate human behavior and human thought is to me a departure from the whole theory of democracy. I believe that a liberalization of sex laws is desirable. Such a course is backed by some of the greatest authorities in the world.

HE NEVER HAD A CHANCE / FRED J. COOK AND GENE GLEASON

A light flashed on the central switchboard of the New York Telephone Company office in Forest Avenue, West Brighton, S.I., at precisely 2:04 A.M., Sept. 2, 1958. Mrs. Catherine B. Thompson, one of the operators on duty, plugged in on the line. She heard the sound of heavy breathing. "Hello," she said, "hello." There was no answer, just that heavy, breathing sound. Mrs. Thompson turned to another operator, Mrs. Florence Parkin, and asked her to trace the call. Mrs. Parkin quickly found that it was coming from a house at 242 Vanderbilt Avenue. Then she cut in on the line, holding it open, while Mrs. Thompson notified police that something appeared to be wrong.

Even as Mrs. Thompson was speaking to the desk sergeant at the St. George police station, Mrs. Parkin heard the labored breathing on the line turn into a voice. A woman gasped: "I've been stabbed."

The operator immediately cut the police in on the conversation, and both she and the desk officer heard the woman repeat: "I've been stabbed. I've been attacked with a knife." A second later, the voice added: "My husband has been stabbed, too."

Then there was silence. It lasted only a second. Then a new voice, a little boy's voice, came on the wire.

"My mother is bleeding," the voice said.
Mrs. Thompson told the boy police already were on the way.
"I'll wait for the police outside," he said.
"No," she told him, "you better stay with your mother."
Such was the beginning of a drama that was to shock the nation.

THE CURTAIN LIFTS

Just six short minutes after that first warning light flashed on the Staten Island switchboard, at exactly 2:10 A.M., Patrolmen Vincent J. Meli and Henry Tyson pulled up before the two-story house at 242 Vanderbilt Avenue in the Fox Hills section, an area that in olden days had been known as "The Witches' Field." The house sat on a steep little hill. The patrolmen climbed seven steps, went up a ten-foot walk, climbed three more steps and entered the front door. Waiting to greet them, clad only in pajamas, was a small, slender, tow-headed boy, Melvin Dean Nimer, aged eight. Behind him in the silent house was a scene of blood and brutality.

The patrolmen found the boy's father, Dr. Melvin A. Nimer, thirty-one, a physician at the nearby Marine Hospital of the U.S. Public Health Service, sprawled on the kitchen floor, covered with blood from deep stab wounds. In the master bedroom upstairs, they found Mrs. Lou Jean Nimer, thirty-one, slumped on the floor between the bed and the wall where she had collapsed while telephoning. She, too, had been badly stabbed.

An emergency call went out for an ambulance and detectives. The ambulance arrived promptly, and at 2:18 A.M., Mrs. Nimer was placed in it to be taken to the Marine Hospital, just three blocks away. She was still conscious. Significantly, in the light of future developments, she still retained her presence of mind. As she was being placed in the ambulance, her thoughts obviously turned to her younger children still asleep in the house—Melvin Dean's brother, Gregory, two, and his sister, Jennifer Jean, just five months. The baby especially was on the mother's mind, for she told police: "Please feed the baby plain milk. No formula."

Even as the ambulance left, in the house, on the kitchen floor, Dr. Nimer was dying. Blood was welling up from his wounds. "I'm choking, I'm choking," he moaned. But he, too, still retained his faculties. He warned police against moving him or raising his head, and told them simply to brace his feet against the wall until the ambulance returned. When it did, within a few minutes, he too was rushed to the hospital, and there he died shortly after he was admitted.

154 *A View of* **THE NATION**

Mrs. Nimer lived a few hours longer. An emergency operation was performed in a desperate attempt to save her life, but at 5:30 A.M. she died while still on the operating table.

Staten Island authorities had a sensational double murder on their hands, and investigative forces were quickly marshaled. District Attorney John M. Braisted, Jr. and his assistant, Thomas R. Sullivan, were notified. Deputy Chief Inspector Edward W. Byrnes and Inspector Carl I. Blank assumed command of the police investigation. Detectives and technical experts swarmed over the house at 242 Vanderbilt Avenue. From the outset, they had one thing going for them. They had an eye-witness—Melvin Dean Nimer, known as Deany.

DEANY'S STORY

The boy told this story:

He had been asleep in his bedroom across the hall from his parents' room when he was awakened by something touching the bed, disturbing the bed clothing. Startled, Deany woke, looked up, saw a man looming above his bed. The man, he said, wore a white mask, like a sheet, that covered his entire head. Deany screamed.

The masked man grabbed him by the throat, tried to choke him. Across the hall, Mrs. Nimer, hearing her son scream, rushed to his aid.

"Mommy came and the man hit her with something and she started bleeding," Deany told police. "Then Daddy ran in and they started fighting and Daddy started bleeding."

The struggle between his father and the masked intruder took place in the hall outside his bedroom, at the top of the stairway, the boy told detectives. The prowler, he said, was "a little bigger than Daddy," and he broke away and ran downstairs with Dr. Nimer in pursuit.

Mrs. Nimer had gone to her bedroom and sat down on the edge of the bed to use the telephone and call for help. She slid off the bed, moaning faintly, "I'm dying. . . ."

This was Deany Nimer's story. Based upon it, police sent out a thirteen-state alarm for the prowler who had slain Dr. Nimer and his wife: "Unknown male, white, wearing blue dungarees and blue-striped shirt. May have blood on his clothing."

THE CLOTH STRIPS

Right at the start there was one bit of undeniable physical evidence that seemed to lend substantiation to the story Deany Nimer had told. Only vague hints of this appeared in the press at the time, and its significance was quickly forgotten. It was mentioned that police had found a piece of cloth (some accounts said two pieces) that had been left folded on the boy's bed. Actually, we are told, there were about half-a-dozen strips of cloth torn into handy lengths that suggested they had been intended for gags or bonds. The cloth was a faded, odd-colored, cotton ticking—the kind of coarse, heavy material that was often used for old mattress covers—and the strips, according to those who tested them, were strong. The material matched nothing else found in the house, and police at first thought that the strips might have been ripped from an old hospital mattress. The nearby Public Health Service Hospital was checked on this supposition, but the cotton ticking evidently hadn't come from there. It never was traced and identified.

Indeed, the mysterious cloth strips soon were forgotten as investigators concentrated on two other elements of the mystery. How had the prowler entered the home? And where was the murder weapon?

Again these key questions were never to be answered, but the first one, from a combination of circumstances at the murder scene, appears to have assumed from the early moments of the investigation an exaggerated importance in official minds. An examination of the house showed that a cellar window had been left open. A water hose led out the window into the driveway, where Dr. Nimer had washed the car the day before he and his wife were murdered. An intruder could have slipped into the house through this window, but technical experts examined the window sill and quickly discounted the possibility. Minute particles of dust and dirt on the sill had been undisturbed, and this would hardly have been possible had a full-grown man squeezed through the comparatively narrow opening.

Yet this appeared to be the only easy means of entrance. Elsewhere in the house, a screen on one of the downstairs windows was unhooked, but again there was nothing to indicate an intruder had crawled through the window. The inside front door had been partially open when the first patrolmen arrived, but the aluminum screen door had still been latched and Deany himself had released the catch to admit police. It almost seemed as if no one could have entered the house—and, especially, that no one could have departed in the kind of hasty flight that Deany Nimer had described, *if* Deany's story were true.

BEGINNINGS OF MYSTERY

This, it became obvious later, was the first fork in the road the investigators were to take. A second element involved the location of Deany's

Boy Scout knife. In searching the house for the murder weapon, detectives discovered that apparently none of the kitchen ware had been used. But Deany's Boy Scout knife was missing. The boy was positive it had been in a pocket of his trousers, hanging on the knob of his bedroom door. Detectives looked, but the knife wasn't where Deany had said it was. A thorough search of the house finally turned up the potential weapon, hidden between the covers of the Mormon magazine *Era*. A laboratory analysis—the kind of minute examination that can reveal droplets of blood not perceivable by the human eye—soon established that the knife was absolutely unstained. Still, could the knife have been cleaned? Could it still be the murder weapon?

These questions were hovering unasked in the air, unknown as yet to press and public, when the first reporters converged upon the murder scene. Even though the early roadblocks, the early forks in the investigative pathway, were not clear, there was about this investigation from the start a disturbing overtone. One of the first reporters on the scene was scrambling for information when he was elated to receive a high-sign from a high-ranking detective whom he knew. The detective drew him aside, and the reporter was all anticipation.

"I thought he had something he wanted to tell me," the reporter recalled later. "But do you know what he said? He pointed to District Attorney Braisted, and he asked me: 'You've been around quite awhile. You've seen Hogan work. How do you think he compares with Hogan? Is he as good?'"

This early, it would seem, some minds were already more preoccupied with the question of the reflected public image, the question of their own reputations, than they were with the baffling details of the horrible crime that cried out for solution.

FINGER ON THE BOY

In the succeeding days, the investigation followed the usual frenetic course of sensational headline crimes. A number of suspects were picked up, questioned, released. The ground around the Nimer house, the streets in the area, were searched and searched again. In all of this just two discoveries were made that seem of significance now. Detectives disclosed that they had found two footprints—the footprints of a man—in the soft earth at the left rear side of the Nimer house. Plaster casts were taken of them in the hope that they might ultimately serve to identify the foot that had made them. The second discovery involved a knife. About 6 P.M. on Sept. 3, the day after the murders, two patrolmen found a sharp-pointed knife, with a five-inch blade and a wooden handle, in a hedge about 1,000 feet from the Nimer home. Under laboratory analysis, the knife revealed traces of blood, but they were so faint that it could not be scientifically determined whether the blood was animal or human.

Both of these discoveries, if they meant anything at all, seemed to point away from the suspicion that already had taken root in the minds of officials. This suspicion involved Deany Nimer. Newsmen, under a pledge of confidence, were told that the boy was a suspect in the murder of his parents. He was undergoing psychiatric examination.

While the public still had no suspicion of the sensation that was about to burst, journalists who had been given the tip dug energetically into the background of the Nimer family. The parents had been Mormons. They had been married in September, 1946, in the culmination of a childhood romance that had begun back in their home town of Orem, Utah. Dr. Nimer had received his medical degree from the University of Utah, had served in a Public Health Service Hospital in Seattle, Wash., and had come to Staten Island only a few months before to start a three-year surgical residence at the Marine Hospital. Intimates of the family had considered their home life ideal. There had never been a hint, prior to the murders, of any mental problem involving Melvin Dean Nimer. He was an open-faced, smiling, attractive boy. Indeed, he and his father had seemed to have great affection for each other. Neighbors recalled how, when Dr. Nimer came home from the hospital, Deany would run up to him and throw his arms around him.

Was it possible that such a boy, at so young an age, could be a veritable Dr. Jekyll and Mr. Hyde? Even if he were possessed by a dark soul-demon hiding under the smiling face, was it physically possible for such a tiny lad to murder *both* of his parents? After all, Deany was only 4 feet 4; he weighed only sixty pounds.

The authorities obviously decided that he could. Relatives of the Nimers had been notified promptly of the tragedy. Mrs. Bertha Park, mother of Mrs. Nimer, and Dr. Harold Nimer, Deany's uncle, had flown to New York immediately. With Dr. Harold Nimer's consent, District Attorney Braisted sent the boy on Friday, Sept. 5, three days after the murders, to the Staten Island Mental Health Center for analysis. The clinic, under the direction of Dr. Richard M. Silberstein, examined the boy in just two days, Friday and Saturday. It was after these examinations, it was to be disclosed later, that Deany changed his original story and gave a statement confessing that he had committed the murders. This was still not known, even to reporters, when Deany left on the weekend, accompanied by his uncle and Detective James Cox, to fly to the funeral of his parents in Orem, Utah.

THE TURNING POINT

The funeral was held on Tuesday, Sept. 9, and on Wednesday, Sept. 10, as Deany was returning to New York with his uncle and Detective Cox, the New York *Journal-American* broke the story and announced in sensational headlines that the boy was a suspect in the murder of his parents. What happened next has to be considered of the greatest significance. For this was the crossroads, the point at which the life and the future of an eight-year-old boy were going to be protected—or he was going to be pilloried in public.

The *Journal-American*'s story was damaging, but it was not official. Other newspapers did not touch it until District Attorney Braisted had been given an opportunity to comment, and on what he said depended the extent to which the story would be used, the credibility that would be attached to it. The district attorney, quite obviously, had several courses of action open to him. He could have denounced the published story as a violation of confidence and refused to confirm it; he could have refused flatly to comment, as district attorneys often do, because the case was under investigation and still unsolved; or he could have confirmed the fact that the boy had been under suspicion—and at the same time pointed out all of the solid facts in the case (as yet unknown to the public) that seemed to negate that suspicion.

District Attorney Braisted did none of these things. He gave the impression of a public official who was glad the story was out. He refused to be quoted on the fact that he had required a pledge of silence from newspapermen about the suspicions that had been focused on Deany; he refused to criticize publication of a story that had tarred an eight-year-old boy as a suspect in the murder of his parents. He said, on the contrary, that preliminary psychiatric examination to which Deany had been subjected had shown the boy was suffering "from a paranoid type of schizophrenia and that the boy's illness and basic personality were compatible with the commission of a crime of violence."

While thus throwing the prestige of his office behind the most horrible and harrowing suspicion that could be leveled at a child, the district attorney left himself an out in carefully expressed reservations. He pointed out that the boy's uncle, Dr. Harold Nimer, was not satisfied with "the statement"—he refused to say confession—that Deany had made. He added, "I am not satisfied, either," and said the boy would be subjected to more extensive and more thorough psychiatric tests.

DRAWING THE NET

The district attorney's statement made the story official. Press services spread it nation-wide. And in the next hours it seemed that the last room for doubt had been banished. On the evening of this day of horrible revelation, little Deany was taken back to the house of tragedy on Vanderbilt Avenue, and there, in a pattern reminiscent of the one followed with all-but-convicted criminals, he "re-enacted" the crime, authorities said. The next day, Thursday, Sept. 11, he was sent to Bellevue Hospital in New York for psychiatric examination. And that same day, in an extended press conference, District Attorney Braisted was subjected to searching questions by reporters about the circumstances that pointed to young Deany Nimer's guilt or innocence.

On the side of innocence, District Attorney Braisted listed just one theoretical proposition. "The one important thing that would negate" the idea of guilt, he said, was that the statement came from an eight-year-old boy. On the side of guilt, he listed an impressive array of supposedly solid facts.

The most important factor pointing to the boy's guilt, he said, "is the statement by the Medical Examiner that the wounds, their location, etc., could indicate they were received while the victims were in a prone position in bed." The first autopsy report (it was later revised) by Assistant Medical Examiner Dr. Dominick DeMaio disclosed that Dr. Nimer had a superficial wound on the back of the left shoulder and a fatal wound "in the upper abdomen under the left chest cage." Mrs. Nimer, Dr. DeMaio's report said, had a superficial wound of the right breast and "a lethal wound of the upper abdomen under the right chest cage." The medical report added that "the thrusts all were direct downward thrusts," supporting the theory that the Nimers were surprised and stabbed while lying "in a prone position in bed."

This scientific documentation seemed to offer a rational explanation for the incredible. Conceivably, even an eight-year-old, 4 foot 4, 60-pound boy *could* stab both of his parents to death if he surprised them as they slept and stabbed them in the soft flesh of the abdomen before they were aware of what was happening. The medical report seemed almost to explain how the crime *had* happened; but even so—and even though there were vital facts in this case that were still being kept from the press and public—there were a few obvious pieces that did not fit into this almost-final solution.

SOME AWKWARD FACTS

One dealt with Deany's person. Authorities said he had admitted he had washed his hands, and so, of course, there was no blood upon them. But what of his pajamas? They had, according to Dr. DeMaio's report, only "one or two" small bloodstains on them. Then there was the peculiar matter of the bedclothing. The murder night had been an exceptionally cool one when, almost certainly, the Nimers would have had covers over them. Yet there were no knife rips, no tears at all in the bed sheets.

These minute flaws in the case did not seem too significant at the time, but reporters questioned District Attorney Braisted closely. And everything he said built one picture, a dark picture for Deany Nimer.

Asked about reports that the boy had changed his confession, the district attorney said: "No, he has not changed his story." Then he admitted that the boy, in answer to a question from his uncle, had said that his original story about an intruder was the true one. The district attorney was asked whether there were discrepancies in the boy's story. He said flatly: "No discrepancies." He added that Deany had had a motive and that it lay in "an attitude he had toward his parents." He explained, "I would be inclined to say they (the Nimers) were very strict." Of Deany, he said: "He has never shown any remorse."

Braisted was questioned about the absence of blood on any of the knives in the house, especially on Deany's Boy Scout knife. Assuming that the knife had been washed off, had detectives examined the drain traps to see if they could find any traces of blood? They had—and they found no blood. Only six minutes had elapsed between the first winking alarm light on the telephone switchboard and the arrival of police. Could Deany have rushed downstairs, washed off the knife so perfectly that it retained no trace of blood and hidden it in that short time? "It is possible," said District Attorney Braisted. "The time limit is conceivable?" he was asked again. "It is possible," he said.

THE BOY'S "CONFESSION"

The effect of all this was to accuse and damn Melvin Dean Nimer in the public eye without accusing him in court. The story touched a sensitive nerve of the times and was a sensation across the nation. Parents everywhere have been concerned in recent years about the increasing frequency of violent and bloody youth crimes, and the case of Melvin Dean Nimer seemed to touch a new nadir. If so young and so attractive a boy could have committed so heinous a crime, then there were no limits to youthful depravity. No New York crime case in our experience caused such deep and widespread agitation among parents.

Yet all the time there were vital elements of the case that had been kept secret—elements that did not fit into the picture of a little boy's seemingly almost-certain guilt. They were vital facts that supported the story Deany originally had told about a masked intruder. For the plain truth was this: *virtually every word that he had uttered had been corroborated from the mouths of his dying parents.*

Though District Attorney Braisted had been questioned with the utmost thoroughness, he had given no hint of this. The district attorney had insisted there were "no discrepancies" in the boy's confession—nor, presumably, in the case against the boy. It was left for newsmen to drag the truth out into the light of day. On Friday, Sept. 12, Vincent E. Sorge, a painstaking and tireless reporter for *The New York World-Telegram and Sun*, broke through the veil of official reticence. He revealed the verbatim question-and-answer exchange between a detective and Mrs. Nimer before Mrs. Nimer died. This was the exchange:

> Q. Can you tell me anything about the case? A. A mask . . . a mask.
> Q. Can you tell me anything else?
> A. A hood . . . a hood.
> Q. What kind? A. White.
> Q. Slits in the eyes? A. Yes, covered full head.
> Q. How tall? A. Tall as my husband, same build.
> Q. Why did you get up? A. Heard boy scream.

District Attorney Braisted was in the midst of another press conference, discussing Deany's motives, when *The World-Telegram and Sun* broke the story. Asked if Mrs. Nimer had made a statement before she died, Braisted said he understood she had described the killer as about the size of her husband and added: "We believe she might have seen her husband and no one else, but this matter is still being investigated."

Thomas Sullivan, Braisted's assistant, came into the room at this point, leaned over and whispered into the district attorney's ear. Braisted paled noticeably. Then he turned to reporters and said: "Mrs. Nimer did mention the words 'white mask and hood' to Detective John Morgan, but you must remember that she was in shock and was put under sedation . . . and [her statements] were made in dribs and drabs. . . . She also said, 'tall as my husband, same build.'" Pressed for further details, he said abruptly: "I will make no comment on any published statement attributed to victims of this crime. I am declining comment because I sincerely believe that comment would impede our investigation."

The lid had been lifted. Answers that did not answer no longer satisfied. More and sharper questions were asked. What about Dr. Nimer? He had lived for some time after the stabbing. Had he, like his wife, identified his assailant? "He didn't give us anything you would call useful information," one high police source said. "He made no positive identification of the assailant," said District Attorney Braisted. It took reporters three days to pierce this screen of non-answering answers; but finally, on Monday, pressed again and pressed harder, District Attorney Braisted admitted that Dr. Nimer, too, before he died, had used the words "prowler" and "mask."

FIRST VERSION SUBSTANTIATED

The picture that then developed was this: Little Melvin Dean Nimer's first story that he had been awakened by a masked prowler, that he had screamed, that his parents had come to his aid—all of this had agreed in exact detail with the statements his dying parents had made to police. His description of the mask, his description of the intruder as a man "about Daddy's size," agreed perfectly with his mother's dying statement. Why, in the face of all this, had authorities concentrated such strong and harrowing suspicion upon the boy?

The answer may be found, perhaps, in District Attorney Braisted's admission of official investigative frustration. Three things, he said, led authorities to suspect Deany, and he listed them: "1. Our inability to establish with any certainty that there had been an entrance to and an exit from the house. 2. Motive—we couldn't settle on a motive. 3. A few statements by the boy which did not conform to the facts. Adding it all together—though we, like many other people, just couldn't believe it— we had no choice."

The only way, seemingly, that the positive statements of the dying parents could be explained away lay in the assumption that, to protect the son who had stabbed them, they had conferred and concocted the story of the masked intruder. Yet Mrs. Nimer had collapsed in the upstairs bedroom, Dr. Nimer in the downstairs kitchen, and there was absolutely no proof that they could have talked with each other in those six short minutes before police arrived. Anyway, in logic, the whole idea appeared preposterous, and in an analytical article on Sept. 19, 1958, the writing half of this team tore into the case against Deany Nimer and asked this question:

> Is it conceivable that a dying mother who thought enough of her children to warn about her daughter's formula would make up a story about a prowler and a mask to protect her son—and endanger the other two children—if he were a killer?

The day that question was asked District Attorney Braisted was not available to reporters, and Sullivan, his assistant, said: "No comment."

And with that story, the Nimer case virtually died. Melvin Dean Nimer's psychiatric examination at Bellevue was concluded. The report, as relayed to the public, was vague. Psychiatrists said they found evidence of "a personality disorder predating the tragic occurrence on Staten Island." Deany needed continued psychiatric treatment, they said; but clear evidence that the boy was not considered dangerous was seen in the fact that he was released and allowed to go to his grandparents' home in Orem, Utah, there to attend school and mingle with other children. Deany left New York for Orem on Oct. 23, 1958, and on Nov. 3, the forty detectives who had been working on the mystery were called off. The case was as good as dead.

AT LAST THE ANSWER

But the damage had been done, and a haunting, horrible suspicion still remained—the suspicion that Melvin Dean Nimer, only eight, might have committed one of the most horrible crimes of the century. Everywhere a reporter went, even in towns miles away from New York, he was asked: "What is the truth about the Nimer case? Did the boy really do it?" It was a question to which there was no official answer, but one to which we can, we feel, give a positive answer now.

It is an answer that was obtained by the reporting half of this team only after weeks of exhausting and meticulous leg work. Every inch of the murder scene was re-examined. Every person who would talk, even many who didn't want to talk, was questioned. The picture that emerged grew more shocking every step of the way. For as we dug more deeply into the mystery, it became apparent that there wasn't a chance, *there never had been a chance*, that Melvin Dean Nimer could have committed the murders. Only the most incredibly slipshod investigation that proceeded in blind defiance of some facts and in blind ignorance of others could have resulted in even the vaguest suspicion being cast upon the boy.

THE BLOOD CLUES

We began with the house at 242 Vanderbilt Avenue. Any supposition of Deany's guilt rested upon the belief—in all logic, the only possible belief—that he had surprised his sleeping parents in bed and stabbed them there. But once we got into the master bedroom and examined the mattress on the bed, we found this: there was just one splotch of blood on the entire mattress and that was on the side of the bed on which Mrs. Nimer sat when she used the telephone.

The traces of blood still discernible in the house indicated clearly that the crime had been committed elsewhere. Across the hallway, there was a splash of blood on the door jamb of Deany's room, and there was a large amount of blood around the light switch in the hall nearby—an indication perhaps that Dr. Nimer, his hands already bloody from his wounds, had fumbled desperately for the switch in an effort to turn on the light so that he could see his assailant already fleeing down the stairs. It was significant to us that signs of blood in massive quantities appeared first in the hallway and trailed down the stairs through the house—just as would have been the case if the first story Deany told were the right one.

Downstairs, we faced the problem of the front door. It was obvious that a key angle had been the conclusion by the police and the district attorney that no one could have come in—or, even more significantly, could have left in haste—through the aluminum door with its spring lock. Yet aluminum doors with this kind of latch often give under pressure. Gene Gleason set the catch, then gave the door a slight tug—and open it came, easily, without damaging door or lock.

MRS. NIMER'S EVIDENCE

Turning from the mute evidence of the house, we sought information of a more positive kind in the records of the Marine Hospital, where the Nimers had been taken. Mrs. Nimer, the records showed, had been placed in a recovery room at 3:05 A.M. Personnel of the hospital who knew her had talked with her. She was fully conscious, fully coherent. When a nurse giving Mrs. Nimer oxygen mistakenly placed the mask on backwards, Mrs. Nimer reached up with one hand and said: "It's on backwards." This was not a woman, obviously, who was in such a state of shock or under such sedation that she did not know what she was saying when she talked about a prowler and a mask.

The vital questioning of Mrs. Nimer had been overheard by hospital personnel. Two detectives were present, and they questioned her gently, carefully, hospital personnel said. They heard Mrs. Nimer tell about the mask-hood, the slits for the eyes; heard her describe the intruder as "about the size of my husband." And they heard her say: "I met the man in the hall."

Every effort was made to save Mrs. Nimer's life. Dr. Norman Tarr, deputy chief of surgery, was summoned to perform an emergency operation. He knew Mrs. Nimer personally, and she recognized him. Before he operated, the records show, he examined her carefully and turned her body over gently so that he could see if she had any wounds on her back. Mrs. Nimer told him that she had not been stabbed there and, indeed, she had not—a sequence again that seems to demonstrate that this was a woman still in possession of her faculties.

In his examination of his patient, Dr. Tarr discovered that she had three wounds. There was a slight knife wound on the heel of her right hand, received apparently when she had tried to ward off a blow. She had a one-inch stab wound in the upper right chest above the breast. And she had a mortal wound, not in the abdomen as the official medical examiner's report had said, but in the right chest between the sixth and seventh ribs.

The location and nature of this last wound assume vital importance. The presumption of Deany Nimer's guilt had been based to a large extent upon the autopsy report that placed the wound in the abdomen and described it as a direct downward thrust. This enabled officials to envision a boy stabbing his parents in bed, *but Dr. Tarr's reports show conclusively that this was a completely inaccurate impression, that the stabbing did not and could not have happened that way at all.*

POWERFUL THRUST

The blade of the knife had been driven through the rib cage and muscles with terrific force. It had gone in at an angle, slanting down and towards the center of the body. So vicious was the thrust that the blade had penetrated about five inches, and there was evidence that the blow had been struck by an experienced knife-wielder. The wound on the outside was small, only about the width of the knife blade; but there was evidence that the knife tip had been flicked on an arc inside the body, the trick of an experienced killer. The flicking tip had slashed through the diaphragm, had severed the major blood vessel going into the vena cava, and had inflicted a cut about five inches long and very deep in the liver.

Dr. Tarr knew that only a miracle could save Lou Jean Nimer, but he attempted to perform that miracle. He made an incision, beginning approximately at the navel and proceeding upward to the bottom of the breast plate. He mopped up the blood and tried to staunch its flow. His patient was sinking fast. Her pulse and breathing faded. She was only a whisper away from death. Dr. Tarr reached into her chest cavity and tried frantically to massage her failing heart. He tried for twenty minutes, but he failed as he had known, almost from the first, that he must fail.

All during this grim drama of the operating room, Dr. Tarr detailed every step in operative notes that he dictated as he went along. Realizing that he would have to cut through the original wound, he was careful to describe its location, its size, its depth. All of this detail, so vital to any understanding of the murder case, was in Dr. Tarr's operative notes when Mrs. Nimer's body was released to the city morgue for autopsy at 7:05 A.M., Sept. 2, 1958.

What happened next seems fairly obvious. The medical examiner, Dr. DeMaio, confused the incision which Dr. Tarr had made with the fatal wound. Only so could the wound have been erroneously located in the abdomen instead of between the sixth and seventh ribs; only so could it have been described as a direct downward thrust when Dr. Tarr, the only man who could know, described it emphatically as an angled, downward-slanting blow. How could this confusion have occurred? Quite simply. The autopsy report was ready the day after the murders, but Dr. Tarr's operative notes were not transcribed and forwarded to authorities for four days! And in the meantime, nobody asked. It was not until "about ten days" after Mrs. Nimer's death that detectives came around to question Dr. Tarr and hospital personnel—and learned, presumably for the first time, one of the most elemental facts about the crime they were investigating: the nature of Mrs. Nimer's fatal wound.

DEANY'S THROAT MARKS

This sequence, revealing enough is not quite so shocking as one other medical fact that until now has been buried from the public. Deany, it will be remembered, had told authorities originally that the intruder had grabbed him by the throat and tried to strangle him. During the period when suspicion was being focused on the boy, District Attorney Braisted had been asked about this. Had there been marks on Deany's neck? He had replied: "There might have been one or two little marks on the boy's neck. There were no lacerations or deep marks. The boy was examined superficially on the night of the murders, but was not given any medical treatment."

This account simply does not agree with specific reports that show conclusively that a man *had* tried to strangle Deany Nimer!

The story of the evidence that was plainly visible on Deany's throat comes from Dr. William Smith, an associate of Dr. Nimer and a neighbor and friend of the family. He hurried to the Nimer house early on the morning of the tragedy. Deany had already been questioned, had been sent back to bed to sleep and had only just reawakened. Dr. Smith and Ralph L. Perkins, administrator of Marine Hospital, were present when detectives began to question the boy again about 6 A.M. Even then, police were saying that the boy's "story doesn't conform with the facts." And even then the trend of the questioning indicated that they suspected Deany. The questioning went on and on for nearly two hours, and considering the circumstances, the age of the boy and the horror of the night, it impressed observers as excessive, as constituting a virtual verbal third degree.

Finally, about 8 A.M., in the kitchen of the Nimer home, police asked Dr. Smith to examine Deany's throat. The doctor turned a sunlamp on the boy, and this is what he found:

> On the right side of the boy's neck—to the rear of the midway point—four fingerprints. On the left side, in approximately the same position, a thumb print and the curvature of a thumb nail mark. Clusters of petechia, more commonly known as pinpoint hemorrhages caused by the rupturing of the capillaries.

Dr. Smith said he told police and the D.A.'s men present: "The marks are more than halfway back. He could not have done it himself. The hand was too big."

This positive finding, it would seem, should have put an end to all suspicions of Deany Nimer. But as the sequel was to show, it did nothing of the kind.

Obviously, police and investigating officials were not listening to facts that they did not want to hear. Their attitude even at the time, even when one could not know what was to come, must have been obvious; for Dr. Smith, when he left the house and took Deany home with him, was so worried that he did an unprecedented thing. He discussed the situation first with his wife, then he called in a second doctor to examine Deany's throat again. This second examination corroborated Dr. Smith's findings, and both doctors wrote out formal reports of what they had found and filed them in the hospital records.

"A ROTTEN DEAL"

It was not until some weeks later that Detective James Cox, who appears to have taken a more realistic view of the case than some of his superiors, came around rechecking evidence and discovered that two formal medical reports establishing beyond doubt Deany Nimer's innocence, showing that a man *had* tried to strangle him, were reposing in hospital files like a couple of concealed time bombs. Cox was visibly disturbed. But no one else appears to have been. At least no one in official position to this day has had the grace publicly to admit the horrible sequence of blunders that ended in the pillorying of an eight-year-old boy. The pretense has been maintained publicly that the investigation is still open; that anyone, including Deany Nimer, could conceivably still be a suspect. *But privately a high police official has since admitted to the reporting half of this team, "We know that the boy could never have done it."*

Out in Utah, Deany went back to school last winter like any other eight-year-old boy. According to his grandfather, Dean E. Park, he appeared normal and bright in every way. There had been no trouble, no need even for Deany to make regular trips to a psychiatrist. But, understandably, there was bitterness. Dean Park, speaking of New York, put it well. He said: "We think we got a rotten deal back there."

WAR, PEACE, AND THE MILITARY

THE ARMS RACE: COUNT-DOWN
FOR DISASTER / **WALTER MILLIS**

The frequent question: "Has there ever been an arms race which did not end in war?" is scarcely answerable, since before the latter part of the nineteenth century there had never been an arms race in anything like the modern sense. There had, of course, been earlier instances of competitive arming and fort-building in peacetime, but the deadly modern competition in armaments is essentially a product of the technological revolution in warfare (in turn a gift of the Industrial Revolution and the coming of the age of steam), which began to become prominent only after the Franco-Prussian War. It was the longer time required for the design and production of the new weapons, the necessity for elaborate advance mobilization and strategic planning imposed by the speed and volume of rail transport and telegraphic communications, which began to produce the huge standing and instantly ready military systems, developing competitively against each other with relatively little regard for contemporary political or economic issues.

The modern concept of the arms race scarcely entered the international consciousness until 1898, when the Czar of Russia issued his famous appeal to suspend the competition, by that time well developed. Those who prepared the documentation for the ensuing Hague Conference could find nothing in the diplomatic record bearing on the idea beyond a suggestion, tossed out by the British Prince Regent just after Waterloo, that peacetime military forces should be regulated by international agreement. By 1898, however, the notion that the "progressive development" of armaments was not only loading the peoples with insupportable financial burdens, but would probably end in the war which the armaments were supposed to prevent, was taking shape. "It appears evident," as the Czar's ministers put it, "that if this state of things were prolonged, it would inevitably lead to the very cataclysm it is desired to avert."

The Russians proposed a thoroughgoing attack upon the problem, not only through an experimental freezing of then-existing force-levels and military budgets, but through halting the scientific and technological competition which even in that day was seen to be one of the worst sources of the disease. In a manner prophetic of our own efforts to deal with the atom and the ICBM, they proposed to prohibit the use of "any new kind of firearms whatever and of new explosives, or any powders more powerful than those now in use," and to "restrict the use in military warfare of the formidable explosives already existing." They wanted to ban the submarine (then only in embryo) and all forms of aerial bombardment.

It was easy then, as so many times later, to point out that the aggressively expansionist but technologically backward Russians were simply trying to defend their gains while restraining the competition. The other powers readily found this kind of problem so "very difficult" as to be insoluble; nothing could be done, and the European arms race swept on to end "inevitably" some fifteen years later in the "very cataclysm" which had been so accurately predicted. It not only "ended in war"; the sober post-mortems after 1918 made it clear that the race had been in itself an important cause—perhaps the most important single cause—of the disaster. The rapid rebuilding of the Czar's own military establishment after its collapse in Manchuria; the really pointless Anglo-German naval rivalry; the competitive Franco-German army increases, had produced the overgrown, over-sensitive and hair-triggered military establishments which rendered the 1914 crisis unmanageable by diplomacy or statesmanship and so made the resultant cataclysm literally "inevitable." The "classic" pattern of the arms race itself leading direct to war had been established.

But after 1918 the arms race was not really revived (though publicists in the inter-war years often talked as though it had been). In the grim and impoverished morrow of the First World War, the conditions for it did not exist. An incipient Anglo-American-Japanese naval race was wisely canceled, so far as the Americans and British were concerned, while the Japanese, confronted by the two others, prudently withdrew their challenge for the time being. The statesmen who labored so long and so ineffectively in the League of Nations disarmament conferences were not trying to halt a race, but to prevent one. They were trying to balance the tired and static military systems of the victors of 1918 against the developing military ambitions of the powers for whom 1918 had represented a defeat. Even when Japan at the end of 1934 claimed her privilege to denounce the naval limitation treaties and Hitler in 1935 tore up the disarmament clauses of the Versailles Treaty with the declaration that German rearmament was already under way, no arms race immediately ensued. Not until the Munich crisis of 1938 did France and Britain make a serious effort to regain the relative military power which they had lost; the United States did not start in earnest to rearm until the Allied catastrophe of May, 1940.

As the Second World War was ending, there was some reason to hope that it might lead to a military stabilization of sorts, comparable to that which appeared after 1918. The hope was destroyed on August 6, 1945. It is fair to say that the most unsettling element of World War II had been the long-range strategic bomber—of necessity carrying its terrors directly against enemy civilian life and the industrial and transportation resources upon which they, like the enemy armies, depended. This was military power in a new form, terrible in its implications, against which defense was difficult, and hard to fit into the kind of rough balances which had been possible at times with the conventional forces of fleets and armies. But its performance, while often significant, had been on the whole disappointing; so long as it was armed only with TNT and incendiary weapons, it labored under severe limitations and might conceivably have been confined within the framework of conventional war, restricted to strategic theories less dreadful and less unmanageable than those which its advocates were perforce obliged to adopt. Unhappily, with the Hiroshima bomb, the power of the long-range bomber was suddenly expanded by a factor of from two thousand to twenty thousand. This destroyed all calculations which might have been drawn from the experience of World War II. It meant that unless something could be done, the strategy of mass extermination must dominate the whole modern war problem and (since the United States then held a monopoly of the weapon) that a race in the new armament was inescapable.

The United States with her Allies tried to do something. They made the famous gesture of the Acheson-Lilienthal-Baruch plan, which looked to the complete elimination of atomic energy as a military weapon and its development for peaceful purposes under an ironclad form of international control. Stalin's government is still castigated in this country for its rejection of the plan; and the President, in his recent letter [1958] to Bulganin, could still speak as if it were only the inexplicable recalcitrance of Moscow which has condemned the world to the present "balance of terror." Yet at the time the Baruch-U.N. plan was offered, many were sure that the Russians could not and would not accept it; some even wondered whether the United States could do so.

If one tries to look through the eyes of Stalin, it is not difficult to see why the plan was fated. The United States, believing itself to hold monopoly control of an almost absolute military weapon as well as of a newly-discovered energy source of immense significance, was offering to yield both into the hands of an international authority in which the United States would have a permanently dominant influence, while both Russia and her Communist international system would be at a permanent disadvantage. The offer was surrounded by conditions as to inspection which might seriously imperil both the internal power of the Communist dictatorship and its political freedom on the world stage. It was clear that the United States would make no actual surrender of the military power until the Soviet Union had demonstrated its loyal acceptance of what was a Western solution of a problem now common to both great systems. Stalin may or may not have realized how enormous would have been the gain, for the Soviet Union no less than for all other powers, if nuclear weaponry could once and for all have been abolished. In other respects, the offer was unattractive by comparison with the alternative, which was simply to wait until the Soviet Union had also grasped the Promethean fires, and then use them to bargain on equal footing for their control and elimination. Moscow decided to wait.

Had the positions been reversed, it seems highly probable that the United States would have done the same. Today, when the Soviet Union seems well "ahead" of us in ballistic rocketry, we make gestures about the mutual control of "outer space," but put our true reliance on renewed efforts to catch up, so that the bargaining—if any—will be equal. Stalin's position in 1947 was doubtless much the same as ours is now. He had every reason to trust our protestations that we would never initiate a preventive war, so he had plenty of time; just as we show, if not by our words, then by our actions—programs and projects that will take years to bring to effective results—that we think the same thing. He may have known that he would not have to wait long, just as we feel that we are behind the Russians in rocketry by only a few months or maybe a year.

The Baruch plan, after all, was rooted in the assumption that the United States possessed a great and dread secret which others would certainly unravel but only over the course of years. Herein lay a motivation that would secure acceptance of the plan—or so we thought. The assumption may have been mistaken. Russian science and technology—of whose power we have lately come to have a better understanding—may have been much farther along the road in 1947 than we supposed. They fired their first bomb only two years later. After all, we pressed on our own atomic development under a desperate fear that the Germans would beat us; we now know that the Germans were not even seriously trying. But the Russians must have been, and may well have been progressing only a little less rapidly than we were. In such a frame, Stalin's rejection of the Baruch plan is not only understandable but must seem inevitable. To throw it now in the face of the Soviet Union may feed our sense of moral superiority; it can in no way contribute toward the control of the appalling new arms competition in which we have been entangled.

The peculiar horror and peril of the current arms race seem to me to derive from two facts. *First*, it centers almost exclusively on weapons of mass extermination which no ingenuity has as yet sufficed to reduce to the useful political and social purposes which war (an "instrument of policy continued by other means") has immemorially served. *Second*, it is almost wholly a technological race. The race in mobilizable numbers, exemplified by the Franco-German army increases before 1914, was at least theoretically subject to some kind of balance. The technological race seems almost impossible to balance. An early, and celebrated, example is "Jackie" Fisher's introduction of the dreadnought battleship after 1904, which rendered obsolete the whole apparatus of British naval supremacy, in order to prevent the Germans from doing it first. The result was to upset whatever naval balances existed at the time and seriously to dislocate the whole structure of naval power. This kind of thing is now happening every year or every six months. The atomic bomb produces the hydrogen bomb. We establish intermediate-range bomber bases around the Soviet Union in order to make sure that we can deliver our deterrent on Russian vital centers; the Russians are pressed to push forward their intermediate-range rocket development so that they can make sure of "taking out" the air bases before the planes are launched. The inaccuracy of even intermediate-range ballistic missiles means that they will have to be armed with megaton bombs to take out the bases. We propose to put megaton-bomb missiles into Europe which can take out Soviet cities in reprisal. We also develop atomic-powered missile-carrying submarines which can substitute for fixed air bases in an attack on the Soviet Union; this means that the Soviet Union will develop similiar weapons which can assault the whole huge population complexes on our two seaboards with the power of total destruction. The "answer" to that is both a $40 billion shelter program and an anti-missile missile which "may" be able to intercept. And perhaps the worst of it is that most of these fiendish devices do not represent existing and usable weapons—like the pre-1914 German and French infantry divisions, for example—but are only prototypes, just as *HMS Dreadnought* was when she came out in 1906. We cannot neglect their potentialities, yet for the present we cannot build rational military policy upon them. They compel us to live simultaneously in the shadow of the past (the older concept of war as an instrument of policy), the shadow of the present (ominous and unmanageable enough with the weapons actually in existence in quantity) and the shadow of a future of unbelievable terror, cost, complexity and inapplicability to any valid human purposes, Communist or non-Communist.

This is the arms race today, which seems fated to end in the same kind of disaster as did the race before 1914, only infinitely worse in its effects. Perhaps there is one difference. I believe that this time both the two great contenders are equally aware of the lethal nature of the dilemma in which both are trapped. I doubt that either a Russian or an American general staff today would make the same kind of mistake committed by the German General Staff before 1914. Von Schlieffen and his followers knew that the explosive potentials which they commanded were so great that any war would put a frightful strain upon all contenders; even Germany, they thought, could not long sustain such a conflict; therefore, any war would have to be a short one, which in turn meant that Germany would have to amass so overwhelming a striking power that victory would be attained in weeks. This was the foundation of the war plan employed by Germany in 1914; it was a concept which led in fact to four years of war ending not in victory but in calamitous defeat. Presumably, both Russian and American staffs are planning today upon quick victory, because total extinction seems to be the only alternative. I doubt whether either believes that its plans are adequate, as the Germans in 1914 thought that theirs were. Both know that they are really in a common dilemma—the inapplicability of any present or future form of military force in resolving the world problem.

Is there any escape from the dilemma? The Russians certainly have been able to offer none. It is curious how many good ideas have proceeded from Russia. In 1898, they proposed an arms "freeze." In 1918 (under the Bolsheviks), they proposed "peace without annexation or indemnities." In the inter-war years, they advocated total abolition of all national armaments. From the beginning of the atomic age, they have proposed total abolition of all nuclear weapons. They are now proposing the abolition of nuclear testing. It is hard to deny that if any or all these proposals had been acceptable at the time they were offered, the world would be a happier and much safer place than it is. Why, then, did they so uniformly fail? The best answer seems to be that the Russians were never able or willing to make a realistic analysis of the power factors with which they were attempting to deal, and consequently were never able to advance any of these ideas except under the appearance of being merely a way of expanding Russian imperial interests or Russian security at the expense of the security and interests of the rest of the world.

Today, the Russian "peace offensives" still have the same character and are therefore similarly abortive. Unfortunately, the responses from the West, or from the United States as its leader, too often are of the same kind. Our own analysis of the place of military power in the international world often seems as defective, or myopic, as that of the Kremlin. Our own "peace offensives" are not very different from those emitted by Moscow, though they seem to be rather less successful with the uncommitted world to which they are supposed to appeal. Mr. Stassen, while earning an A for effort, does not seem to have been able to do much more than Secretary Dulles toward altering the essential dynamism of an arms race, the horribly lethal character of which must be apparent to all—in Moscow as well as in the United States.

Given the fact of a common dilemma, a common peril, a common necessity for substantial peace if any of the objectives of either the Communist or the Western world are to be achieved, it does seem that there is some better way than a continued building of what General Bradley has called "this electronic house of cards"—a technological arms race pyramiding in ever greater instability and uncertainty to the point of a collapse in which a thousand years of civilization are likely to perish. A "summit" conference will probably not be of much help at the moment; whatever small gains may be possible from continued "disarmament" negotiations are unlikely greatly to affect the nuclear-arms race which has been sweeping on as if the disarmament negotiators did not exist. But surely it is practically possible to reduce the tensions and the tempo of the competition. It is possible to return to the point achieved at Geneva in 1955, when each superpower declared, not only that it did not intend to wage war upon the other (the small-change of diplomacy), but that it believed the other did not intend to wage war upon itself. Nothing has really happened since to alter that fundamental statement of belief; if it is true on both sides still, as it seems to be, it should furnish a powerful foundation on which diplomacy might operate to reduce the nonsense (apparent in our own country as well as in Russia) generated by the idea that aggressive war is the most imminent danger now facing our two systems.

THE AIRPOWER LOBBY / AL TOFFLER

On a hot day in mid-July this year [1957], a man named Joseph F. Quilter climbed up the stone steps outside the Washington office of the Friends Committee on National Legislation. Quilter had come all the way from Sunnyvale, California, to this small house around the corner from the Senate Office Building to discuss prospects for disarmament. Quilter went elsewhere, too. He was collecting, from all sources, the best possible estimates of the degree of disarmament, if any, which could be anticipated in the next ten to fifteen years.

Quilter is with the Product Planning Section, Missiles Divisions, Lockheed Aircraft Corp., and Lockheed has a right to be worried about disarmament. Since 1951, no year has passed in which less than 69 per cent of Lockheed's sales has been military. In some years the proportion has been as high as 92 per cent.

Quilter's trip here, in itself unimportant, symbolizes the understandable anxiety with which the aircraft industry—the nation's biggest employer—views any relaxation in international tensions.

Other evidences of this anxiety abound. Said the San Francisco *Chronicle* on June 30: "Aircraft stocks have been in a nosedive. . . . Villains of the piece are the trend toward disarmament and the increasing competition from missiles."

By August, disarmament talks in London had cracked wide open. On Aug. 30, *The New York Times* reported "a spurt in demand for aircraft issues. . . . The renewed interest was attributed by some observers to Russia's flat rejection of the West's disarmament program. . . ."

Few (and the author is not among them) would urge that the United States disarm unilaterally as long as the Soviets remain strong and antagonistic. On the other hand, as the recently formed National Committee for a Sane Nuclear Policy has pointed out eloquently:

> The test of a nation's right to survive today is measured not by the size of its bombs or the range of its missiles, but by the size and range of its

concern for the human community as a whole. . . . The earth is too small for intercontinental ballistic missiles and nuclear bombs, and . . . the first order of business for the world is to bring both under control.

This is a large order of business and the Russians do not always make it easier of accomplishment. But under the Dulles regime we have deliberately by-passed several opportunities for at least partial disarmament. Disarmament need not depend on the good faith of Moscow. Negotiated properly, it can be made to depend on Moscow's self-interest as well as our own.

However, a climate has existed in Washington which made it almost inevitable that we would pass up the limited opportunities. If we are ever to move on to "the first order of business," this climate must be altered, and to be altered it must be understood. It is within this context that the amazingly frank remarks of former Secretary of Defense Charles E. Wilson before the House Appropriations Committee last January 30 take on special significance. Wilson confessed that during his more "adventuresome" moods he has talked to his friends about the relationship of industry to the cold war.

> One of the serious things about this defense business [Wilson testified] is that so many Americans are getting a vested interest in it: properties, business, jobs, employment, votes, opportunities for promotion and advancement, bigger salaries for scientists and all that. It is a troublesome business.

Later Wilson observed that "If you try to change suddenly you get into trouble. . . . If you shut the whole business off now, you will have the state of California in trouble because such a big percentage of the aircraft industry is in California."

The vested interest of which Wilson speaks is no will-o'-the-wisp. It extends, of course, far beyond California and far beyond the aircraft industry. But this particular industry is something very special. An excrescence of the cold war itself, it has become the biggest single employer in the nation, with over 900,000 workers in its cavernous installations. Its member-firms, like Boeing Aircraft Corp., top the list of all defense contractors, in contrast to a traditional industrial giant like Mr. Wilson's own General Motors. During the Korean War, G.M. was the country's biggest war-material producer; today it has given ground to the aircraft and missile makers, having dropped to sixteenth place.

The political power exercised by the industry cannot be measured exclusively by the handful of giant firms which control it. The system of subcontracting gives the industry roots in thousands of communities over the nation—and each community thereby shares a vested interest in its continued well-being. In an article entitled "Small Business and the Cold War," *The Nation* pointed out on June 30, last year:

> Fifty producers of airplanes, engines and component parts reported that they had negotiated 60,000 subcontracts. The geographic spread of these subcontracts is as significant as the number: nearly every Congressional district is represented.

In short, the vitality, growth, profit—the very life—of the aircraft industry, more than any other, is inextricably intertwined with United States military and foreign policy.

The importance of this is twofold. The industry, with its insatiable needs and shrill propaganda, contributes significantly to the creation of the anti-disarmament climate. Secondly, even if disarmament is considered out of the question, as it is by many, then the influence of the aircraft industry still needs careful examination. For just as the industry has a vested interest in continued international tension, it also has a vested interest in particular military strategic concepts. These may, fortuitously, be correct; but of this there is no guarantee whatever. Whether or not one agrees with the charge that we have been disarming unilaterally, everyone ought to agree that military policies should be shaped by military needs and not by commercial considerations.

Yet the fact that the aircraft industry and the United States Air Force are partners in advocacy of a special strategic philosophy, i.e., almost total reliance on air power, creates powerful pressures that distort this basic premise.

The relationship between the aircraft-missile industry and the Air Force is quite different from that between other industries and their military customers. The Army, for example, buys billions of dollars worth of hardware, but the orders are widely distributed through the industrial community. The Navy may subsidize shipbuilders, but it also purchases a great deal from other scattered industrial sources, including the aircraft industry. But the Air Force, while it too needs uniforms, soap, hypodermic needles and milk, channels the overwhelming bulk of its procurement expenditures through the handful of large companies that dominate the aircraft industry. (See "One-Customer Industry," *The Nation*, August 11, 1956.)

The relationship between these firms and the Air Force, therefore, "goes far beyond the normal business dealings of buyer and seller"—to quote the Aircraft Industries Association.

The Air Force and the industry are thus partners. But they are partners with a division of labor. For while the Air Force has its own life and its own interests, it nevertheless functions as the steel-tipped spearhead of the industry's Washington lobby. In this task, it receives civilian support from the Aircraft Industries Association, individual aircraft manufacturers, the Air Force Association and its junior satellite, the Arnold Society, the Air Division of the American Legion National Security Commission, similar veterans' organizations, the International Association of Machinists and other labor unions representing workers in the industry.

The role of the Air Force in this compound pressure group was explained this way by a staff member of one of the Congressional Armed Services committees: "The industry doesn't do much direct lobbying here on the Hill. To sell a project to Congress is the hard way to do it. It's much easier to sell the idea to the Air Force and let the Air Force do the pushing."

How influential the industry is in selling projects—and, more significantly, the policies that justify them—should be of vital concern to every citizen and especially to every Congressional committee interested in national defense.

The delicate feeler at the very end of the steel tip of the Air Force lobby is the Office of Legislative Liaison, presided over by Major General Joe W. Kelly and operating directly under the authority of the Office of the Secretary of the Air Force. At one time, assignment to O.L.L. was considered exile, but no longer. According to the people on Capitol Hill who do business with the services, Kelly is "one of the best in the business" and his office attracts top-caliber people. With over 125 personnel and an annual expenditure of over $700,000, it is the biggest legislative arm of any service—although admittedly not by much.

Kelly's unit maintains a special office in the House Office Building to serve Congressmen. When a constituent writes his Congressman that his son in the Air Force needs an emergency leave, wants a transfer or needs some other form of special attention, the request is passed along to the O.L.L. office. There it is processed with more or less rapidity. This service —which the other military branches also perform—is a necessary and legitimate one. It also makes friends and influences Congressmen.

Back in the Pentagon, Kelly's office helps pick out the right officers to testify before Congressional committees; it helps prepare presentations which are intended to sell Congress one or another program; it keeps a sensitive ear to the Congressional mood and is responsible for keeping the Air Force informed as well as representing it in the halls of Congress.

The O.L.L., it should be noted, does little work on appropriation bills, which are largely handled by the Assistant Secretary of the Air Force (comptroller) and the military chain under him. But O.L.L. does work closely with the Armed Services committees, where the basic lines of military policy are established. These committees clear projects before their submission to the Appropriations committees; their endorsements carry great weight with Congress.

The efficacy of the Air Force's political activity can be measured to a degree in the way the ever-expanding military melon is divided among the services. It is true that technological and other factors have been involved in the ascendancy of the Air Force. But the political footwork of the Air Force and its civilian allies has not been without significance.

In 1950 the still-young Air Force received only 31 per cent of the funds divided among the three services—less than either of the other two. Today, with the total melon more than tripled in size, the Air Force gets 47–48 per cent, more than either of its "rivals" and almost as much as the two combined.

In view of the current furor over missiles and satellites—a furor nourished in part by the aircraft lobby—it is an absolutely safe bet to say that any increase in military spending will widen still further the percentage gap.

The jet-like rise of the Air Force can be measured in other ways, too. In the *Annals of the American Academy of Political and Social Science* in May, 1955, W. Barton Leach, a fervid airpower enthusiast, complained among other things that the air arm was insufficiently represented in the Office of the Secretary of Defense. Of the key men in that office, he charged, none had any Air Force background. Since then, Air Force men have moved into dominating positions in the military establishment as a whole, including the Office of the Secretary of Defense. Donald Quarles, former Secretary of the Air Force, has moved up to Deputy Secretary of Defense, the Number Two civilian job in the whole set-up. General Nathan Twining, former Air Force Chief of Staff, has been elevated to Chairman of the Joint Chiefs of Staff, replacing Admiral Arthur Radford, a Navy man, but in recent years an excellent friend of the Air Force.

This ascension of the Air Force has occurred during a period in which its rationale—airpower as the ultimate deterrent—gained overwhelming acceptance in Washington. The emergence of the concept, of course, can be traced to the astounding series of revolutions which have taken place in the science of destruction since Hiroshima. But strategic theories seldom just "catch on." They have to be helped.

This is where the public-information program of the Air Force and the propaganda efforts of the industry and its organizations come in. The Air Force is allotted $816,667 a year to carry on public-information activity. Thirty full-time and over 200 part-time publicists, in and out of uniform, devote at least a part of their efforts to popularizing the airpower philosophy. Additionally, braided speechmakers brandishing "cleared" scripts appear at civilian conventions and meetings almost every day of the year.

But even if the Air Force were, as Barton Leach inaccurately labeled it, "the silent service," the airpower story would still be drummed into the ears of citizens and Congressmen by other units of the lobby. Around the corner from the White House, for example, is the headquarters of the Air Force Association. This organization, first conceived by General H. H. Arnold, sprang to life in 1945 as a "civilian airpower group." Today A.F.A. boasts over 50,000 individual members, 125 community groups and 300 industry affiliates. A key link between the industry and the Air Force, A.F.A. is a dynamic and aggressive exponent of the all-for-air thesis. Says one of its recruiting brochures:

> A.F.A. headquarters are in Washington so that A.F.A. can keep tabs on what's going on in Congress, at the Pentagon, at every top echelon. And so that A.F.A. can present at the top military and government level an airpower policy that is originated and hammered out by some of the best qualified men in the country—our members.

A.F.A.'s interests are broad. It is not registered as a lobby organization and its staff vigorously denies any such function. But here is what the organization tells its members:

> On everything from pay, PX privileges and housing to logistics and optimum overall air strength, A.F.A. has the information that legislators and policy-makers need. And they appreciate honest, thorough help in working out the problems they've got to solve. They turn naturally to A.F.A. . . .

On a more diffuse propaganda level, A.F.A. assiduously issues information in support of a bigger Air Force budget. Its staff works with Hollywood and the press "to get public appreciation for the needs and status of airpower." It also publishes an expensive monthly magazine which is supported by institutional advertising from the aircraft companies.

If A.F.A. serves as a sounding board—particularly a grass-roots sounding board—for the propaganda of the industry and the service, it also performs another vital function in providing a liaison link between the two. Although it is supposed to be a "civilian airpower group," its board of directors is studded with present and former air generals (Jimmy Doolittle, "Tooey" Spatz, George C. Kenney). It is also weighted with industry representatives. The president is Peter Schenk, a high executive in General Electric's military-marketing operation. Convair, Northrop and Fairchild are also represented on the board.

In its own words, the A.F.A. "provides a meeting place for industry and the military . . . We think and act on issues which are fundamental to business because they are fundamental to security." Pointing out that "the U.S. Air Force is beyond question the biggest business, and the biggest single market in the world," A.F.A. adds unnecessarily that "industry's interest in effective liaison with the Air Force is obvious." An A.F.A. staff man put the relationship more colorfully: "A.F.A. is the catalyst that encourages the Air Force and the industry to make happy music together."

The organization also supervises the Arnold Society, an organization devoted to preaching the airpower line to the country's youth.

Perhaps even more important politically and in terms of liaison is the Aircraft Industries Association, which, although it protests that it is not a lobby, has registered a lobbyist, Harold Mosier, in its name. It claims to "represent the industry's viewpoints and interests to the government. It is vigilant of legislation and regulations that might affect the aircraft industry." It spends $350,000 a year for a high-powered public-relations program (directed by Hill & Knowlton, a blue-chip agency). It has an overall budget of about $1,500,000 a year, according to a spokesman. Its president is a retired four-star Air Force General Orval R. Cook. Its well-illustrated publication, *Planes,* goes to 60,000 readers, many of them in the opinion-making professions.

In addition to these components, the airpower lobby is also backed by the pressures applied by individual companies. When North American Aviation lost its massive Navaho missile contract last summer, an up-in-arms delegation of California Congressmen marched on the Department of Defense demanding to know why. The source of this regional pressure is the industry itself, individual companies and the unions representing the aircraft workers.

Thus no voice has been louder in support of limitless spending for aircraft and missiles than the International Association of Machinists, AFL-CIO, which represents about two-thirds of the organized workers in the industry. As the *Machinists Journal* once put it, "The I.A.M. has ... become synonymous with the aircraft industry." The union's fortnightly newspaper (circulation almost 1,000,000) may attack the companies on collective-bargaining issues, but there is a closing of ranks on the issue of more airpower.

The United Auto Workers, which represents many aircraft employees, has also pressed hard for higher airpower spending, albeit its leadership does so with some sense of private embarrassment. The blush didn't prevent the union's vice president, Leonard Woodcock, from commenting, after the Navaho cancellation, that the government must not be permitted to cancel weapons contracts purely on the basis of national-defense needs.

Labor's concern is natural. Pre-Sputnik cutbacks in defense spending have already resulted in the layoff of about 25,000 aircraft workers in Los Angeles alone, and additional thousands have lost jobs in such aircraft centers as Long Island. Moreover, the outlook is not good; the fabrication of missiles and rockets needs less manpower than that of conventional aircraft, and this is the direction, of course, in which tomorrow's airpower is turning. Layoffs affect whole communities as well as the ranks of labor. Los Angeles, for instance, needs 100,000 new jobs each year to keep pace with its population growth.

So communities join with labor in pressing for a national-defense system that guarantees full employment. National security shapes up as a problem of profits, wages and jobs. Many of the laid-off Los Angeles aircraft workers, sensing the trap they are in, are seeking to get out of the industry altogether and line themselves up with jobs less dependent upon the vagaries of defense spending.

The industry, through spokesmen like General Cook, stridently urges acceleration of spending for both manned aircraft and missiles. The implication is that even if we do not need more planes or missiles at a given time, the industry ought to be fed with contracts just so that it will remain on the alert. Meanwhile, the Air Force presses its own political struggle with the other services.

Sputnik's effect on the politics and mentality of America will be profound. But its impact on the economy will be no less important. As a spokesman for a major aircraft and missile company told me a few days ago [1957], "The boys are going to be jumping all over themselves to see who'll get in the first bill to increase funds for missiles and manned aircraft after Congress reconvenes." There were no perceptible tears streaming from his eyes as he spoke.

The remark dramatizes the fact that no segment of our economy has more at stake than the aircraft industry in the explosive events triggered by the Sputniks. The industry's powerful lobby is aware of both its responsibilities and its opportunities. Current events are going to shake the industry and force at least a conditional settlement in the sputtering feud among the nation's three military services. If the showdown is to be resolved rationally, on the basis of achieving the best defense for the smallest dollar, the military issues must not be obscured by the internal needs of a single industry or a single military service, no matter how vocal.

To understand the stake of the aircraft and missile-makers in all this, a few statistics are in order. The industry consists of many companies, but it is substantially dominated by thirteen: Bell, Boeing, Curtiss-Wright, Douglas, General Dynamics (Convair), Grumman, Lockheed, Martin, McDonnell, North American, Northrop, Republic and United Aircraft. In 1956, the industry sold $9,496,000,000 worth of goods, an annual turnover exceeded only twice during World War II: in 1943 and 1944. Over 75 per cent of the total was sold to a single customer, the Department of Defense; and of this, most went to the Air Force, although some went also to the Army and Navy. (The Navy's air arm, incidentally, is the third biggest air force in the world; only the United States and Soviet air forces are larger.)

As of March, 1957, six of the above companies—Grumman, McDonnell, Martin, North American, Northrop and Republic—were devoted virtually 100 per cent to filling military orders. The other major firms ranged in degree of dependence on the military from about 60 to 95 per cent. Between October, 1950, and May, 1957, the thirteen companies, in view of their defense nature, received from the government a total of 573 certificates granting rapid amortization privileges on $370,000,000. The Hebert subcommittee in the House reported in 1956 that twelve of the firms were using $895,000,000 worth of government-owned plants, machine tools and equipment, compared with their own total private investment of $394,000,000 (a large part of which represented retained profits).

The war nature of the industry was capsuled simply by the Hebert subcommittee: "There is not enough commercial business in this country *nor in the world* to justify the utilization of all the facilities now 'in being.'" (Emphasis added.)

Representative Martha Griffiths (D.-Mich.), a former defense procurement officer in Detroit, referring to the firms which do nothing but military work, told her colleagues: "They—the management, and the employees and, to the extent they participate, the stockholders of these companies—are just as much federal employees as you are or as I am. Every dime that they are paid comes from the taxpayers' money." In view of this, she said, the government, in determining prices it was ready to pay, ought to scrutinize closely the profits and remuneration of aircraft companies and their officials. She had in mind that North American, for instance, in 1955, had paid its president a nice round $147,000 in salary and extras and had paid its chairman $201,000.

The six companies dependent exclusively on government contracts paid out $694,000 to their six presidents in 1955, not including stock options and dividends. The remuneration of their top executives, including presidents and board chairmen, totaled $3,468,000. And the total paid out in this fashion by the thirteen companies whose work is principally for Uncle Sam came to $9,838,000. Evidently air-industry executives are the highest paid "federal employees" in the history of the nation.

As for profits, in 1956 twelve of the big thirteen made a net, after taxes, of $156,000,000, according to the Aircraft Industries Association. This was the third best year on record for the industry—five times as much as was made in the Korean War year 1951 and almost twice the net profits of 1952. Such statistics are admittedly slippery; but these are industry figures, and possibly conservative.

Employment in the industry has risen from 237,700 in 1948 to about 900,000 today. This makes the industry the nation's biggest private employer, with almost 5 per cent of the country's total manufacturing work force on its payroll.

Statistics aside, the fact of key significance about the aircraft industry is the intimacy of its relationship with the Air Force, its biggest customer. The two are almost parts of an organic whole. Liaison between them occurs on many levels. Company salesmen beat a well-scuffed path to the Pentagon. Airpower organizations provide numerous forums for social and business contacts. Even more important is the startling osmosis of Air Force brass into the company hierarchies. General Ira C. Eaker, formerly vice president of the Hughes Tool Co., recently moved over to the Douglas Aircraft Corp. Convair is headed by General Joseph T. McNarney. Boeing and Convair each at one time reportedly had sixty-seven retired officers on their payrolls. The Martin Co. has had at least fourteen.

The Hebert subcommittee in 1956 charged that "the presence of retired military personnel on payrolls, fresh from the 'opposite side of the desk,' creates a doubtful atmosphere." The Congressmen were chiefly concerned with the influence such men could wield on procurement. But there is another, more important and more dangerous aspect. The purchasing done by the Air Force depends to a great extent on its underlying military philosophy, its strategic outlook. Theoretically, men in uniform determine basic policy subject to the general approval of civilian authority. But the osmosis process raises the question to what extent Air Force policy is molded by ex-officers whose outlook is colored by interests of the companies they serve.

Liberals have long felt that the presence of businessmen in key government posts has frequently resulted in harm to the public interest. Right now a House subcommittee, under liberal leadership, is exploring the reverse situation (a parallel of which exists today in the aircraft industry): the employment by industry of former commissioners and other top personnel of the independent regulatory agencies. In many of these agencies, it is possible for a man to leave his job as a commissioner and within twenty-four hours, to appear as counsel before the commission in behalf of a regulated industry.

If the influence of industry on government policy in civilian areas is a continuing source of concern, is not the possibility of similar influence on military policy even more alarming? This is not a charge that military policy has been determined by the aircraft industry. Nor does it impute conscious selfishness or lack of patriotism to the industry and its hired generals. It is, however, a suggestion that the unique relationship between the industry and the Air Force not only makes possible, but actively encourages, the exercise of private influence. What's more, the stakes are high.

These, then, are the essential characteristics of the aircraft industry: low investment, low working capital, high remuneration for executives, direct dependence on military purchasing, intimacy with a particular branch of the armed forces, dependence on a variety of federal subsidies, absorption of military personnel, interest in strategic policy. Its two major problems are (1) disarmament and (2) the rise of the missile.

When Germany first began pouring V-2 rockets upon Britain in World War II, military men were impressed. But they considered the missiles an expensive way to deliver a small warhead. It wasn't until the genius of humanity had produced nuclear weapons that it became "economical" to invest heavily in such complex delivery systems as are required by missiles.

Ever since, the handwriting has been on the wall for the fliers and manufacturers of manned aircraft. Industry and Air Force spokesmen tend to sneer at Khrushchev's post-Sputnik description of manned aircraft as museum pieces. They speak in terms of producing at least one more "generation" of long-range, manned bombers. But no one should understand better than they how rapidly aeronautical technology changes. As *Look* magazine put it not long ago. "The death rattle is in the throat of the flying Air Force."

For the industry, this has posed critical issues—and especially for the makers of tactical fighters and bombers, since these appear to be destined for quickest obsolescence. In simple terms, the industry's problem is how to capture complete, irrevocable and unchallengeable control over missile-making.

The proportion of Air Force spending on guided missiles has risen steadily. In fiscal 1951, it was less than 1 per cent of the total spent for aircraft procurement. By 1952 it rose to 4 per cent; a year later, to 12 per cent. In fiscal 1957, according to the latest estimates, it was 20.3 per cent and it was expected to be 35 per cent by 1959, according to a 1956 estimate by the Aircraft Industries Association. With today's Sputnik furor as a propellant, the missile proportion of a total military spending should streak heavenward much faster than expected.

The aircraft firms are not merely fighting for contracts to develop, partially produce and assemble missiles; they are reaching out into related areas. North American, for example, has moved into the manufacture of rocket fuel, and its Rocketdyne division already accounts for 18 per cent of sales. Another area of interest is the electronic industry, which is responsible for about 50 per cent of the cost of any missile as opposed to 35 per cent of the cost of a plane. The industry, accordingly, has prospered on subcontracted work from the aircraft industry, and as the president of the Radio-Electronics-Television Manufacturers Association said last spring, "The ceiling is not in sight." Now, however, aircraft companies are also reaching into electronics.

The aircraft industry is in transition, and Wall Street analysts, ever sensitive to shifting industrial patterns, expect a "shakeout." The number of firms will be smaller, and those which remain will be bigger. Last year a quarter-million workers for small, scattered subcontractors produced nearly a billion dollars worth of goods and services for planes and missile-makers. According to the *Wall Street Journal*, these "corporate satellites" are already being squeezed as the giant aircraft firms go increasingly into the "parts" business. And the squeeze will tighten in the months ahead.

In the race for missile work the aircraft manufacturers see no major competition from any other industry. Even the electronics industry hardly falls into the competitive category; as long as the aircraft makers remain the prime contractors, they can control the degree of subcontracting. What the industry fears is competition from the government as represented by the tendency of the Army and the Navy Bureau of Ordnance (but not the Navy Bureau of Aeronautics) to place contracts with non-profit institutions like universities, or to assign projects to government-operated arsenals using government employees.

It was industry disapproval of this trend that lay behind the furious battle over the Air Force's Thor missile as against the Army's Jupiter. This, in turn, formed the backdrop of the court-martial of Army Colonel John Nickerson.

Jupiter was developed by the Army at Redstone Arsenal in Huntsville, Alabama. Component parts were made by aircraft companies, but if the missile ever goes into production, it will be built not by an aircraft company but by Chrysler. Meanwhile, the normally highly lucrative development work and the overall supervision were performed by government employees rather than privately-employed workers. In contrast, the comparable Thor is being developed for the Air Force by Douglas Aircraft.

It was not surprising, therefore, that a fever-pitch propaganda battle developed over the two missiles. Air Force supporters opened a campaign to discredit Dr. Wernher von Braun, the Army's German missile expert. *Aviation Week*, one of the industry's chief publications, in mid-September attacked the Army for a "vicious" campaign against the Air Force. At the same time, General Orval Cook, head of the Aircraft Industries Association, insisted that the "government arsenal has outlived its usefulness." Moreover, Cook told newsmen, the universities should stick to teaching and basic research, leaving development work for industry.

Advocates of the arsenal, however, point out that research and development are the fuzziest of all cost items. By doing some of both at arsenals, it is possible for the government to gain some notion of the real cost factors involved. In effect, the arsenal can function as a yardstick.

The controversy also revealed the increasing importance of research and development from a financial point of view. The industry is not kicking up a squall about peanuts; big money is involved. It is estimated that the Department of Defense this year will spend over five billion dollars for research and development. However, only about 40 per cent of this sum is directly appropriated; the rest of the amount is scattered through other budgetary compartments. The result is that concrete figures are hard to pin down. Even the A.I.A. isn't sure of the size of the nugget involved. The organization is making conditional use of a partial breakdown issued last September by the National Science Foundation, which shows that of the identifiable $2,000,000,000 which the Defense Department will obligate for research and development in fiscal 1958, nearly $1.3 billion will be spent on projects handled intramurally or by non-profit agencies.

This is a rise of almost $400,000,000 since 1955 in expenditures withheld from private enterprise. The A.I.A. believes that there are additional millions hidden away in less identifiable appropriations. In all, the A.I.A. scents a minimum of around a billion dollars which could be smoked out by its members if the Army and the Navy were as cooperative as the Air Force.

A decade of intimate association with an "understanding" Air Force has given the aircraft industry a stake in the outcome of the continuing interservice warfare. Congressman George Mahon (D.-Tex.) set this rivalry in its proper perspective last spring when he told his colleagues:

> Able and ambitious officers have devoted their careers to one of the three services. Will they have a place in the sun in the 1960's or will their careers go into decline? The present assumption is that any service which fails to have a part in the utilization of intermediate range and intercontinental ballistic missiles will be relegated to a lesser role. . . . The stakes are high. . . . The desperate struggle for power and position among the services is quite understandable, and real, and quite expensive and wasteful.

The conflict among the services revolves around this hard core of truth. But it is clothed in all kinds of strategic rationales. Thus the Air Force has taken the position that the nation cannot afford continued maintenance of strong "conventional forces" (read Army). General Twining has told the Senate that the country cannot have military forces for both "the old type of warfare plus those for atomic warfare . . . and our mind is made up." Certainly his mind is made up—and made up in favor of the Air Force.

The Army, seeing in all this a relentless diminution of its role, prestige and budget, counters with the sophisticated argument that reduction in conventional forces raises the "level of provocation" necessary before this country would respond militarily to defend its interests. We must, argue the Army theorists, be prepared to dole out retaliation in measured, and not merely in massive, doses.

There are many other points of conflict between the Air Force and its one-time parent, the Army. On a military-technical level, they focus on what kind of missiles the Army will be permitted to develop and use. Essentially, the Air Force argues that missiles are air weapons. They fly, don't they? The Army counters by noting that they are basically an extension of artillery, a traditional Army function.

Meanwhile, the Navy has its own air and seapower interests, which it is jealously guarding.

These may sound like questions which the generals and admirals ought to settle by themselves. However, they are questions which citizens in a democracy cannot shrug off or simply refer to the military men. The weapons involved are too big and too dangerous. The stakes affect everyone—including the aircraft industry. Any shift of "roles and missions" which gave the Army primary responsibility for missile warfare would make the Army, rather than the Air Force, the Number One customer of the aircraft industry. This would shatter all the business, personal, social, political and economic relationships which have grown up between the Air Force and the dozen or so key aircraft companies. From the industry's viewpoint, it would mean dealing with a service which has shown much less readiness to "cooperate." And it would render obsolete the services of all the Air Force officers recruitd by the industry to do its bargaining.

In short, if the Air Force fails to come out on top in the inter-service Armageddon which is in the offing, the results could be very serious for the aircraft makers. So once again the industry finds it necessary to support the particular strategic reasoning of a single branch—to support, publicize, and perhaps to refine, stiffen or otherwise influence it.

Thoughtful aircraft men must recognize the dangers that grow out of this kind of relationship. The perils should be even more clear to outsiders. And as for remedies, perhaps the only real one is relaxation of world tensions and the planned replacement of arms production by something more constructive. Short of this, however, Congress and the people ought to give thought to the implications of the fact that the nation's biggest manufacturing industry is now a kind of mutant in our capitalist society, dependent almost solely on public funds for its day-to-day existence.

SMALL BUSINESS AND THE COLD WAR / CAREY McWILLIAMS

"Russian smiles and the coming of the H-bomb," reports the *Wall Street Journal*, have created new pressures in Washington for the curtailment of military spending. But any attempt to cut military appropriations will meet with stout resistance and increasingly so if the economic outlook does not improve. Oddly enough, the resistances are stronger in the Democratic Party, the party of labor and small business, than in the big-business GOP.

This is not as paradoxical as it sounds. Big business, of course, gets the lion's share—80 per cent or more—of defense contracts. But since the Korean War, small business has been encouraged to believe that the competitive advantages of big business might be offset if only a larger slice of defense work went to the smaller firms. In point of fact, however, every expansion of the military budget only intensifies the forbidding disparity between them. It has been expectation of *more* defense work, rather than any actual benefits received, that accounts for the surprising number of cold warriors in the ranks of small business.

But if small business has played a small part financially in military procurement it has, in the words of the Select Senate Committee on Small Business, "played a large part numerically." There are 4,000,000 small businesses in the country [1956] and 300,000 small manufacturing concerns ("small" meaning here an establishment with 500 employees or less). On one contract, Pratt and Whitney gave out 5,278 subcontracts to firms located in twenty-eight states. RCA Victor reported it had roughly 5,000 suppliers in forty-two states. Fifty producers of airplanes, engines and component parts reported that they had negotiated 60,000 subcontracts. The geographic spread of these subcontracts is as significant as the number: nearly every Congressional district is represented.

The industrialization mobilization that preceded but was rapidly accelerated by the Korean War found small business no more anxious than big business to abandon rising consumer markets for defense production. Even before the outbreak of the Korean War, business was recovering from the 1949 recession and the civilian market was on the upgrade. A great many GI's had set up firms of one kind or another in the post-1945 period and by 1950 were just beginning to "get on their feet." An older generation had vivid memories of what happened to small business during World War II: from Pearl Harbor to the middle of 1943 the number of small establishments declined by 16 per cent. Big business could be induced to superimpose a military program on existing consumer production schedules by the government's offer to finance, under the accelerated tax-amortization program, the construction of new "standby" or "parallel" plants to take care of defense work. But with small business the government had to use a stick as well as a carrot.

Washington's reconversion carrot for the small-business man was an assurance of preferred treatment. This time, the government said, he would get his share of defense work. The Select Senate Committee on Small Business was set up a few weeks before the outbreak of the Korean War to encourage "the participation of small business in military procurement." A similar intent was manifest in the Defense Production Act of 1950 and, under a July, 1951 amendment, the Small Defense Plants Administration had been created to give more prime contracts to small business. Various executive orders were issued aimed at "broadening the industrial base" and "encouraging subcontracting." Small-business defense clinics—designed to show the small-business man how to get defense orders—were held across the country. The armed services set up special small-business divisions and added literally hundreds of liaison officers to encourage subcontracting. With much fanfare, the air force launched Operation Pacemaker—a special program designed to give small business a larger share of aircraft procurement. Seldom has small business been catered to in this fashion.

If the "carrot" proved to be an illusion, the stick was real enough. Even before the outbreak of the Korean War it was virtually impossible for small business to obtain scarce materials, particularly copper, steel, aluminum—precisely the materials that most small manufacturing plants needed for their civilian or regular production. Even if a small plant got a DO—a defense-order priority—it could not always get scarce materials. Most small plants are not diversified; they purchase materials, for the most part, through jobbers and warehouse suppliers, not from prime producers. Caught in the materials squeeze, small business had to bid on defense work as a condition of survival. But the prime contracts—the so-called "hard core" of the defense effort—went to big business, which alone had the necessary productive and financial resources. A hundred large corporations received 62.4 per cent of the value of all prime contracts awarded from the outbreak of the Korean War to June, 1952. In 1951, the three services awarded small business about 20.8 per cent of the total dollar value of procurement; but for the year ending in June, 1950, the average figure was 24.5. During World War II the figure had been as high as 34.5 per cent (small business, after all, accounts for something like 40 per cent of the nation's productive capacity).

Much of the politics of the cold-war period is implicit in the vicissitudes of the Master Freeze Company of Sister Bay, Wisconsin, as related to the Senate Committee on February 12, 1952. The company manufactured prefabricated refrigerators, food freezers and milk coolers for the civilian market. The number of employees varied from twenty-five to 225. Founded in 1946 with family funds—the outside capital amounted to only $4,000—the company managed to show a net worth of $79,000 by 1949. The materials squeeze forced it to enter a bid for defense work. The bid—the lowest—was opened on May 3, 1950. With the Korean War, prices for materials and labor skyrocketed. Net result: the company lost $81,710.10 on its first defense contract and was forced to lay off all but six of its employees. The impact on the economy of Sister Bay can be readily imagined. Master Freeze was the only industrial plant in the peninsula of Wisconsin where Sister Bay, population 500, is located. With the backing of the community, officials of the company had come to Washington to seek an adjustment—and more defense work. That is how the story came to light.

In this and many similar situations one can see how it came about that the Democratic Party's efforts to win a larger share of the arms pie for small business created an enormous mass pressure at the grass-roots for larger military appropriations. Although the relative position of small business was weakened, many small firms did enjoy, for a time, a delirious interlude of prosperity. With from 40 to 60 per cent of their entire productive capacity devoted to defense work, many small firms could afford to dismantle sales organizations. Profits soared as sales costs declined. One firm reported $4.2 million worth of business with sales costs of only $10,000 (later the same firm spent $24,000 to get new civilian business which grossed only $450,000). It is not surprising, therefore, that a kind of March-on-Washington—from Main Street—should have taken place. Five per-centers thrived and the sale of mink coats and deep freezes boomed. A small-business man told the Senate committee that, in one year, he had spent $20,000 and twenty-two weeks of his time in Washington chasing defense orders.

The chasing, however, was mostly waste motion; small business got a steadily diminishing percentage of defense work. It received 51 per cent of the total dollar value of *advertised* procurement but managed to get only 18 per cent of the dollar value of *negotiated* procurement. Procurement-by-negotiation tends to be noncompetitive; procurement officials naturally find it easier to negotiate with one large corporation than with many small firms. And vague phraseology in executive orders and legislation made it possible for department heads to decide that more and more items were best procured through negotiation. "A great many small concerns," one witness testified, "find that negotiated prime contracts are very hard, I might say almost impossible, to find." Later the Defense Department prepared a list of "preferred firms" for a great many "essential items"; even the Senate Committee was unable to pin down the precise meaning of the preference. In resigning as head of the Small Defense Plants Administration, Telford Taylor charged that the Defense Department's delay in implementing directives in favor of small business reflected an "apparent hostility." Then and since, small business has complained about the ambiguity of the phrase "or equal quality" in advertised bids; of unrealistic delivery dates; of tricky specifications; of its inability to secure progress payments; of Pentagon red-tape. At one hearing, former Senator Benton remarked that a small-business man was one who could not afford to keep a lobbyist in Washington. This remains an excellent "operational" definition.

Now and then a small-business man appeared before the Senate committee who was able to take a detached view of the position in which he and his colleagues found themselves. One of these—John Orchard—told the committee that it was "like fifty people at a picnic going after twenty-eight hot dogs. . . . If there are small boys among those fifty people—and lots of us are small boys—then it is kind of rough, particularly when the big boys are in the first row around the barbecue pit." Remember, the total military budgets of the cold-war years were never more than about 50 per cent of the peak World War II budgets and America's productive capacity had greatly increased in the meantime. Three years after Korea, the Senate committee reported that "thousands of small businesses" were "still feeling the pinch." There just didn't seem to be enough defense work to go round.

But small-business interests failed to appreciate the meaning of the accelerated tax-amortization program which enabled big business not only to walk off with most of the defense work but to enlarge its share of the civilian market. Since this program was initiated in November, 1950, fast tax write-offs have been authorized covering private-capital outlays of $36.3 billions. For the whole period, November, 1950, through 1956, the program has resulted in an estimated tax loss of $2.8 billions and, should taxes be reduced now or in the immediate future, the government will never recover this amount or anything like it.

The great bulk of the write-off certificates have gone to big firms. In 1954 only 11 per cent of the proposed capital investment authorized under this program went to small business; for 1955 the small-business share had dropped to 8 per cent. In theory, write-off certificates are issued only in connection with needed defense facilities; but, since 1950, certificates have been *concentrated* in primary metal manufacturing, private utilities, railroad transporation, chemicals and allied products, and petroleum and coal products. Oddly enough, there has been *a sharp rise* in certificates in the past six months despite official assurances in 1951 and again in 1952 that the program would soon be terminated.

The effect of the amortization program has been this: government has largely underwritten a huge plant-expansion program which has enabled big business to take on defense work without cutting back production for the civilian market. Small business had an equal right to apply for certificates but obviously failed to come off with its share. But the taxes paid by small business have helped to support the program. And now that the emergency is about over, what assurance does small business have that the vastly expanded industrial plant operated by big business will not be used to its competitive disadvantage? Small wonder that Secretary Humphrey, in urging a cessation of the program, should have characterized it as "an artificial stimulus of a dangerous type" and then gone on to say that encouraging industrial production by an inducement of this kind "is not the American way." More ironic than the fact that this stricture on the accelerated amortization program should have been voiced by the spokesman for a big-business Administration is the circumstance that this remarkable giveaway to big business should have been sponsored by a Democratic one.

By 1952 the Korean panic began to subside and the cutbacks began. Big business, of course, could afford to be philosophical; in the post-

Korean period it had gobbled up the major share of the civilian market and accumulated huge cash reserves. But small business had not been able to operate "parallel" plants for military orders; reconversion for small business often meant starting from scratch, reassembling a sales force, reentering the civilian market against formidable odds. Then, too, the profits of small business, after taxes, had shrunk, while the profits of the largest corporations had increased. Small business lacked funds to convert or expand. The larger firms had prepared for the cutbacks by diversifying their holdings and operations and by using mergers to strengthen their competitive position. But the relative position of small business was weaker than before the Korean War.

The Senate committee lost little time in pointing out that the cutbacks "began to play havoc with many established prime-subcontractor relationships as the primes . . . pulled increasingly large amounts of work under their own roofs and cut out many of their suppliers completely." The committee found, for example, that a 20 per cent cutback in the amount of prime contracts usually means "a hundred per cent cutback of that corporation's subcontractors." "Experience shows," to quote the Senate report, "that when there is a decrease in general military buying, the subcontractors will feel the impact more acutely than the prime contractors."

In the period since Korea, rapid technological innovations have greatly changed the military needs of industry's biggest customer. Even before Korea, the army was the best bet for small business (it buys caps, shoes, shoe polish and brass buttons as well as guns, shells and tanks), the navy next best and the air force a poor third. Today about 90 per cent or more of air force procurement is handled by large companies; thirteen of the fifteen top suppliers of war materials from July 1, 1953, to December 31, 1954, were aircraft companies. In the first year of the Korean War, the air force spent $6.3 billions, a shade more than the navy and a little less than the army. Two years later the air force spent $15.2 billions and this year will spend about $16.8 billions (much more than the army or navy). In a year or so the air force total may well jump to $20 or $24 billions. Army expenditures for the current year are estimated at $8.6 billions; the navy, $9.6 billions.

The shift in the dollar value of procurement from the older services to the air force has a special significance to small business. The steady decline in the small-business share of the military procurement dollar since Korea has reflected, in part, the expansion of the air force and the relative decline of the other services. Here were the percentages of total dollar volume which the three services allocated to small business in 1951: army, 28.6 per cent; navy, 16.5; air force, 11. Today [1956] the percentages are estimated approximately as follows: army, 29.8; navy, 13.6; air force, 9.8. The fact is that none of the services has ever managed to award small business the full percentage of procurement for which it has been found to be "suitable" by Defense Department experts. And when the navy, in a realistic move aimed at helping small business, attempted arbitrarily to set aside a fixed portion of its business for the little guy, it was promptly told that the practice violated basic government policy.

As the air force expands, big business will increasingly monopolize procurement. The "empire builders" in the armed services are acutely aware of the problem this poses: small business, which has provided so much of the political support for cold-war policies, may become disaffected—the more so as cold-war tax policies have favored big business. Hence political strategists in the three services are working overtime to convince prime contractors that they must be more generous with subcontractors. They exhort, they argue, they issue directives, but the outlook for small business is not good. Indeed, it is clear to almost everyone except the small-business man that his real interests lie in the direction of a curtailed arms economy and an expanded civilian market. Not many B-52's are being made; they cost about $8 or $10 millions each. This is not the kind of production in which small business can compete.

Unfortunately, small business is shot through and through with contradictions. It is badly organized. Its spokesmen, too, are mostly cold warriors. At a recent House committee hearing in Los Angeles, one small-business man said: "the small-business man does not want charity—he just wants equal rights with the major companies." This he will never get. Indeed, an arms economy directly menaces small business. To the degree that the small-business man profits from procurement, his competitive position is usually weakened; what he gains on the military side, he loses on the civilian. Small business is invariably hardest hit when industry converts to war production; it is hardest hit also when the cutbacks come. The Senate committee sums it up this way:

> Small business thrives in a free economy. Statistics show that small concerns fare best in open competition. When materials and equipment and all the other necessities of commerce are available to all, large and

small alike, small business can more than hold its own. Its size is no handicap. In fact, its size in many instances gives small business certain advantages of fast changing conditions and opportunities. . . . The ability of a small concern to concentrate and specialize on one product or one particular type of service also has its advantages. When a national emergency requires that controls be placed temporarily on the economy, however, many of these advantages are lost.

Yet it has been the pressure of small business for defense orders that largely accounts for the Democratic Party's consistent attempts to increase military appropriations. Although they berate the Republicans for advocating a "trickle down" theory of prosperity, the Democrats favor a trickle-down procurement policy. The small-business man is supposed to become a subcontractor. Recently Senator Chavez, who heads a Senate Appropriations subcommittee, succeeded in getting an extra billion for more B-52's. Other Democrats, notably Senator Symington, have been equally active in urging larger aircraft appropriations. In terms of strategy, it may be wise to increase aircraft appropriations, but it is not the way to help small business.

At the moment, big business is less warlike than small business; it can afford to be. But what would the outlook be if the consumer side of the market should shrink? Would big business then insist on an expansion of the military side of the government's spending? Dangerous vested interests have been created in our $39 billion defense budget. To be free from these pressures, American policy-makers should devise alternative means by which this country's vast productive machine can be fully utilized. It may not make much difference to the company that holds a defense contract—or to its stockholders or employees—whether the plant is used to produce milk-storage tanks or shells. But it makes a great deal of difference to the rest of us. In the one case we are asked to support production that is wasted; in the other—even if we were taxed to support it—we would be adding to the world's store of wealth and resources.

In the long run, production-for-waste cannot benefit any section of the economy—large units or small. Today, for the first time since the inception of the cold war, there is reason to hope that the waste of arms production can be curtailed. But the vested interests that have been created in a large military budget will continue to resist cutbacks unless an economic alternative is provided. Small business remains one of the most potent of these interests despite the fact that the likelihood of small firms getting a larger slice of defense work is even less now than it was at the outset of the cold war.

THE AMERICAN LEGION DIES LAUGHING / HARVEY GLICKMAN

On September 16 [1957], in Atlantic City, New Jersey, over 3,000 middle-aged male Americans will observe their annual organized outdoor catharsis. Shipments of water bags, cap pistols, horns and whiskey are already piling up in the basements of the Boardwalk hotels, and desk clerks, no doubt, are renewing the locks on fire extinguishers. Each year the American Legion announces that its convention will be less raucous than in the past, but the "regulars" respond with knowing winks.

These annual high jinks provide the Legionnaires with their only opportunity for free expression in the internal affairs of their organization. Apart from this useful social therapy, the convention is mere sound and fury, for the Legion itself is dying as an important social force. True, the organization continues to perform such desirable welfare services as the sponsorship of boys' baseball tournaments and high school essay contests, and the printing of about 400,000 pamphlets a year on how to display the American flag. But as for exerting any significant influence on most Americans, or even on the country's 28,000,000 ex-servicemen, it is well-nigh finished. Possessed of a gradually diminishing proportion of the nation's veterans—the membership has remained stationary for five years at 2.8 million—the Legion is well on its way to becoming a paunchy and rather less useful edition of the Boy Scouts.

A concerted membership drive in the last two years, aimed at a total membership of 5,000,000, proved a dud. Even more alarming to the Legion's officials is the fact that since the 1946 peak, membership has dropped 600,000, or almost 20 per cent. From 1951 to 1956, despite strenuous efforts to recruit new blood, the Legion added but 67,000 members. The dues coming in hardly cover the expenses of recruitment. Last year the Legion officially admitted that its membership situation was certainly "unhealthy and most discouraging."

Probably the main reason for the organization's dire straits is, ironically, that there are just too many veterans. Today just about everybody is a wartime or peacetime ex-serviceman of one variety or another, and in general it may be said that the desire to commemorate an experience is in direct ratio to its uniqueness. So, unless a veterans' organization continues to advance the interests of ex-servicemen on a massive and ever-widening scale, its *raison d'etre* is shaky indeed. Today, once the ex-serviceman absorbs the initial bounty of benefits, the Legion's exertions in this direction rapidly reach the point of diminishing returns. Nobody gets excited any more about promises of postwar bonuses, pensions, loans and other benefits. As far back as 1951, the *Army Times* detected a feeling among veterans that Congress had closed the books on veterans' benefits. Having already reached the limits of what is practical and legitimate in behalf of its membership, the Legion must now push beyond. For example, how is one to regard the Legion's recent proposal for special pensions for all veterans over sixty-five?

In kind and in degree, the Legion can do less for servicemen than ever before. This fact in itself tends to discourage new recruits; any suspicion that the Legion is deserting its self-assumed position as defender of the interests of the nation's veterans surely would be enough to lead to a wholesale exodus from its ranks. Many veterans take a dim view of the 1953 decision by the Legion Executive Committee to permit an increase in interest rates on G.I. loans for private homes. The decision coincided with the demands of the National Association of Home Builders and the Mortgage Bankers Association of America; John M. Dickerman, executive director of the N.A.H.B., himself credited the Legion with breaking "the log jam" on the issue. Moves like this reinforce the notion that the Legion listens to the voice of organized business with as much care as it does to the voice of its own constituents.

Most of us know the Legion for its extremist political views, which in recent years have grown increasingly strident and ridiculous. (For many years nobody has taken seriously the clause in the Legion's constitution which states that the organization shall be "non-political and shall not be used for the dissemination of partisan principles.") The Legion has consistently equated both free speech and internationalism with subversion. As long as the Legion's policy-makers confined their attacks to Communists, Socialists and New Dealers, they were supported by conservatives who wanted to get rid of a Democratic Administration. But since 1952 much of this conservative support has disappeared. "Modern Republicanism" has brought a new outlook to the business community and to conservatives in general; the Legion remains a defiant dog-in-the-manger, still fighting McCarthy's long-lost battles. Not unnaturally, the Legion's leadership has responded to mounting public indifference by screaming louder than ever. Today many veterans regard the Legion's views as not only wrong, but stupid and silly as well. Perhaps they agree with Harry Truman, himself a Legionnaire, who remarked in 1955 that the Legion had "gone haywire in the last three or four years."

Signs of imbalance began to appear as early as 1947, when National Commander J. F. O'Neill charged the late Senator Robert Taft with "making common cause with the Communists" because he had opposed universal military training. In 1955 the Legion really went wild. The Illinois Department asked the organization to withdraw support from the Girl Scouts because there were "un-American influences in the Girl Scout handbook." Former Illinois State Commander L. J. Fenlon remarked, "How screwy can we get?" But his comrades responded by asking that the United States approve "a declaration of independence from the U.N." The Westchester County American Legion reported to the National Executive Committee on diabolical doings in upstate New York, where the League of Women Voters had distributed six pamphlets on civil liberties financed by the Fund for the Republic. The Un-Americanism Committee of the Westchester Legion declared that the pamphlets were "designed to delude the public into believing Communism is a red herring." The Legion National Executive then took on the League of Women Voters, asking it to disown the pamphlets, particularly one on freedom of speech by the late Harvard Professor of Law, Zechariah Chafee, Jr. This assiduous Westchester group also protested the showing of a film in the Pleasantville High School and in the Katonah Village library, in which Edward R. Murrow interviewed Dr. J. Robert Oppenheimer. In this affair, the Westchester Un-Americanism experts gained the support of T. E. Paradine, the Legion's national vice-chairman of public relations and a former national vice-commander. Movies were also the target of a Legion protest in Briarcliff, New York. This film starred Dr. Mortimer J. Adler; G. F. May, commander of the Briarcliff post, denounced the practice of exposing public school children to "controversial intellectuals."

The climax of uproarious 1955 came at the national convention in Miami, where the Legion "deplored the continued economic aid by the United States to India," recommended that the United States withdraw from the Korean Armistice Commission and allow the South Koreans to settle things "in their own way," and urged Congress to take the United States out of UNESCO. The *New York Times* called this last suggestion "a prize example of sophomoric xenophobia." No doubt many Legionnaires felt the same way, but dared not speak up. The origins of the Legion's anti-UNESCO campaign may be traced to the American Flag Committee and W. Henry MacFarland, Jr., a professional patriot who has also been active in the National Renaissance Party and the Nationalist Action League. Both organizations have been named as Fascist, the former by the House Committee on Un-American Activities and the latter by the Attorney General.

A quality of silent suffering has long marked the rank and file of the Legion. Control over policy, as well as over elections, is exercised by a small number of "regulars" who, until recently, were all of World War I vintage. The "regulars"—the delegates and the small-time officials—of any mass organization tend to be the traditionalists, the fellows who are always sticking to outworn principles; and the most outworn principle of the Legion is its own peculiar brand of "Americanism." As the supply of genuine talent diminishes, a display of the virtues of "Americanism" becomes the chief test of ability. The old-timers hand-pick their successors, perpetuating images of themselves at the top. Some years ago, when the Legion commanded such powerful support that, as Bernard Baruch once said, it can make office boys out of Congressmen, the organization produced national commanders with some claim to national stature—men like Louis Johnson and Paul V. McNutt. In the past few years, however, the national commanders have been as uniformly undistinguished as they have been indistinguishable. The commander this year, Wilbur (Dan) Daniel, barely qualified as a war veteran, his service consisting of some months in basic training.

But more important than considerations of individual talent is the age group of the Legion's leadership. Only in the past few years have veterans of World War II managed to win high position in any numbers. For many Legionnaires, undoubtedly, it took far too long for the "second generation" to reach the higher echelons; by the time it did, thousands of their fellows, impatient under the unrelenting tutelage of the men whose last service experience dated back at least thirty years, had left the organization.

The difficulties of the rank-and-file Legionnaire of either generation in influencing Legion policy are underlined by the experience of the supporters of the Murphy Report on UNESCO. In 1955, Ray Murphy, a former national commander and not a dissident upstart, headed a committee of six which exonerated UNESCO, and the Americans associated with it, of charges of atheism, un-Americanism or Communism. The committee's report went to the National Executive Committee and subsequently was shunted to the Legion's Foreign Relations Committee. After much wrangling, this committee and the Americanism Committee considered the report together and directed a subcommittee of ten to prepare a joint report of its own. A summary of the subcommittee's findings criticized UNESCO for disseminating "subversive educational materials." This summary accompanied the resolution denouncing UNESCO at the Miami convention in 1955. The national leadership not only brushed aside the Murphy Report, it did not even permit any of its proponents to address the convention when the resolution reached the floor. In a matter of minutes, without floor debate, the die-hards had rammed through their resolution by a voice vote.

As for the choice of his leadership, the ordinary Legionnaire is in precisely the same position. Both 1955 and 1956 provided striking evidence of the prevalence of boss rule. The executive committee of the Forty and Eight, fun-making organization of the Legion, in 1955 decided to renounce its connection with the parent body. It charged that a group of unnamed "kingmakers" distributed committee appointments and used funds to benefit those "who do their bidding." Immediately the Indianapolis *Star* discovered one of these kingmakers, one J. P. Ringley. In 1956 Ringley turned up again as the target of similar charges, this time levelled by C. M. Blackburn, a candidate for national commander during the Los Angeles convention. W. C. Daniel, Ringley's candidate, won handily, almost as easily as had his predecessor, J. A. Wagner, who managed to provoke thirty-five opposing votes the year before. "If you fail to support the wishes—and the candidate—of the kingmaker, your department doesn't get any appointments that year," remarked the defeated Mr. Blackburn.

Two other factors in the decline of the Legion deserve some attention. There is some evidence that membership in the Legion today is decidedly *déclassé*. One suspects that the solid supporters of the Legion—the regular convention-goers and the Fourth of July paraders—belong increasingly to the lower middle class. The executive type leans toward membership and participation in more sedate groups, such as Rotary and Kiwanis. After all, today's American Legion represents a peculiar non-conformity; it is out of line with the smooth, conservative mood of our time. To the man who aspires to a niche in suburbia, the Legionnaires resemble backwoodsmen. Secondly, there should be an interesting correlation between the number of rural and semi-rural counties which have gone "wet" in the last five years and the geographical distribution of the drop in Legion membership. The American Legion Post bar has always been the only place to secure liquor by the glass in the numerous "dry" counties and "dry" states that dot the country. The Post bar stays open almost day and night. What better reason for a virile ex-serviceman to keep his membership in the Legion up-to-date? Recently, where they could exercise local option, the voters in many of these sections have gone "wet" for a variety of reasons—principally to attract tourists. The Post bar now has lost much of its unique attraction.

Most people, when they think of the Legion, associate it automatically with isolationism and super-patriotism on the one hand, and parades and high jinks on the other. In a short time, these notions will express the total essence of the importance of the Legion on the American social scene. Already most of the Legionnaires are content with the high jinks, while 90 per cent of America's veterans don't care about the Legion at all.

THE MILITARY RESERVES: LEARNING THE CANNONEER'S HOP / RICHARD ELMAN

Anybody who has ever been in the army must realize that his training period revolves around the verb "simulate." Except for a week of marksmanship competition on the rifle range, the new recruit, during his first eight weeks of basic training, is expected to simulate practically everything: fear, respect towards his officers, wonder, even a degree of interest.

Once basic is over, if the recruit enters one of the service branches as a supply clerk, or goes into Intelligence, Graves Registration or Personnel, he will probably have to simulate very little. He will also, it may be noted, have to do very little. But if he enters one of the combat arms, whether it be infantry, the armored cavalry, or the artillery, he will only just have begun to simulate. Almost everything that occurs during the training in one of these branches is like the twenty-second inning of a nothing-to-nothing ball game. It all involves what the Army has labeled a "simulated tactical situation." The idea is to make individual training more practical and to make unit training seem more real. This may mean anything from standing on the chow-line five yards apart from one's neighbor to the camouflaging of a bivouac in such a way that only the battalion commander's shiny new jeep is visible from the air. It covers a variety of discomforts.

To the two- or three-year man stationed overseas, or who is on a tactical maneuver with a regular TO & E [Table of Organization and Equipment] outfit, this kind of simulation will very shortly become dreary and routine and therefore bearable, but in the career of the new six-month reservist (or short-timer), the act of simulation and the "tactical situation" seem to be a pathetic waste of his time and energies.

The alert short-timer reasons that he is in the service to be trained, or that he has pulled a fast one on the government and he wants to get it done with even faster. In either case, although he may be prepared to waste time and even to goldbrick, he is unprepared to waste his time simulating, or, as is so often the case, simulating the wasting of time. For he wants to learn as much as possible about many different aspects of his branch of service, so that when he returns to his Reserve unit he can gain a certain amount of rank and status and thereby narrow down his chances for future inconvenience. But the men in the Pentagon and at the different training camps throughout the nation do not see the problem of training the reservist in quite this light. They probably decided that training a man to be versatile would be at best a kind of military dilettantism (already plentiful in the Reserves) and at worst would create an unruly mob of 400,000 "jacks-of-all-trades." Thus they decided to use the Regular Army system of drilling a man in one particular specialty until he knew it like the callous on his palm. To do this, steady, harassing simulation was deemed absolutely essential, and the results often turn out to be quite interesting.

For instance, let us consider the Field Artillery. Even the readers of the tabloids know that field artillery is fast becoming obsolescent for any future large-scale war. However, even its most vituperative detractors have to admit that it would still be of great utility in another limited conflict such as Korea. Furthermore, as a result of Korea, the Army Ordnance is overstocked with guns and howitzers. So they still find it necessary to train gun crews and detail crews (wiremen, surveyors, fire-direction computers) for the field artillery. One of the most active training grounds for reservists in the Field Artillery is to be found at Fort Chaffee in the scraggly, eroded hill country of Southwest Arkansas.

Fort Chaffee is one of the newer Army posts. Named after General Ada Chaffee, one of the pioneer American advocates of mechanized warfare, it was for a long time an armored center. Then, with the expansion of Fort Knox in Kentucky, and after the lessons learned in Korea on mountainous terrain concerning the relative inefficiency of tanks, it was converted to artillery. During the last few years (aside from a small basic-training complement and a specialist school command of about the same size), artillery crimson has been the order of the day at Chaffee; and, since the passage of the Reserve Forces Act in 1955, it has trained mostly short-timers.

It is estimated that 50,000 reservists have been instructed in the Artillery Training Center. By far the largest percentage of these have been trained as cannoneers. Now this training can be broken into two uneven parts. After basic, there is a second eight weeks of individual training, followed by six weeks of unit-training in a somewhat abridged and simulated TO & E outfit. For these fourteen weeks a rigid training schedule has been developed which accounts for every hour of the day. Aside from classes in sex education, citizenship and character guidance, and simultaneously with duties in his home battery—such as KP or latrine orderly—the reservist is oriented first in the mission and purpose of the artillery; then he is shown some quasi-technical movies on the basic functioning mechanism of the howitzer; he is next trained step by step as a cannoneer; and lastly he is led through a series of drills and simulations. This might be an excellent method of teaching something as complicated as anti-aircraft detection or the firing of liquid-fuel missiles which require long, complicated count-downs and safety checks. It might even be a desirable program for the weekly training sessions of those reservists who are not on active duty, so that they can maintain themselves at some level of readiness. But the young reservist who is on active duty very soon discovers that the care and operation of a howitzer is plainly not the most abstruse of subjects. In those moments when he is not aggravated by the pompous assertions of his superiors that he is basically unteachable, he is overcome by an immense ennui.

The "cannoneer's hop," you see, is not a difficult step. In fact, one need only to have the use of two arms and two legs to master the "laying of the piece," as the setting of deflections and elevations is called. What little brain work there is belongs to the fire-direction computers. Thus a fantastic division of labor occurs. If it takes only two to tango, it takes twelve to do the cannoneer's hop. In a howitzer training section, there is one man who merely sets the fuse; another loads the gun; still another removes the empty cartridge casing and stacks it neatly along the side for Ordnance to collect; another pulls the lanyard. . . . (One old sergeant, a veteran of both Korea and Normandy, once confided to me that he had never had more than four men on his gun in all the time that he was in combat and that they still fired an awful lot of rounds.)

The idea is to get quick precision registration and firepower out of light artillery. The system probably originated with Lord Nelson or with

Michael Kutusov; or perhaps it is something left over from those days before the Reserve Forces Act when mostly draftees were being inducted and when those who scored lowest on their GT scores, or who had no other usable training, qualification or aptitudes, were sent either to the infantry, the armor, or the full artillery like lambs to the simulated slaughter. This is no longer the case. Our present reservists are not receiving Military Occupation Specialities (MOS), or job-titles, because of their test scores; they do so on the basis of the Reserve units from which they come.

But when a man joins a reserve program nowadays it is usually because his draft board is in hot pursuit of him, or because he is eighteen and a half or under and wants to get his time in before going on to college. In either case he is recruited by the Reserves, assigned an MOS, and sent off to active duty without any of the usual processing or interviewing that takes place in the Regular Army and, in some cases, without even taking a physical. (There were boys at Chaffee who suffered from 60 per cent blindness or a severe lack of muscular co-ordination [two of the usual 4F categories] but because they had technically enlisted and because they were only short-timers, it was not adjudged desirable to process them out. Some were made permanent latrine orderlies, but some are now serving in your ready reserves.) The reserve officers neither know nor care to know of a man's potentialities until he returns from active duty. So he is merely fitted into the first available slot in their TO & E roster; and the very first available slot in the TO & E roster of a line battery of a field artillery battalion is usually as a cannoneer.

The man who is thrust so awkwardly into such a gap might very well be capable of performing a more complicated and useful function for his country. It was not surprising to discover at Fort Chaffee the shocking number of college graduates, or even men with graduate school training as lawyers, architects and, of course, writers, doing the cannoneer's hop in any one of the multitudinous training compounds.

To any sensible civilian the sight must be disquieting. Imagine a huge compound, about 500 yards square, surrounded by high wire fences. In one direction there are drab rows of narrow, rectangular classroom buildings. In the other direction are the even longer rows of howitzers with their muzzles pointed at low elevation. The area is neatly policed; the buildings, although buff-colored, are immaculate; and the guns have been freshly painted olive drab. It is a cold, gray afternoon, or else it is blistering hot and dusty (it is always one or the other in Arkansas). There are groups of trainees at attention behind each howitzer. They are trying to listen to the hoarse commands of a large, enthusiastic sergeant who is wearing a red helmet liner and a red scarf along with his fatigue uniform, and who is mounted on a small podium to their front.

It is very much like a game of musical chairs with a little roughhouse thrown in. The first command is: "At ease, you goddamn Cannonballs. At ease!" The men's bodies stiffen with anticipation and worry. There is a moment of dreadful silence broken by the command, "CanNonEeers Post!" At this, the Number One man goes through his simplified duties one at a time. Then he moves down the line to become the Number Twelve man; the Number Two man takes his place, and everybody else moves up a slot. Sometimes the wind howls or it begins to drizzle. Sometimes the sergeant has to bark "At Ease!" even louder to demand attention. But the big switch continues, rain or shine.

This grotesque ballet goes on for eight uninterrupted weeks in the short army career of a short-timer. Only then are the men moved out into the field for live firing and for their training in RSOP, or bivouac. But before this transfer can take place, they are supposed to pass what is known as a proficiency test. Those men who are not bored senseless, and who meet the minimal requirements for belonging to what the zoologists call the primates, pass easily. But a surprising number of the brighter sort do not. I suspect that many of these, after eight weeks of tedium, are interested either in making fools of the army by deliberately failing, or else they have had resort to the subterfuge of one almost continual sick-call for the eight weeks of their training. Even so, the numbr of men who fail is usually admitted to be quite negligible. There would certainly be many if the men were not threatened as they are. But the threats are also negligible, and for cycle after cycle the rigid monotony of the cannoneer's hop continues, while thousands upon thousands of young men are trained to be bored, to be insufferably lazy, or to be, at best, somewhat reluctant automatons servicing a somewhat inefficient weapon.

I was one of the luckier ones. So that this won't seem like just another case of sour grapes, let me state right here and now that I was privileged because I was not chosen to be a cannoneer. Instead, I was given the opportunity of going to Radio-Telephone School. In fact, the only real contact I had with the cannoneer's park was when I was ordered to walk guard around it late one wintry evening. I suppose I shall always keep this image of myself circling that empty compound with an empty rifle over my shoulder, trying to find an empty boiler room to hide in and warm up, as a symbol of the inadequacies of the training program. For, if somebody had come along that evening and had tried to steal some of our priceless equipment, I think I might have welcomed him with open arms. I know that I certainly would have been hesitant to call the Commander of The Relief, because he would have been sound asleep and would have been very angry at being disturbed.

I was about to discuss my eight weeks in Radio-Telephone School. The words "radio" and "communications" are given a high priority in the Army's vocabulary; they would seem to indicate skilled labor of a sort, and when I was notified that I was to go to the school, I must confess that I was excited with my prospects. I had visions of myself with that intense look on my face, adjusting my ear phones, trying to detect dit from dot, flashing frantic code messages around the world. I bragged to my wife about the hi-fi system I would be able to construct for her—and I went to my first few classes in a real state of anticipation.

Being a short-timer, however, I was not to be trained as a code operator or as a radio repairman. I learned very soon that my course was to be no more esoteric than that of my colleagues in cannoneer park. I discovered, in fact, that the radios which we were being trained to operate were about as difficult to handle as my little Philco portable at home. I was to learn nothing more than how to turn a radio on and how to shut one off, turn it on, shut it off, on, off. It required simulation, dedication and no skill.

But in my case it paid to be ignorant. At least I didn't have to do the cannoneer's hop and, because I was going to school, I was considered a specialist by the cadre. Thus I was able to miss bivouac and a host of other nasty details. Nevertheless, I couldn't help sharing the guilt of my superiors for having let me get away with all this; and, as I used to sit and look about my classroom at the many B.A.'s and M.A.'s and L.L.B.'s who were turning on and shutting off their radios, or as I looked through the window at the even greater number who were policing the area outside, I couldn't stop myself from thinking what a waste of talent it all was. I suppose the Army thought differently.

After all, we were only in for six months. Six months wasn't like being in the *real* Army. It was only a simulated army experience. So what more could we expect?

THE ECONOMICS OF LIFE

RECIPE FOR PROSPERITY: ''BORROW. BUY. WASTE. WANT.'' / KENNETH BURKE

Some years ago, in fact just before the stock-market crash of '29, I wrote an article entitled "Waste—or the Future of Prosperity." It was a burlesque, done along the lines of Veblen's ingeniously ironic formula, "conspicuous consumption," as used in his *Theory of the Leisure Class.* The article worked up several variants on this theme, finding much merriment in such paradoxes as the fact that our people, who had been systematically led to believe that the maximum use of new manufactured objects is a sure sign of one's moral and social election, were kept frantically busy turning out labor-saving devices, that the more our consumers wasted the more they could buy (hence the greater the waste the greater the prosperity), and that, insofar as people failed in their economic function as wasters, there could always be recourse to wars, since in wars and the preparation for wars the amount of production for waste is prodigious. In sum, our position was: "We realize now that culture resides in *prosperity*, that prosperity is the outgrowth of *production*, that production can only follow *consumption*, that the maximum consumption is made possible by the maximum possible *waste*, and therefore that *culture depends upon a maximum of waste*. (At least until there is nothing more to waste.)"

In particular I centered on the automobile industry, taking Henry Ford as the symbol of that industry.

I think it's the only article I ever made any real money out of. In fact, I have sold it several times, and once a part of it was reprinted without consulting me. One sale (psst!) actually was to *Reader's Digest.* That was the most remunerative; but I should add: the sale was to a *Reader's Digest* then in a mood much different from its moods now. But, alas! I, too, am in a mood much different now from my moods then; and I couldn't now, for the life of me, stir up the spirit, not even out of a bottle, to cavort hilariously about such matters now as I did then.

Hegel remarks somewhere that all great, world-historical facts and personages occur, as it were, twice. He has forgotten to add: the first time as tragedy, the second as farce. And I nearly forgot to add that I am quoting from the opening sentences of *The Eighteenth Brumaire of Louis*

Bonaparte, by one K*rl M*rx. However, in accordance with my nature, I would use the words revisionistically: for I am dealing with the fact that, whereas over twenty-five years ago I considered the so-called Higher Standard of Living fit subject for a farce (insofar as this mode of life relied so heavily upon scientifically organized methods for goading the citizens of a great nation into a frantic scramble to buy unneeded things), now, in the years of my decline, I would look upon this same state of affairs as material for an almost awesome tragedy (albeit a tragedy that lends itself, in flashes, to such shrewdly morose and wincing appreciation as can at times go with high comedy).

The terror derives from the fact that, to a great degree, unless we can somehow mend our economic ways and modify our naive and even crude response to the range of things made possible by applied science, there is no other solution for us but to persevere in the current frenzy, a frenzy largely maintained by the paid priesthood of advertising and by the corresponding paid or unpaid priesthoods of the arts.

My article—like all burlesques—was based on what I thought was a grossly exaggerated statement of my case. But recently (in their May 5 and June 16 [1956] issues) *Business Week* published two articles that startled me, and even nonplussed me, by offering as simple gospel a line that, if I could have thought of it when I was writing my burlesque a bit more than a jubilee ago, I'd certainly have used as the perfect frisky summing-up of my thesis "Just past the midmark of the 20th Century," we read, "it looks as though all of our business forces are bent on getting every one . . ." (and here is the notable slogan) to "Borrow. Spend. Buy. Waste. Want."

I would then have looked upon such a slogan as ideal material for a farce. Now presumably it is to be taken in full earnest.

In my original article, also, I thought I was making much sport of the trick psychological devices whereby a customer with a perfectly serviceable car was persuaded that he should get rid of it because there was a newer model available. In particular, I guyed the doctrine of "obsolescence" that was implied in such high-pressure selling tactics. But now I find *Business Week* referring quite respectfully to the way in which General Motors "adopted the annual model change, helping to establish the auto industry's renowned principle of 'planned obsolescence.'" I had mistakenly thought that the principle was a joke; by now it has become "renowned."

A correction of another sort is in order, too. I had featured Henry Ford as the person most responsible for this type of economy. However, the articles in *Business Week* point out that, on the contrary, Henry Ford was an old-timer ("the archetype of the production man") with an antiquated Puritanical notion that, if you gave people a serviceable car at a price made progressively lower by increased sales, a car that the buyer might use for several or even many years before it needed replacement, you would have done enough. According to *Business Week*, it was General Motors that freed us of such old-fashioned nonsense, and started the rat-race of the annual change-over, plus the inducements of ever-lengthening time for payment on the installment plan; and Ford was reluctantly driven to the same methods by the pressures of the situation, with its technologically and financially Darwinian competition for survival.

The articles help us see how, when other industries such as appliances and plastics developed by following the same marketing procedures as General Motors, we finally came to have, in all its perfection, "the Consumption Economy," the "age of distribution, of the consumer and his foibles," in brief the Grand Convergence or Fatal Confluence of the factors that make up what now usually goes by the honorific title (and perhaps partial misnomer) of "The Higher Standard of Living."

This, then, according to *Business Week*, is the age in which "Consumer is King." And I'd like to round out my statement by meditating briefly on that resonant formula.

First, I couldn't help recalling the gnarled philosopher, Friedrich Nietzsche, who went crazy at the thought that the modern world was undergoing a moral upheaval, a "transvaluation of all values." But if these articles in *Business Week* are reliable evidence, then the Nietzschean supermen of our modern sales philosophy can take a revolution in moral standards simply as a matter of course. Many people, we are told, "are upset by what they see as an enormous emphasis on materialism and triviality" in the contemporary scene. Whereat the articles accurately pit their bright new asyndeton ("Borrow. Spend. Buy. Waste. Want.") against "all the old admonitions" that "appear to have been outdated," such *Poor Richard* proverbial saws in behalf of frugality and thrift as "Neither a borrower nor a lender be.... Waste not, want not.... A penny saved is a penny earned.... A fool and his money are soon parted." Discussing the "danger in thrift," the articles note that if the typical consumer should take it into his head to buy only the things he really needed, "he would scare the life out of business men and economists."

But fortunately (and we seem to have here a modernized variant of the paradox in Mandeville's *Fable of the Bees*, whose individual greed brought prosperity to the hive), the typical consumer "seems to prefer living just barely within his means. This may be profligate and short-sighted of him, in some people's eyes, but it is a powerful stimulus to the economy,"—and the statement looks to me as though it could be fairly translated: "This may not be morally good for the individual, but it is good for business." Or, more bluntly, the obvious *ethical* question which should always guide a state, "What is business good for?" is almost imperceptibly translated into a quite different *economic* counterpart, "What is good for business?" For the *Business Week* version of a business ethics would seem to be somewhat like the ethics of a tavern-keeper who thought it his business to get us all stinko drunk and keep us so. But surely ethical business admonishes a buyer, and does not merely seek to make a fool of him. Meanwhile I begin to fear that what I thought was pardonable in my burlesque only because burlesque is by definition a playful exaggeration, is now presented to us as the Ideal Norm. But that can't be business ethics. Here it looks to me as though the congregation is being wronged by its priesthood. Business helps supply us—and that's a good job. And surely we don't have to become damnfool spenders for business to carry out its role.

As a matter of fact, one might even go a step further and ask whether, over the long run, promiscuous spending really is so good for business if, as tested by the rule of the Higher Standard of Living, the economic function of business is to see that the maximum amount of money is being spent on the output of our mines, mills, factories, farms and the like. For when a buyer is induced to buy on credit, then in proportion as his indebtedness increases, more and more of his income must eventually go to pay the interest charges on his loans. Thus eventually his creditors are taking a handsome cut out of his income; and thus, to the extent of that cut, in the long run a buyer cannot buy as much as he could have bought had he proceeded at a slower pace and bought always for cash.

However, the argument in behalf of systematic goading of the people into long-term installment buying may be that, had they bought purely on a cash basis, they would never have bought as much unnecessary goods in the first place. For when credit terms look easy, presumably there will be a greater temptation to adopt an easy-come-easy-go attitude that takes on obligations as lightly as the supermen of the *Business Week* articles seem to have taken on a reversal of moral values.

But maybe we have been proceeding too fast. For maybe, in trying to get an accurate insight into the possible cultural issues involved here, we should take a closer look at the assumption that this really is the Age of the Consumer. True: this "age of plenty" does contain a whole new wilderness of machine-made innovations available for a customer to buy if and when the fancy strikes him. But we should also remember that, at the same time, even greater mountains of productivity have gone into goods such as munitions, about which the individual member of the mass-market has no say-so whatever. And in the search for the exact proportion among the motivational ingredients in our culture, we should not allow ourselves to be too distracted by the gaudy stuff in the store windows on Main Street.

Indeed, it's fortunate for our economy that a vast proportion of our productivity does go into goods not accessible to the fluctuations of the mass-market. (I refer to such resources as investment by private corporations in plant expansion, but above all to the vast sums spent by the government for defense, rivers, harbors, dams, reclamation, highways, housing, crop subsidies, direct or indirect subsidizing of exports and the like.) For insofar as the Higher Standard of Living involves the mass-production of goods for sale to individual customers in mass-markets, it is necessarily synonymous with maximum instability.

What we might call the "Inevitability of Instability" in the Higher Standard is inherent in the fact that, by definition, the Higher Standard is preponderantly a realm of "conveniences" or "improvements" rather than basic "necessities." And even where they are "necessities" (as with automobiles in many cases) they may be "postponable" purchases (as our old car may do well enough for a while yet, if we decide that at present we can't afford a new one). As a result, "business men and economists are much concerned with what is now frequently called 'discretionary' spending, or the outlay on things which there is no pressing need to buy." And though one expert is quoted as thinking that "the whimsical nature of consumer spending" is likely to be exaggerated, we also note: "Since each shift of a percentage point between spending and saving can mean a difference of $2.5 billion in the nation's expenditures on goods and services, it is no wonder that business men and economists have been nervous about the personal-savings rate."

The articles say nothing about the kinds of production and consumption that, in falling outside the power of the individual consumer to cast an economic vote by buying or not buying, can counteract the instability natural to such a situation. The omission in itself is no scandal, since the articles were not on the subject of production as a whole. They were dealing only with production for mass-consumption. But in their engrossment with their subject, they make the individual consumer loom too large, even in his role as member of a great homogeneous band of similar consumers who tend to buy like him if they have the same income. And above all, the articles can make us overlook the cultural possibilities of stabilization in this other kind of production and consumption that lies beyond the consumer's direct jurisdiction.

True, such stabilizing kinds of production have various problems of their own. The most obvious instance would be the case where in times of peace a threatened sag in the civilian economy is prevented by an increase in spending for war goods. The surest way to make the citizens concur in such expenditures would be by working up a large measure of international ill-will. And while such a procedure might seem to some the patriotic thing to do purely from the standpoint of an armaments race, it can have an unsettling effect upon the national psychology, since a permanent state of systematically coached ill-will is not a sound basis for moral discipline or peace of mind. And the maintenance of peace productivity by war productivity obviously has a bad effect upon a nation's reputation abroad, where the citizens are not given the same slant by press and radio as in their own country.

My own particular fond dream along these lines is of a dispensation whereby the federal government would undertake to reclaim our streams by equipping all towns and cities, and even private industries, with sewage disposal plants. If such a mighty cleansing operation were set up, to purify the very symbol of purification itself, and thus to give us back our miraculous rivers, to reconstitute as trout streams and pleasure spots what are now but excremental drains and chemically-laden sewers, then indeed technology could by its own technological devices transcend itself—and we could begin to correct the most drastic ill besetting our culture, those grim conditions whereby "progress" equals *pollution*. Far from being expended in a cult of waste, with the almost diabolical ingenuity that must sometimes be exerted to goad our citizenry into frantic efforts at exhausting our national resources as rapidly as possible, a vast project in national reclamation could be undertaken to the profit of us all.

Then, as patriots, we could have the maximum grounds for congratulating ourselves on our citizenship. And far from cramping the consumer, such improvements would but extend the range of opportunities for the consumer to disport himself, just as government-built dams but increase the opportunities for private enterprise.

SIOBHAN McKENNA AT THE N.A.M. / DAN WAKEFIELD

In the three short days of its sixty-first convention [1956], the National Association of Manufacturers was exposed to the assorted heretical doctrines of God, the Irish poets and American youth, in that order. It is not so frivolous to say that the NAM, after those frightening visitations, owes its collective sanity to the lavishly padded interior of its meeting place, the Waldorf-Astoria, where nothing that happens seems to bear any relations to reality; and the speakers drawn from its own membership, who managed in spite of the convention theme of "New Dimensions for America" to convey the warming impression that everything was still as it always was and ever shall be—except, of course, for the growing menace of labor and socialism (and they, after all, are old and comfortable menaces to the NAM). The real menaces were the guest outsiders (religious, poetic and young), for the logical conclusion of their combined messages could only be the dissolution of the NAM and a mass return to the soil by all its members.

These subversive messages came at the rate of one each day—each more surprising than the last. The first was from God, who is rather expected to throw a note of warning around at such occasions. It was delivered this time by The Very Reverend William A. Donaghy, S.J., president of Holy Cross, who turned out to be an unusually articulate and menacing messenger of the Word. He took as his text the decline and fall of Rome, Carthage—and possibly New York. He quoted to the manufacturers from Polybius:

> The Romans do not trouble about the moral decline of the empire. All that they ask is that it should be prosperous and secure. "What contents us," they say, "is that everyone should be able to increase his wealth so that he can afford a lavish expenditure and can keep the weak in subjection."

He recounted the tale of the tank-corps soldiers in the African campaign of World War II who rumbled past the mute sign in the wasted desert that read "Carthage"; and warned that if America did not return to the ways of the Spirit there could some day be "a similar bleak deserted plain and a similar pathetic sign—New York." He called for a new dimension of Faith and a rejection of the purely materialistic way of life which put men in "a world bounded on the East and West by birth and death, on the North and South by Dun and Bradstreet."

The NAM applauded warmly as the Father finished, and one delegate was heard to remark as the session broke up for lunch that the Father was "a very forceful speaker." Technique, not philosophy, was all that had left its impression. The prophet was accepted by the business men as a competent—nay, talented—craftsman. The message itself was blunted by the reality of a manufacturing magnate's life and by the mass of words which had preceded the Father's speech and had affirmed that the delegates were there once again to beat the old drums.

". . . I wonder," said NAM president Cola G. Parker in the keynote address that began the day, "what is meant by such expressions as 'enlightened capitalism.' To the extent phrases like this mask a retreat from the ancient virtues of self-reliance, self-determination and self-responsibility, I for one cannot go along with them."

Let no one be deceived by the title of the keynote speech and the convention theme, "New Dimensions for America." The boys were back for their annual return to the nourishing earth for root-holds in the ancient values.

But respect for the theme did stimulate some real soul-searching among several of the NAM's own gospel carriers. Imagine the moral agony of Merle G. Jones, president of the Store-Kraft Manufacturing Company, as he sat in his study in the God-forsaken flats of Beatrice, Nebraska, this fall and got his mandate to speak in New York on "New Dimensions for America." Introduced to the assembly as a Sunday School teacher as well as a successful manufacturer, Mr. Jones took the stand, unbuttoned and rebuttoned his blue double-breasted suitcoat and began with this thought that must have come to him at the time of agony in Beatrice: "I am told that Abraham Lincoln once gave a very simple analytical outline that could be applied to many situations. He asked these questions: 1. Where are you? 2. In what direction are you going? 3. How will you get there?"

Mr. Jones asked himself the first question, and wrenched out this conclusion: "Well, at least we are not in the past. Whenever I am tempted to live in the past, I am reminded of a comment that was often made by W. B. Morton, the founder of the Store-Kraft Manufacturing Company:

'Things aren't what they used to be and never were.' No, we are not living in the past."

The New Dimensions for America were taking shape, and the NAM pressed on down the trackless red-carpeted frontiers of the Waldorf, rising Thursday morning to the Starlight Roof for a session of the wives sternly titled "Women Mean Business." The Starlight Roof suggests the scene of a funeral that might have been staged by Jay Gatsby in his headier days. The ladies, heavily hatted and furred, moved in quietly to expose themselves to the promised enlightenment.

They were told in the twanging tones of Walter G. Koch, president of the International Steel Company, that "Women Mean Business"—didn't they own 54 per cent of all stock, 65 per cent of all savings accounts and the deeds to 40 per cent of all homes in America? In recognition of their great role in the economy, president Parker would speak to them on the subject "You and Your NAM" and pull no punches—it was time for women to share the responsibilities and know the truth. He told them that the NAM "stands for freedom."

The ladies raised no argument to that, and seemed willing enough to accept Mr. Parker's subsequent challenge that they learn about economics, politics and such matters, and keep right up there with the menfolk. As a first step in their education, a style show was presented with costumes "from many lands," and a chatty commentary informed the girls as a model floated up the aisle in a German peasant costume that "Germany is a land of romantic scenery and wonderful castles—seemingly unchanged through the centuries." So much for Germany.

But the hard facts of current problems were brought to the fore at the end of the session by Henry J. Taylor, radio commentator and prophet. Mr. Taylor rambled around the Suez question without much response and finally got down to Korea, which drew a good hand from the ladies in praise of General Douglas MacArthur. After a rather sketchy summary of the world's pressure centers, Mr. Taylor prophesied that business, in general, would be good next year. There would be "some uncertainties in certain industries," he said; but he felt that there was "no need to spell it out."

Thus armed, the ladies exited for lunch in the Grand Ballroom, evidently meaning business.

The program had said that Siobhan McKenna, then starring downtown in *St. Joan*, would be the "feature" of the luncheon entertainment. It did not say what she would do. And who among us, either the NAM folks or we few visitors of little faith, suspected that she would read to the National Association of Manufacturers from the poetry of James Stephens and William Butler Yeats?

With waiters still rattling silver in the background, the spotlight struck the darkened stage and the figure of Miss McKenna, straight and poised in a plain black suit, appeared before the manufacturers armed with the volumes of Stephens and Yeats. The room gradually quieted and the audience sat in respectful silence, applauding at appropriate intervals. It was, after all, being "entertained." Miss McKenna pronounced to this concentration of country-club, Junior League, Chamber of Commerce leadership the words of James Stephens that "all that is lonely is beautiful"; and out of Yeats, from *The Ballad of Moll Magee*, the notion that "God lights the stars, his candles, and looks upon the poor."

In the main section of the ballroom, the audience continued their mechanical cycle of silence and applause, but around the tables at the edges certain gentlemen began to show signs of restlessness. They were the older ones, who resembled *Pravda*-conceived cartoons of fat-cat capitalists, red-necked and recently heavy with poppy-seed rolls, no doubt wondering what the state of the world had come to. A gentleman whose name card placed him as a citizen of Two Rivers, Michigan, asked a colleague from Marion, Indiana, "What's this all about, anyway?" The Hoosier gentleman evidently wasn't up on his early Yeats, and suggested they "get outta here," which they did. A man whose tag identified him as the president and treasurer of the Abrasive Machine Tools Corporation of East Providence, R.I., wondered when the main speaker would come on. It was then that Miss McKenna was reading her final selection, which ended with the lines

> But I, being poor, have only my dreams;
> I have spread my dreams under your feet;
> Tread softly because you tread on my dreams.

The lights went on, chairs shifted and the main speaker, Keith Funston, president of the New York Stock Exchange, was reminded of a story before plunging into his text ("Needed: A Fair and Warmer Investment Climate"). It seems there were two fellows in some pretty hot spot, and the first fellow said to the second fellow, "Gimme something tall, cool and loaded with gin," and the second fellow said, "Careful what you say, you're talking about my wife."

Yeats was gone; the program was back down to business.

But the sixty-first convention of the NAM was not yet free of the voices of heresy. On the third morning the student winners of the NAM's annual scholarship awards were billed on a panel discussion with six industrialists to discuss "New Dimensions for America." The official program reported that "These students were invited to attend all sessions of the three-day meeting so that they could observe at first hand industry's thinking and philosophy."

The six industrialists were evidently unprepared for the possibility that the kids might not have dug the "thinking and philosophy" of the industry which they had just observed at first hand. After all, they were getting their scholarships, a trip to New York and a chance to talk to these prime movers of production. But the questioning had no more than gotten underway when it turned out that Alexander M. Clarke of Virginia Military Institute had some grave worries about the future of capitalism.

"We know that another depression would ruin capitalism," he said. "If we fall down like they did in the thirties, the plants'll close up and we won't be able to open up again. NAM says it doesn't like government centralization, but without government controls, what does NAM propose to do about the business cycle going another way? If the government takes off controls, what does NAM propose to do in place of them?"

Cadet Clarke was assured by one of the industrialists that the NAM "has more confidence in a free market than it has in the decisions of the bureaucrats"; that it has "tremendous faith in the overall ability of the American consumer to spend his money."

One of the panelists, becoming aroused, asked Cadet Clarke if they didn't teach him over at that military academy how to get out there and fight for what he wanted, and not have the other fellow do it for him. Cadet Clarke, replied that at the military academy they taught him to obey his officers. The matter was dropped.

It was then that Rosemary Lee of Chatham College, Pittsburgh, wished to put the question of federal aid to education before the industrialists. She wished to quote from Peter Marshall that "Liberty is not the right to do what you please, but the opportunity to please do what is right." "Would it," she asked the panel, "be more democratic for a certain business to decide what is right—or for a whole government, representing all the people, to say if we need federal aid to education and ought to support it?"

Dr. Ralph Robey, economic adviser to the NAM, explained that he had no use for federal aid to education, that it would mean complete government control and that students ("just like you!") would be told what to study and would have to do it, just as they did in Russia.

This evaluation drew the wrath of a young man listed as Lloyd G. Becraft, a student at Montana State College. "I disagree with you," he said. "I go to school at Montana State College and we get federal aid and our president says there are no strings attached and we do what we want, study what we want, think what we want. As for me, I'd be in favor of accepting money from the Communist party as long as there were no strings attached to it."

The audience was suddenly shifting, buzzing and laughing. The industrial panelists were beginning to raise their voices more than was necessary to be heard on the public address system. One blurted out that "Your parallel between taking money from the Communist party and the federal government is very apt."

The interlocutor, sent for the occasion by NBC, looked for the next question. It came from Daniel S. Kemp of Reed College, Portland, Oregon. He wanted to know about the dangers of overproduction and its consequences to future generations. Wasn't it the responsibility of the manufacturers to consider these consequences now? One of the industrialists answered him with the words of a popular song: *Que sera, sera*, the man said.

Feeling perhaps that this was not enough, Cola G. Parker leaned to the microphone and explained to the lost young man from Oregon that the reason business failed, after all, was that they didn't do what the consumer wanted.

Dr. Robey, getting more excited, moved to the fore and pounded out the philosophy of mass consumption. There was no need to worry about overproduction, he said, because of the wonderful phenomenon of consumption, which resulted in this saving line of thought, as summed up in a little story: "Anything I have one of, I'd like a second one of—at the right price—including my wife."

Thus introduced to the mystique of the American economy, the college students were told by the NBC man that the game was up, thanks for the questions.

The audience was loudly astir as the curtains closed. What was it creating with its national scholarships? One NAM staffer who has been through several of these annual rites said they always had the student quiz, but the students had never been so "enthusiastic" before. There was the feeling that given another hour of questioning the industrialists would have had no choice but to ring down the curtain and revoke the scholarships.

The world of the NAM conventions, usually bounded so safely (to use the imagery of Father Donaghy) on the East and West by Lexington and Park avenues, on the North and South by the laws of supply and demand, below by the Grand Ballroom and above by the Starlight Roof, had been badly violated. God and William Butler Yeats might be dismissed as "unrealistic." But who could account for Lloyd G. Becraft, the boy from Bozeman, Montana?

MADISON AVENUE JUNGLE: ADMEN AND MADMEN / DAVID CORT

One of the most significant and quietly sensational stories of 1956 has remained relatively inconspicuous in the pages of American newspapers. The reason: the story was a lawsuit against an important advertising agency.

This treatment of an important news story brings into focus a basic fact of American journalism. In telling about a murder, adultery, drunken misbehavior, tax evasion, American newspapers seldom identify the criminal as an employee of any large corporate advertiser, department store, chain store or, most particularly, any advertising agency.

The reader has no grounds for complaint about all this exquisite tact in his paper, because in most instances he does not pay for the publication. The advertiser pays for it. The citizen pays a symbolic tip to get in on a free ride. All he really has to contribute is his response to the advertising pages. You don't imagine, do you that your twenty cents pays for the eighteen pages of four-color pictures in *Life?* Count the full-color advertising pages: in the issue I am looking at they come to forty against eighteen. That should tell you how you rate against the advertiser in *Life's* love-life.

The existing press is primarily a vending machine. "Freedom of the press" is 90 per cent a beautiful parrot cry by which we seek to identify ourselves with the Founding Fathers. Indeed, it is unfair and irrelevant to criticize this vending machine because it dispenses Coca-Cola instead of truth. Should the American people ever decide that it wants the whole news, it would have to begin paying for the whole magazine or newspaper. Meanwhile we must settle for what we get.

The lawsuit that the press ignored revolved around the advertising account of American Airlines (president: C. R. Smith), which rose rapidly from a trifling $7,000 in 1938 to over $4,000,000 last year. The selling of air travel was pioneered for American Airlines and to some extent for the whole airline industry by a man named P. P. ("Pete") Willis. In 1938, American Airlines gave Mr. Willis the power to choose an advertising agency. For the then small account, the agency of Ruthrauff & Ryan gave Mr. Willis a "lifetime, irrevocable" contract paying him $1,000 monthly and a third of all gross agency commissions on the account exceeding $18,000 in any six-month period.

On December 14, 1955, Llewellyn A. Westcott, Master in Chancery in Chicago Superior Court, ruled on the facts in a suit for an accounting between Ruthrauff & Ryan and Mr. Willis. Not a newspaper reported that the Master had found that Ruthrauff & Ryan had tried to harass and "dominate" Mr. Willis, offering him small "loans" to be repaid at interest, trying to get him to sign cancellations of the contract, reneging on a plan to pay his back income taxes and ultimately suing him for $5,000 that the Bureau of Internal Revenue had returned. Mr. Willis launched his countersuit in November, 1954.

The Master in Chancery's report described the testimony of the company officers, F. Barry Ryan, Jr., and Ralph Van Buren, as follows:

> I find that Mr. Van Buren's testimony must be disregarded in its entirety as being untrustworthy and unreliable. . . . Mr. Ryan, Jr., exhibited a reckless disregard for the facts in permitting himself to swear falsely to two affidavits. . . . Mr. Van Buren and Barry Ryan, Jr., betrayed the confidence and trust that Willis placed in each of them by displaying a lack of good faith and fair dealing. . . . I find that the statements of both Messrs. Ryan Jr. and Van Buren are unreliable and untrustworthy and should be disregarded. . . .

The full story appeared in only one American publication, *Advertising Age*. Soon Afterward Barry Ryan, Jr., surrendered his job as board chairman to Paul E. Watson, uncle of the company's president.

Superior Court justices will normally accept the findings of Masters in Chancery. But on June 4, 1956, Judge Marcovitz in Chicago reversed the Master's findings and ruled for the defendants. This sort of news the press was able to handle, though still furtively and cryptically. In the back pages of the New York *World-Telegram and Sun* of June 5, near the bottom of an advertising business column, was an item noting that Ruthrauff & Ryan were very happy that day because the court had "nodded favorably to them in the million-dollar action by Paul Willis in connection with the American Airlines account."

Included in the trial evidence was a letter to Mr. Willis from the man who replaced him as account executive for American Airlines: "I am not the type of person who turns around and cuts a friend's throat. . . . Throughout this whole mess, I have felt that our interests were more closely related than apart, yet you call me every kind of blackguard imaginable. In this racket that's comparative (sic) to two inmates on a penal jute machine calling each other crooks." The helpless immorality expressed in this pathetic letter reflects a world in which the immorality seems to some inhabitants conventional and necessary.

To explain this I am led to a brief survey of the advertising business. There is too much money in it for too little effort. In the present phase, there is very little pioneering toward the creation of new American habits and a gigantic brawl to pander to established consumption habits. A campaign or layout costing perhaps $50,000 to create is duplicated in media whose billing runs into the millions, theoretically profiting the agency perhaps $500,000 at the 15 per cent commission for billing. One TV commercial may be repeated $10,000,000 worth (agency commission at 15 per cent: $1,500,000).

What kind of money are we talking about? In 1955 the billing in magazines, TV networks and newspaper sections alone for the top one hundred advertisers came to about $2 billion. Add to that oddly limited statistic all radio and local TV time and newspaper space for all advertisers and a much better figure, according to *Tide*, is $8 billion. The pregnant 15 per cent of that figure comes to $1.3 billion in commissions. Some 3,000 agencies (excluding 1,800 one-man operations) divide it for an average of $444,000. Actually, only sixty-six agencies do $2.5 billion of the billing. J. Walter Thompson should keep about $35 million on its billing of $220 million; Young & Rubican, $27 million on $182 million. McCann-Erickson and B. B. D. & O. should keep about $25 million. Next in order come N. W. Ayer; Foote, Cone & Belding; Leo Burnett; Benton & Bowles; Kenyon & Eckhardt; Grant and Kudner.

More interesting is where all the money comes from. A breakdown of that unsatisfactory $2 billion total shows the giants among the advertisers (figures in millions of dollars): General Motors, 44; Procter & Gamble, 42; General Foods, 30; Chrysler, 27; Colgate-Palmolive, 25; General Electric, 19; Gillette, 19; Ford, 18; American Tobacco, 17; Reynolds Tobacco, 15; Lever Brothers, 14; General Mills, 14; American Home Products, 11; Campbell Soup, 10; National Dairy Products, 10; Bristol-Myers, 9; Liggett & Myers, 9; Lorillard, 9; Distillers-Seagram, 8; Pillsbury, 7; Goodyear, 7; A. T. & T., 7; Swift, 6; Borden, 6; Kellogg, 6; Westinghouse, 6; R. C. A., 6; and duPont, 6.

A lot of money is moving around. But do the advertisers actually let the agencies keep all of that enormous 15 per cent? If not, do the agencies bid competitively for accounts with promises of ever-larger "kickbacks"? If so, where does the backflow disappear to? Is the United States government missing out on its tax cut?

Constant flirtation by agencies with the accounts of other agencies is the present foundation of the advertising business. The "kickback" is a very seductive form of flirtation. Every week several accounts change agencies; yet there is rarely any sensible apparent reason for the change. However subtle the flirtation, in the minds of the two parties involved it has all the dignity of a trollop's wink.

The reason for this unattractive and unnecessary relationship is an odd one, and the whole vice of the advertising business. It is just the opposite of the trollop's practice of getting paid. In this case, the client—the advertiser—never pays the strumpet. He pays the business man at the other end—the newspaper, magazine, TV or radio network. The poor trull gets to handle the money briefly and takes off her huge commission; but it is not morally her money for real services rendered. She passes it on minus her cut, and may even give back some of that to the heartless client to keep his favor.

This system is the disease that turns men into hucksters. The agency's charge does not really add a great deal to the cost of a product to the consumer. But the agencies constantly advise the manufacturers how to get more and more out of the consumer. The current conspiracy against the American consumer, disguised as a shower of free-enterprise blessings, is quarterbacked by the agency.

The days are past when every agency employed a few men solely to butter up the clients' sales personnel. They produced the tickets, reservations, women and liquor, and sometimes have been known to secure a contract with a well-placed tape-recorder. But if the practice is now largely extinct, there are certain interesting exceptions. One applies to the lower echelons of executives in the transportation corporations—automobiles, airlines, railroads and shipping. The more conspicuous exception is the hard-liquor industry, some of whose proprietors today are Capone-era graduates now surrounded by C.P.A.'s as well as charcoal-gray hoods. Here again only the lesser executives can be so easily seduced.

However, there are many real friendships in the business. The social palships flourish between the client's sales manager and the agency's account executive, or at a lower level between the agency's media buyer and a magazine's sales manager. In New York they can all be found lunching at Twenty-One, the Stork Club, the Ritz Bar, the Cloud Club, the Waldorf Men's Bar, Christ Cella's, the Divan Parisien and the Park Lane, often at their own expense. They may be telling the joke, six months late now, about the account excutive who lost his account and whose hair turned charcoal-gray overnight. Not a very good joke, it is hilarious to agency men because they read the agony beneath it. An account executive in the same situation, telling his hundred subordinates about the lost account, choked up and burst into tears. The best story right now is about Milton Biow who, on dissolving his great agency and throwing hundreds out of work, told them, "I've saved my money, old friends. Please don't worry about me. I'll be all right." This was really funny because Biow's whole career had clearly told everybody they need never worry about Milton Biow. A few days later, according to the New York *Herald-Tribune*, he was dining in Paris with Art Buchwald.

The huckster's love for the 15 per cent commission system within the advertising agencies seems to me to separate the men from the hucksters. *Tide* and the Association of National Advertisers generally seem to regard it as sacred. Others within the business have attacked it for forty years as senseless, humiliating and obsolete. The Grocery Manufacturers' Association debates it at every meeting. The late Albert Lasker got around it by buying control of a company before he advertised his products. One agency, Cowan & Dengler, managed to do business on a flat retainer fee. The U.S. Justice Department recently got a consent decree against advertising associations for conspiracy to make the 15 per cent commission standard.

The hucksters' love for 15 per cent is compounded of belief that they are getting something for nothing and a groggy conviction that they are already running the United States. One agency man recently proposed to solve farm surpluses by "awarding wheat to McCann-Erickson, corn to J. Walter Thompson, cotton to Cunningham & Walsh and butter to B. B. D. & O." Sometimes advertising men feel capable of repealing the law of supply and demand, or even the law of gravity, for a 15 per cent commission.

My own suggestion, if a percentage system is preferred, is that an agency, like a lawyer, playwright, novelist or inventor, take a contingent fee based on a percentage of sales income rather than a percentage of billing costs.

Perhaps the present system is irrestible to the business man because he, too, thinks he is getting something for nothing and if he gets a "kickback" he is getting it for minus nothing. It is tempting to analyze the attitude as the ancient and consecrated contempt that the man of business has always accorded the man of talent. The advertising talent does its work with such ease and enjoyment that the business man finds it somehow obscene, hardly worth paying hard dollars for. Make no mistake about the talent in the advertising business. Compared to most other editorial work in America today, advertising offers more jobs, more scope, more research, more challenge and more money. It draws some of the best people in the United States, along with the dull boys and the connivers. They certainly deserve an honest day's pay for an honest day's work.

But the commission on billing is not an honest day's pay. The only reason it exists now is that the advertising business started that way, under circumstances very different from the present ones.

In 1880 there was mass production in the United States, but the problems of mass distribution and mass consumption had not yet been solved. The chief consumer goods were "do-it-yourself" necessities such as sewing machines, bolt cloth, pins and needles, tools, rifles and revolvers, and the unique swindle of patent medicine. They were sold by drummers, door-to-door salesmen, peddlers, pitchmen, fairs and local newspaper advertising. In this situation, the forerunner of the advertising man bought space in the newspaper and resold it for whatever he could get from the advertiser. Sometimes he helped to write the copy.

National advertising did not arrive until after the invention of the mass magazine by *Munsey's, McClure's,* the *Ladies Home Journal* (1883) and the *Woman's Home Companion* (1893). Now the first advertising men, like J. Walter Thompson and Frank Presbrey, bought space in the magazines and sold it at a mark-up to the first true mass-commodity producers. The earliest fortunes were made by the patent medicines; the attitude that advertising was a bare-faced swindle lingered on, not in the minds of the readers but in the minds of the advertisers and agents. Oddly, the agents rarely went into the magazine business. They evidently liked the something-for-nothing illusion; the advertisers liked it, too.

American periodicals in 1908 numbered 5,136. In 1955 there were 6,092 consumer magazines, 8,525 country weeklies, 1,870 business newspapers, 1,765 daily newspapers, 2,698 radio stations, 412 TV stations and three TV networks, nearly all living on advertising revenue. The fleshpots were very enjoyable. In 1955, *Time Inc.* netted $144 million in advertising, the *Saturday Evening Post* alone took in $83 million, the Hearst magazines $119 million, Crowell-Collier $24 million and U.S. newspapers $695 million.

Even at these prices, it is sad and unnecessary that the magazine be so servile to the advertiser. Any communications medium that can prove it has a relative monopoly on a particular audience may charge anything it likes, up to taking over ownership of the advertiser. The medium makes the mass corporation possible—not, as so many advertising people believe, the other way around. If there were no way to speak to the consumer, consumer goods would become local or homemade again. The trouble is that everybody in the act of selling, from the editor to the business man, is ashamed of selling. They all think they are getting something for nothing, try to get something more for less than nothing and end up with less than they are actually entitled to.

The consequent demoralization in American culture is most apparent in radio, TV and magazines, in that order. Magazines do not accept much interference with their editorial matter, though they certainly do not intentionally offend the advertisers. Daytime radio, on the other hand, has long been ruined by the insistence of the advertising agency on writing and producing the whole program for its client, who is usually Proctor & Gamble, Lever or American Home Products. Hence the soap opera, the most abominable art form ever conceived.

The agencies are outraged that they have not yet got the same free hand in TV as in radio. Senator John Bricker's Congressional investigation would challenge the monopoly that networks have in TV. Who would be behind the investigation? Who but the agencies? They have already got their hands, usually in collaboration with "talent-packagers," on such shows as the $64,000 Question (Revlon), Groucho Marx (De Soto) and the Kraft Theatre, while convincing the naive that they want no part of TV. The operation is as impudent as if a political dictator should demand to sit in on *Saturday Evening Post* editorial conferences or, worse yet, "package" the whole magazine.

The agency's dictatorship over what ought to entertain America is not necessary or even useful to the advertiser. The advertiser knows as much about entertainment as I know about dressing hogs. Until the communications medium throws him bodily into the street, he is going to dictate what the people want as long as he can.

And all this is a consequence of the American people's happy abdication of the burden of paying for their magazines, newspapers, TV and radio. The occasional editor who still puts up a suicidal fight for the integrity of the American people's information sources goes unsung and unthanked. The tragedy is all in the closet.

Meanwhile, I must go on getting my pleasure from the advertising-trade publications. The Ruthrauff & Ryan story, which started all this, is not the only good one. In recent weeks Colgate-Palmolive and Mennen lost a patent case to Carter Products on the pressurized shaving cream they have been selling; Toni and Hudnut are at war; Liggett & Myers changed agencies to blended agony and jubilation; and Lucky Strike won its case against a man who claimed to have invented "Be Happy—Go Lucky." Above all, in April there was the crash of the once mighty Biow agency that had once handled $50 million in billings and lost half that in its last six weeks. Its trouble went back to Biow's testimony in 1953 in a tax evasion case against one Arthur Samish. But Biow went down fighting, obstreperous and inscrutable to the last. You miss these great stories in the newspapers and news magazines.

It must be clear by now that a great deal that is both important and invisible bears on the decisive influences that bear in turn on the American people. As I have said before, the invisible man is always unpopular; he has too great an advantage over the rest of us. But in this case the advertising man, who is the invisible one, is not the ultimate villain. Behind the visible pages of consumer-goods advertising, behind the loving gargle on TV and radio, stands the really invisible man, the one with the false face, the man of business who is being given these words for nothing, who did not and could not think of them, who despises everything about them except the sales they bring him, who despises the idiots who believe the words and at the same time cannot help believing them himself, who despises the sycophants who wrote the words for nothing and is constantly looking for new sycophants who will write shiny new words.

If the Revolution or Counter-Revolution should ever come to America, I would not be surprised to find on the first line of barricades none but advertising men and women. I would have to be on the other side, but my heart would go out to them. Certainly if they wanted to change America, they would know well what it is they have to change. Finally, it should be remembered that the Republican National Committee is employing Lee Burnett's advertising agency, and the Democratic National Committee Norman, Craig & Kummel. The advertising people may have already decided on revolution—an invisible one, without the risks of the barricades.

SEX AS A SELLING AID / EVE MERRIAM

Supposedly, Mrs. Samuel Johnson entered her husband's study one afternoon and discovered him with housemaid a-lap. "Why, Samuel," his wife exclaimed, "I am surprised!" "Not at all, my dear," he replied with the nicety of his lexicon background, "it was *I* who was surprised. *You* were astonished."

Many Americans continue to be astonished at the presence of prostitution in our culture, yet rarely is the profession surprised by law enforcement or by a determined citizens' campaign. This is probably not to be deplored, since prostitution per se is scarcely the pillar upon which the whole house of hell hinges.

During recent years the incidence of venereal disease has lessened to a considerable degree. This does not mean necessarily that trade is down, but rather that sulfanilimide is up. How prevalent is the trade as of today, [March 1959], U.S.A.? Statistics cannot of course be ascertained, but New York police records reveal that violations in the three fields that are customarily associated—prostitution, narcotics and gambling—were substantially higher in 1958 than in 1957. Since the total of arrests is always the merest-sized token, it is plausible to assume that unrecorded violations ran into complex figures.

The number of women, however, making their living directly from the life does not constitute a decisive voters' block; nor are call girls as influential as they would seem to be according to the glamorous build-up currently under way to make them out the Auntie Mames of the power trusts. Their work is not always steady, the clientele shifts, fees are erratic, there are obvious hazards, and take-home pay after what is given over to the procurer, pimp, landlord, and fancy and plain-clothes colleagues may average little more than a union job at a soberer trade. Even in the $100-an-engagement bracket, a few may be able to afford the mutation of mink, the culture of pearls and the couch of psychoanalysis, but they have not added to their charm bracelets any international oil combines or railroad and banking mergers.

They are engaged by industry, to be sure: in an age of Organization

Man there is a place for Accommodation Woman. Still, they are only one of many cogs that keep the big wheel spinning. On the whole, the rather commonplace device of using sex to advance business deals has, by now, been put in its modestly proper perspective by the Bureau of Internal Revenue. Deductible or non-deductible? That is the pertinent question about the wages of sin.

Therefore, to the majority of the audience that tuned in, the recent CBS documentary broadcast produced by Edward R. Murrow and entitled "The Business of Sex" came with all the shock value of last year's calendar. The information imparted—about the retaining of madams on monthly corporation payrolls, and the employment of climaxes to relieve tension and help climax sales—was strictly in the this-is-no-news department to any worldly listener. Understandably, the volume of mail and telephone responses ran very little higher than for any other sustaining show the network put forth, and the proportion of 80 per cent commendatory letters to 20 per cent opposed was about normal.

The word *SEX*, though, contains built-in jumping beans, and the morning after the broadcast night, things began hopping. Loew's theatres in New York had a small-time picture, *Party Girl*, playing the neighborhoods. Immediately the exploitation office at headquarters swung into action with streamers and blow-ups proclaiming "All N.Y. Is Talking About That 'Party Girl' Radio Program." Television and night-club comedians set their gag writers to working on variations of what *Variety* referred to as "the three M's of the week—Madam, the Mann Act, and Edward R. Murrow." The Associated Press and United Press International each sent out a thousand-word report of the broadcast to their subscribers, and the New York *Post* published the entire fifty-five-minute script in installments over a four-day period.

Headlines from coast to coast had a gala; as charges and countercharges were hotly flung about, it got to be like real cool. The Hearst papers unleashed a congeries of reporters, columnists, cartoonists and editorial writers to demand that Murrow apologize for defaming business ethics, intimating that he might well be tried for treason, since his "unsupported smear against American enterprise, the prestige of New York City and the reputation of its police force" would be "a prize package for the propaganda machine of international communism." Against the broadcast's "unsupported" smear, they brought forward genuine rebuttal evidence produced by the *Journal-American*'s own poll-taking. "'I have never seen the slightest bit of evidence in my firm or in any firms in the same field to support the statements made on this broadcast,' said one company spokesman." And, "'utterly unbelievable,' said the public-relations representative of another corporation. 'We would not even acknowledge that such unproved practices are encouraged or permitted anywhere.'" Finally, to crown the poll, "A public-relations man with one firm declared the picture Murrow attempted to portray is 'laughable. At the upper levels of big business today, everybody watches his step very carefully,' he said. 'Why, most of us are afraid to go to the races, let alone get involved with procuring women.'"

The senior citizens of the N.A.M. took off on another gambit of outrage. Never mind that Murrow was giving aid and comfort to Khrushchev; there was a more diabolic plot involved. Noting that this "innuendo, smear, snide implication and unsupported accusation" came from the man who had once dared attack Senator McCarthy, they warned that the broadcast was a Machiavellian attempt to divert public attention from the corruption of labor unions.

The Associated Press interviewed a sampling of executives in banking, manufacturing, oil, steel and utilities. Total result: out of twenty-two individuals queried, twenty-two replied that they had never heard of any company's employing prostitutes to increase business.

Lines of inquiry to police chiefs and mayors of cities across the country produced another overwhelming group of nays. On the West Coast, Mayor Norris Poulson of Los Angeles: "I have no knowledge of such practices in Los Angeles"; Milwaukee's Police Captain Harry Kuszewski: "Those who come here for conventions, meetings and on business, and who feel desire for such things, complain that 'there's no fun available in Milwaukee—no girls available'"; Rochester (Deputy Police Commissioner John Rein speaking for the chief): "The call girl situation here is very dim. We have very little, if any. We have a clean town"; U.S. Attorney Hubert L. Teitelbaum, in charge of the Pittsburgh district: "Certainly there are some indications that sex entertainment is afforded for business purposes. How widespread the practice is I do not know. I've never heard of anyone being on the payroll for that purpose."

Meanwhile, back in Manhattan where the broadcast had originated, everybody was, as *The New York Times* said, reacting in character. There was a surety about the step-by-step procedure, as with the dialogue leading up to the song numbers in a pre-*Oklahoma* musical comedy. While the-business-of-sex brouhaha lasted, a sweet nostalgia filled the air; you felt as though you were hearing a tune from the Jimmy Walker era played on an old handcrank phonograph. The players in the charade were lovably familiar. There was the firm-jawed Police Commissioner, Stephen P. Kennedy, issuing a stern warning: "If sufficient evidence can be obtained against any businessman who is using call girls for business, he will be arrested and subjected to prosecution." And to aid in obtaining such information, the commissioner added an urgent appeal to the public: any employees of business organizations knowing of the call girl system in their companies should get in touch with First Deputy Police Commissioner James R. (no relation) Kennedy by telephone or in writing. Dial direct CAnal 6-2491; mail orders receivable at headquarters.

Then there was the judiciously cautious judge's reaction. Said Chief Magistrate John M. Murtagh: "I could not help but feel that at least some of the material was based on impression rather than factual knowledge.... I have sometimes been asked where in the world the best job has been done about combatting the practice, and my answer has always been 'right here in New York.'"

There was the go-for-broke determination of the district attorney's office. Said James O'Leary, press secretary for District Attorney Frank S. Hogan: "We are going over the transcript of the broadcast to determine if anyone involved in the show, or any of those quoted, have any factual information about vice in New York. We're not concerned with vice anywhere else."

There were also the ruminative remarks of Earl Wilson, New York *Post's* conductor of statistical surveys: "Fake! Fake! screamed B'way today about the big vice scandal ... HOWEVER, I know personally that the wife of one Hollywood near-celebrity DID furnish herself and other girls from a deluxe 5th Ave. 'house'.... Another sharp girl 'auditioned' to 'book the talent' for a corporation—and made good, real good. And—for the deviationists—there was a 'call *boy* ring.' Credit cards—billing for drinks and dinners, not girls—were honored." (Mr. Wilson was recuperating nicely from the depressing effects of his recent trip to England, where he had been shocked by the open flaunting of sex for sale. "Brittania no longer rules the waves," he had summed up on his return to these shores. "Instead, she waives the rules—of conventional conduct and decency." Clearly, open solicitation in the streets was no way for a mother country to behave; it was good to be back home again with more daughterly items for his column.)

So the headlines huffed and puffed until even the tabloids got worn out from shouting. The topicality of the subject has palled; about the only place where its newsworthiness remains is in the novelty stores along

Times Square where out-of-towners can purchase made-to-order newspapers with their names included in the headlines. At latest report, the best seller was still "Joe Doakes Hits Town; Call Girls Overworked."

To be sure, the use of sex as a commodity to help sell other commodities is not always a cause for merriment or *laissez faire* on the part of all members of American society. When the General Electric Supply Company sales convention of two years ago in Newark was revealed as having hired Nedda Bogart to furnish call girls as part of the company's standard kit for salesmen, many wives of the men who attended the convention became irate. The human electricity in the air had to be grounded, and it was: a huddle with a firm of top-notch public-relations counselors, and a positive rather than a negative approach was decided upon as best suiting the situation. Plans were formulated for at least one sales convention a year to include the wives from that time on. Moreover, it was arranged that these meetings be held at some fun-in-the-sun spot for the distaff side as well, such as Florida or Las Vegas. (There would be nothing improper about Las Vegas, surely, for the decree of 1906 had long been repealed; no longer did the district attorney's office post notices to the effect that "saloons maintaining or running in connection with places of prostitution or employing women to solicit trade on commission or otherwise, must pay a license of $500 in addition to the regular saloon license." Rather, the wives of the salesmen could enjoy the healthful outlook produced by the advent of cleaner H-bomb testing, where the Chamber of Commerce was sponsoring a young lady known as Miss Atomic Blast, attired in a Bikini, the bra featuring an 88-carat diamond called "Spellbound" and the panties displaying another gem entitled "Spirit of Hope.")

As far as can be noted, internal relations at the General Electric Supply Company are now quite all right. In any case, there was no boycott of any of the company's products on the part of dealers or consumers, and many an American could empathize with the explanation of company executive Lewis E. Rinker, who testified at the court trial in February, 1957: "I did it because it was part of my job"—adding that he understood the girls' services had helped sell seven carloads of appliances.

If the operation had fizzled, and sales had not increased, there might be some justification for complaint. It was evident, however, that this was no mixing of pleasure with business; it was a bona fide business legitimacy. Our salesmanship economy is at a fearsomely competitive level, and ill fares the people's capitalism where wealth accumulates and sales delay. All knights must to the jousting; the lieutenant of General Motors who went buckoing around Madison Square Garden last autumn, blasting a six-shooter and shouting "You Auto Buy More" was hardly in a more dignified position than Mr. Rinker.

In the case of the General Electric Supply Company, all's well that ends well for everybody concerned, since even though there was sufficient evidence to convict Mme. Bogart, the all-male jury acquitted her. As one of the jurors explained somewhat apologetically to one of the reporters after the trial, they felt it wasn't quite fair to convict her and let all the men get off free. This is a radical departure from the prevailing gentlemen's code of conduct where, in any prostitution raid, the women are found guilty and the men released without their names being revealed. This may seem like simple sex discrimination, but it is really noblesse oblige toward women and children. We must at all times maintain the sanctity of the home and protect the institution of the family. Since most of the men who patronize prostitutes are married and fathers to boot—well, as a chivalrous male, you would not want anybody's wife embarrassed at the next P.T.A. meeting. Besides, the notion of the female as a Niagara and the male as the salmon leaping upstream against his will has a venerable and still-revered place in our patriarchally-oriented society. St. Paul was scarcely the original Mister Misogynist, and although we have come far since his burning edicts, advances in morality are not our principal concern. As the latest General Electric advertisements state, "Progress Is Our Most Important Product"—progress in sales. If the hiring of call girls is a helpful adjunct to that progress and can unload seven carloads of appliances onto already overstocked dealers, then may seven times seven fructify your future.

For where, in an earlier, less taxing period of business competition, there could be a postprandial celebration over the fact of the dotted-line signature, today it often has to come before, as the *apéritif*. The use of sex-for-hire as one of the devices to get the stubborn hand relaxed enough to fill out the order pad is merely one of many available aids. Expected bribes and pay-offs run a wide gamut, with "lush entertainment" (feminine companionship there subsumed) only one item in the listing. *Sales Management* reports that in addition to vicuna coats, Oriental rugs and free hotel suites, there are less publicized but more common items of exchange such as guns, whiskey, hand tools, sporting goods, radio and TV sets, fire-protection items, electric shavers, fishing tackle, clothing, appliances, paints, gift certificates, amateur radio gear and vacation trips. The reasons given by *Sales Management* for salesmen extending such bribes sound most plausible: "To retain the business" (29 per cent); "to obtain a bigger share of the business" (51 per cent); "to break into the prospect's firm" (55 per cent).

As the "free world" contracts, and as international trade is curtailed by cold-war policies, the domestic market has to loom larger than ever; it also becomes harder than ever to keep on getting a larger share of that market. If you don't exert yourself to go on making it larger, it will shrink. It is not only in Looking-Glass Land that you have to keep running fast to be able to stay in the same place.

Fortune extols the miracle of "the new All-American market—the moneyed mass middle-class rising"; more customers for what they now refer to as "the wonderful, ordinary luxury market." They find that "millions of Americans enjoy their great Christmas foray into the luxury market, but this market is by no means a seasonal curiosity. What has happened is that luxuries in the U.S. are becoming unexceptional, habitual, functional."

It might be more accurate to note that in the drive to distribute these luxuries, many practices—with the use of sex-for-hire as only one trick under the counter—are becoming unexceptional, habitual, functional. In the shape-up for sales to come, the device of hiring call girls may be one of the most innocuous that will be employed to keep the trade wheels turning on the home scene.

For *Fortune* is forced to recognize that "the wonderful, ordinary luxury market" is not just there for the taking. As they see it, "the challenge to business is to keep up with the market's potentialities not only by making and selling more of everything, but by improving, varying, and adorning everything—by blurring still further the already blurred line that distinguishes Americans' luxuries and Americans' necessities."

It is not so easy to keep blurring that line when four and a half million Americans are out of work, and when a rise to five million or more unemployed is predicted for the future. Salesmanship is going to have a hard sell on its hands.

All kinds of ingenious ways and means will have to be found to fit in with the thesis advanced by John Kenneth Galbraith in a lecture on "Economic Power in the American Setting" before a Polish audience. In what is surely the epitome of understatement, he declared that "Profits are still an important test of performance in our business system." More of a clue may be had in the remarks of Dr. Theodore Levitt, marketing adviser to Standard Oil of Indiana and other corporations. Speaking before the Harvard Graduate School of Business, he titled his remarks, "The Dangers of Social Responsibility," and came swiftly to the heart of the matter:

> The point is this: The businessman exists for only one purpose, to create and deliver value satisfactions at a profit to himself. He isn't and shouldn't be a theologian, a philosopher, an Emily Post of Commerce. His job is ridiculously simple. The test of whether the things he offers do indeed contain value satisfactions is provided by the completely neutral mechanism of the open market. If what is offered can be sold at a profit (not even necessarily a long run profit), then it's legitimate. The cultural, spiritual, social, moral, etc., consequences of his actions are none of his personal concern.

It is rather a relief to know that there need be no further worries about distinctions between okay and non-okay bribes. *Chacun à son coup.* Those with an over-cultivated taste for the spiritual, social, moral and etcetera consequences of actions will simply have to learn to include prostitution as one of the facets of our many-splendored business system.

It should not be so difficult to broaden our threshold of tolerance. In our salesmanship economy, the treatment of sex as a commodity cannot really be interpreted as a perversion of our dominant ethos; it is a pervasion of it. Sex is part of the come-on pitch in everything from automobiles to soup mixes: why should it not be carried to its logical conclusion and be incorporated as part of the business-deal pay-off?

THE CREDIT CARD MILLIONAIRES / RICHARD SCHICKEL

"I've been afraid of this," says one Russian bureaucrat to another as an angry mob mills beneath their window. "The people want credit cards!"

This poignant vision of the Soviet future, as seen by *New Yorker* cartoonist Alan Dunn, may yet become a reality, especially if Nikita Khrushchev achieves his ambition of parity with the United States in the production of consumer goods. The men in the Kremlin might well ponder the experience of the United States in this respect, for it isn't difficult to imagine that once the material millennium comes to pass in the USSR, its people will do exactly what we Americans have been doing since the millennium came here—demand the democratization of conspicuous consumption, a process in which credit cards are extremely useful.

Within the recent memory of most Americans, the purchase of a new car was a great event, a thing that occurred, in most middle-class families, only every five years or so. I can still remember the general swelling of pride in our family when we bought our first refrigerator in the midthirties, and as a child I recall overhearing intense debates over the desirability of various methods of purchasing those capital goods which were, in a sense, luxurious variations on necessities. Things being what they are today, everyone seems to have a refrigerator, and a home freezer, too, and the arrival of the new car has become an annual event, like birthdays. The telephone company, having achieved total saturation of the market, is now telling us that extension phones, "in color, of course," are "a beautiful way to save steps."

In short, most of us have all the necessities we need, perhaps more than we need. So, because there is left-over money burning holes in so many pockets (even with personal savings at a record high) and because, if the economy is to continue its expansion, artificial wants must be created at an unprecedented rate, we are witnessing an awe-inspiring revolution in spending habits.

Luxury-spending and tax-dodging, once the more or less exclusive prerogatives of the classic *nouveau riche*, have been extended to two groups that, since 1929, couldn't afford it—the old rich and the burgeoning middle class. Only the very poor, a dwindling minority group of slackers who simply don't consume good, like Americans should, cannot indulge in this, the biggest fad of our history. (Even they, however, can afford the $2.50 solid-gold sewing needle, or the $2.95 brass belt buckle that cunningly incorporates a can opener, bottle opener and screwdriver—items which did very nicely in last year's Christmas trade.)

There are a multitude of reasons for the new methods Americans have devised to get rid of their money. Naturally, they are interrelated.

Let's begin with the old rich. Quite simply, their prestige has always been closely tied to the ups and downs of the business cycle. With the economy booming, they can now spend as they did in the twenties, without risking public outcry over the injustice of it all. "The rich have been in hiding for twenty years" says an interior designer, who happily adds: "They're coming out of their holes. And they're having a ball." Spencer Samuels, president of an art and antique firm, concurs: "The wealthy no longer worry about what people will think if they spend thousands of dollars on a painting. Being rich has lost its stigma." Meanwhile, it might be noted that the political Left, which used to spend so much time and effort pointing and shaking an accusing finger at the wealthy, hardly has the energy to lift it any more.

But don't get the idea that it's easy these days to prove wealth without being vulgar about it. Notes *Business Week:*

> In a day when plush cars, swimming pools, boats have become commonplace for the middle-income groups, some of the old prestige symbols have lost their hold. Thus pressure from below, as well as the pressures of their own economic circumstances, lead the wealthy to spend—with more restraint perhaps, but with more skill. . . .

What are the things the poor, pressured old darlings are being forced to buy? *Business Week* lists, among others: Caribbean land (no inheritance taxes there); rare books and manuscripts (a way to tie up capital in small portable objects as a hedge against taxes); jewels ("Diamonds may be a girl's best friend . . . but they are the matron's best investment against a rainy day"); and art ("an owner can give a painting to a museum, get a fat [tax] deduction and keep the picture for most of his life").

The skill and restraint of the spending habits presented on the foregoing list should be breathtakingly obvious to all but the most churlish, as should their potential for tax evasion.

But what about those pressures from below? If the *canaille* is riding around in yachts, where can a man go? Africa? Even Kenya is crowded. The *Wall Street Journal* notes that last year 60,000 people spent over $21 million on African safaris, compared to 13,000 spending only $1.5 million in 1949. It adds that "Photo-hunting is on the rise in Africa. . . . The sport can . . . be inexpensive enough to fit even a middle-income executive's purse."

The rich can't even call their dining habits their own any more. Gourmet foods are an interesting footnote to the new American taste for luxury living. Purveyors of these foods, which once exclusively came to rest on the tables of the rich, have seen their retail dollar volume rise 300 per cent since the war, and sales continue to rise 15 to 20 per cent each year. There are now about 6,000 specialty food stores in the United States, plus around 5,000 specialty shelves in groceries and supermarkets. Here, again, we see business opening the prerogatives of wealth to a large group.

Things are just as bad in the urban clubs, where it used to be possible to observe the power elite in repose. The barbarians are within those portals, too. Says one clubman: "I'd guess about 90 per cent of the checks received by my club are company checks—you'd have to look pretty hard to find a personal check." Adds another: "There are some fine clubs whose old-line members are fast dying off and whose only hope is to recruit promising young men who have made a name for themselves in industry. But the old-timers hesitate—they still cling to the idea that only the bluebloods... deserve membership. They fail to see that the so-called social aristocracy has long been on the wane, that the business aristocracy is in the ascendancy."

Reporting all this, the *Wall Street Journal* notes that, with costs up and membership down, the clubs in self-defense are taking in businessmen whose business will pay their dues as well as the checks for the business lunches. Increasingly, the clubs are actively seeking the membership of the type who, as one clubman puts it, "will spread his damned papers all over the luncheon table."

The expense account, of course, is responsible for more than the decline of the old-fashioned club. It is a much-discussed social phenomenon, and we need not pause over-long on it. Its extension and increasing generosity have been caused by a desire to reward executives with non-taxable income—a fact the internal revenue department has at long last noted. Starting in 1959, you have to report expense account receipts.

Whatever the pros and cons of the expense account, it has had one important psychological effect on vast numbers of people. It has turned them into Cinderellas. Take as an example the husband and wife who spend a week attending a convention in Bermuda at company expense. They note that, by scrimping a bit, they can afford a week or so of similarly high living at their own expense. Obviously, they cannot live every week of the year like millionaires, but they can have a day here, a week there, a few hours at another time, of living virtually indistinguishable from that of the wealthy. In our present economy, they can afford an occasional stop at the gourmet food shop, or a dinner-dancing-theatre evening on the town once a month or so. In short, almost anyone can judiciously sample the good life—the really good life—by shopping carefully, budgeting wisely and having a little luck.

Meanwhile, says the *Wall Street Journal*, "an increasing number of business associations are transferring their conventions to luxury passenger liners"—and 92 per cent of the wives go along for the ride.

For the old rich, then, this is the real "pressure from below." Everyone is trying, in some way, to emulate them. American business, ever alert to the national mood, is doing all in its power to make emulation easier—especially since there is now a class that can not only afford, but desperately wants, to engage in this part-time deception. Hence, the credit card, the handy wand that turns pumpkins into rented Rolls-Royces.

The credit-card boom is truly staggering. The Diners' Club started on $20,000 some eight years ago, now bills $91.1 million annually and expects to have 750,000 members this spring, a figure which will undoubtedly be equaled by the relatively new American Express all-purpose credit card. The cards of the Sheraton and Hilton Hotel chains are, meanwhile, coming up fast on the outside. In addition to these there are literally millions of less diversified cards floating around, ranging from the granddaddies of them all, the oil-company credit cards, to those issued by hotels, railroads, airlines, car rental services and the phone company. There is even a yachting cruise club, on whose card you can charge docking fees, repair bills, ice and gasoline when you are away from your home port. *Newsweek* reports that a member recently called the Diners' Club of New York office to ask if it could "recommend some good places to go slumming."

Plainly, the credit card, the possession of which is in itself a status symbol, represents a major artery down which trickle the prerogatives previously reserved to the wealthy. If what we are witnessing now is the democratization of consumption (or at least the outward signs of it), the credit card is the major manifesto of revolution. *U.S. News & World Report* says:

> The credit-card agencies believe a person is likely to spend more money if he buys with a credit card. One of the companies that issue the cards says that, on the average, people who charge purchases spend about 35 per cent more than those who pay cash.
>
> "It has been found that the charge account purchaser does more impulsive buying," it says. "The individual's tendency to buy an article which strikes his fancy is greater if he does not have to reach into his pocket or purse for cash, but can forget about payment until the end of the month."

The democratization of social values, and to a degree of wealth itself, is making it tough for the rich to keep ahead of the middle class. Even the popular press has shifted its spotlight from them to entertainment and sports figures. So, since there is nothing else for it, they are spending a little more conspicuously than they were previously. But not for them the vulgarity of the Robber Barons! The essence of current conspicuous consumption is the soft-sell—the painting quietly purchased for the local art gallery, the quiet (but not quite anonymous) subsidization of a cultural or charitable organization, a new "responsibility" in political and community affairs, a quietness in entertainment and in home decoration—these are the hallmarks the old wealthy are more and more adopting (viz., the career of Nelson Rockefeller).

Today's burgeoning middle class—the chief beneficiaries of the democratization of consumption—really has no time or inclination toward this sort of modesty. For one thing, their pleasures still have the tang of newness about them; for another, it is at least as difficult to learn how to spend with unobtrusive good taste as it used to be to learn how to spend gaudily. You have to have lived with wealth for a couple of generations before you can, as a class, produce many Rockefellers.

Somehow, observing the current social scene, the famous conversation between F. Scott Fitzgerald and Ernest Hemingway, keeps coming to mind. Fitzgerald declared that "The rich are different from you and me," and Hemingway replied, "Yes, they have more money." At the time, Fitzgerald was right, Hemingway merely flip. There were great differences in attitudes, beliefs and behavior between the middle class and the rich. But if uttered today, Hemingway's remark would seem acutely perceptive. Increasingly, you can't tell the rich without a tax return.

Any process of democratization results in a blurring of class lines; and that, of course, is what is happening today. Partly, the old rich have only themselves to blame. It is they, when the heat was on, who adopted middle-class plumage as protective coloring. They began leveling down in the thirties. In the fifties, they have been met by the increasingly prosperous middle-class leveling up. Hence, even though the wealthy are coming out of hiding, it remains difficult to spot them. On a Bermuda beach, in duplicate bathing suits, you can't tell a rich girl from an ad-agency secretary on vacation. Things reached such a pass recently that *Esquire* published an only half-kidding chart on "How to Tell a Rich Girl" (she wears plain pumps, is found on the East Side, goes to Europe with her real daddy and wears white underwear).

This leveling down, of course, makes things ever so much easier for all those—and that includes damn near everyone who isn't on relief—intent on poaching the preserves of the wealthy. The only way you can spot them is by the small, satisfied smiles that hover about their lips as they head toward the Metropolitan Club for lunch, the itineraries for their safaris nestling against the sheafs of credit cards in their pockets.

MYTH OF THE POWERFUL WORKER / HARVEY SWADOS

A small group of unhappy and bewildered Americans is gathered musingly about a little table in a trailer parked beside a gas station on the outskirts of Winchester, Virginia, a quiet, pleasant Shenandoah Valley town. The town, called the Apple Capital by its boosters, is the homeplace of Senator Harry F. Byrd, who owns something like 2 per cent of all the apple trees in the United States. The Americans, seated uncomfortably on a broken-springed couch and three kitchen chairs beneath a couple of girlie calendars and a scrawled reminder of an impending meeting of their local union, munch on hamburgers and southern-style beans (the trailer is mostly a cookhouse, with a refrigerator and a little rotisserie), and ponder the fact that a trial examiner for the National Labor Relations Board has just ruled that they are violating the Taft-Hartley Act [1958]. They have been on strike against the O'Sullivan Rubber Company for over two years, and after having been disenfranchised in a decertification election, they are now advised that they cannot continue picketing the plant down the road, and that their international union, the Rubber Workers, which has been giving them $25 a week strike benefits so that they do not go hungry or lose their homes or possessions, must cease and desist from its nation-wide boycott of O'Sullivan products.

While they stare at each other, lined-faced family men, toothless oldsters, motherly widows and shy young women, wondering how it came about that all the power of the federal government seems to be invoked against them simply because of their desire for decent relations with their employer, a professor of economics from Harvard University is testifying in Washington before the subcommittee on labor of the Senate Committee on Labor and Public Welfare. The nation's capital is only two hours to the east, across a green and lovely Virginia country-side dotted with baronial estates devoted to the raising of fine horses and fine cattle; but those who sit in the high-ceilinged committee room just down the hall from Senator Byrd's office might be on another planet, a million light years from the baffled strikers in Byrd's hometown. Senators Kennedy,

Goldwater, Ives and Morse are listening quietly and politely to a parade of academic and professionally interested witnesses from both sides of the fence expounding their ideas on new legislation affecting the NLRB and the Taft-Hartley Act.

The economist, Professor Edward H. Chamberlin, is telling them that "Organized labor is on the whole rather well up the income scale, yet the anachronism that labor is downtrodden and deserving of some special kind of public sympathy carries on. It derives, in part, from a cultural lag."

The professor may not have the sympathy of all his listeners in the committee room, but there are others besides the National Association of Manufacturers (which commends him to the readers of the N.A.M. *News*) who hold to his position: indeed there are times when one might suspect that he speaks not only for the conservative Right, but also for the host of former friends of labor and ex-radicals who smile wearily when they are informed that there are still embattled strikers in this golden land. And the casual visitor to Washington who pads from one marble palace of labor to another through the acres of broadloom, from the incredible Teamsters Union Taj Mahal to the hardly more credible temple of the Union of Operating Engineers to the plushy International Association of Machinists building to the well-appointed Philip Murray building to the quietly luxurious AFL-CIO building, might be pardoned for thinking—unless he troubles to discover that there are still some dedicated and worried men working for their ideals amid all the opulence—that the professor is right and that "labor"—that great abstraction—has reached the promised land after all.

The O'Sullivan strikers of Local 511 do not think so, but even though they have a clothing depot set up to receive gifts from those who care, they are not pressing the point that they are "downtrodden and deserving of some special kind of public sympathy." They do a lot of hunting for deer and small game, a lot of fishing for everything from herring to trout, a lot of odd jobs around the town; they hold bake sales to raise money for things that the union can't afford to provide, like school books for the kids; and although it is hard to find steady work (always the ostensible reason is that they would be only temporary until the strike ended), nobody is going hungry. But people like Mrs. Martha Webster, a gentle, tired widow who went to work for O'Sullivan with her brother and her brother-in-law twenty-seven years ago, and who had never heard of unions until she joined the one that she now supports ardently, as an embattled striker; Mrs. Carrie Boyd, a jolly widow who is mostly Cherokee, seldom reads the papers but knows what she is fighting for after some fourteen years as an O'Sullivan worker; Arthur and Asa Smith, who helped build the plant back in the twenties and put in about thirty years of their lives there before going on strike; Charles Rittenour, who when he went on strike was making $1.30 an hour after eleven years at O'Sullivan, and whose face is a little more lined now because his oldest boy (he has five children) has leukemia; and Bruce Muse, who started in at O'Sullivan twenty-five years ago at 15¢ an hour, making $1.87 for a twelve-and-a-half-hour day, and going around to his friends' homes evenings to try to talk union after the twelve-and-a-half hours were over—these people are the victims of a piece of legislation most of them had never heard of. After having voted 343 to 2 to affiliate with their union, and 355 to 2 to strike, they found themselves the targets not only of an intransigent company, but also of an apparently implacable and vindictive government as well. What is more, they are not merely the fluke victims of an accidental legal clause (which the new Kennedy bill would repeal): millions of American workers are now being victimized in one way or another by the Taft-Hartley law, which is now being applied so rigorously by the Eisenhower-appointed NLRB that even back in 1954 *Business Week* was saying, "from a practical standpoint, it's obvious that T-H has changed in operation."

To understand why, it is necessary to recapitulate a bit of the Winchester experience, as well as that of workers in other places and other industries who are suffering as a result of legislation and administration which had hitherto engaged their attention less deeply than had the private life of the Prince of Monaco. It is difficult even for a more sophisticated individual than a Virginia worker-housewife to understand what Section 9(c)(3) is going to mean personally until the paychecks stop.

In April, 1956, the NLRB certified the United Rubber Workers as exclusive bargaining agent for O'Sullivan workers, after the 343-2 election. Negotiations followed, but there was disagreement on the question of a general wage increase (the company average was 40¢ to 60¢ an hour below similar organized shops), and the employees struck the plant on May 13 after the 355-2 secret strike vote. The company immediately began to recruit strikebreakers from the West Virginia hills (it is a commentary on conditions in the area that people were willing to scab on their neighbors for $1.25 an hour), and to pepper the strikers with telegrams urging their immediate return on penalty of job forfeiture.

At this point the strikers—the vast majority of whom had never before belonged to a union, paid much attention to politics, or even voted—

had their first collision with the majesty of the law. The State of Virginia, not ordinarily noted for its social pioneering, had been one of the first to pass a "right-to-work" law. Under its terms, the strikers were hardly allowed so much as a frown as they stood at the gates, surrounded by state police, and watched the sheltered newcomers going in to take over work that they had been doing for upwards of a quarter of a century.

"We never thought that it would last more than a day or two," says one of the lady strikers, "or that the company would be so glad to be rid of us after all those years we put in for them. Actually, we should have given the scabs the same reception that Nixon got down in South America —but then, there was the right-to-work law, and those state police."

From that point on the company was in the driver's seat. It prolonged negotiations, broke them off, rejected the assistance of the Federal Mediation and Conciliation Service, resumed negotiations, stalled again, meanwhile hiring about 200 new employees. In January, 1957, the Rubber Workers Union inaugurated a consumer boycott of O'Sullivan, the first such boycott ever undertaken by the union in all its history. The company, which had obviously been reading the fine print, filed a new election petition with the NLRB in April and a decertification petition in May.

Now, according to Section 9(c)(3) of Taft-Hartley, "No election shall be directed in any bargaining unit or any subdivision within which, in the preceding twelvemonth period, a valid election shall have been held. Employees on strike who are not entitled to reinstatement shall not be eligible to vote. . ." Thereupon, the year having elapsed and the strikers having been replaced, the NLRB disfranchised the O'Sullivan strikers and, with majestic impartiality, proceeded to poll the strikebreakers, who voted 288 to 5 against the union.

This may seem a little unfair. Indeed, this peculiar provision in a law ostensibly designed for "encouraging the practice and procedure of collective bargaining and by protecting the exercise by workers of full freedom of association, self-organization, and designation of representatives of their own choosing," was so designated by President Eisenhower. He pledged an A.F. of L. convention in 1952 (six weeks before Election Day, to be sure): "I know the [Taft-Hartley] law might be used to break unions. That must be changed. America wants no law licensing union-busting. Neither do I."

Even if the President were to strain every nerve and sinew to keep this pledge, which is not exactly what he has done, it is an open question whether the Congresses which have followed his noble words would have contented themselves in their labor legislation with simply striking out the ineffable Section 9(c)(3), which had distressed even Senator Taft himself.

But this was only the beginning of the education of the O'Sullivan strikers. In October, 1957, the O'Sullivan company returned to the NLRB to charge that the union, by conducting its picketing, and engaging in its consumer boycott of O'Sullivan products, was in violation of Section 8(b)(1)(A). This section reads: "It shall be an unfair labor practice for a labor organization or its agents to restrain or coerce employees in the exercise of the rights guaranteed in Section 7...."

So, in February of this year, the NLRB issued a complaint and on May 15, the trial examiner, finding no merit in the union's claim that it was no longer seeking recognition, but was simply exercising its right of free speech by displaying such picket signs as:

> WARNING
> PENALTY FOR STRIKEBREAKING
> A LIFETIME OF SHAME AND REGRET
> URW   ON STRIKE   AFL-CIO
> ON STRIKE MAY 1956 to ?
> DON'T BUY O'SULLIVAN PRODUCTS
> HEELS MADE BY A COMPANY WITHOUT A SOUL

recommended that the union cease and desist from "restraining and coercing employees of O'Sullivan Rubber Corporation in the exercise of rights guaranteed by Section 7 of the Act by picketing said Company for the purpose of obtaining recognition and a contract...", cease and desist from "conducting a boycott campaign against the Company's products...", post in conspicuous places a formal notice that they are so ceasing and desisting, mail such notices to the NLRB for posting on O'Sullivan bulletin boards as well, publish in the *United Rubber Worker* a notice that the boycott is over, and notify the Regional Director of the steps taken to comply.

In Winchester, the strikers drift in and out of their trailer on their way to go fishing or to look at the picket line down the road in front of the plant where they had put in so many years, and they wonder aloud why their noses are being rubbed in it.

"I never was one for politics," muses a gray-haired lady as she bends over the icebox to get out some food for the menfolks. "It's a little hard for me to understand why the whole government seems to be so determined to be against us. I know the company would do most anything, but the government...."

But by and large the strikers are more sophisticated now. They know that the trial examiner's recommendations must go to the NLRB in Washington, that their union will appeal, that the case will probably wind up in the courts, and that precedent is against them. They know that all they can do is grit their teeth and hang on; they are caught in a box, and thank God for the union. They also know that in a sense they have themselves to blame for never having bothered all their lives to pay their poll tax.

"What for?" demands Maurice Miller, president of the local. "To vote for Byrd and his boys? We never had a choice, so we never bothered with the head tax. But now we've learned the hard way—I'd say we're close to a hundred per cent registered, and we're paying our COPE dollars so the unions can get into politics and see if we can scare up a couple pro-labor men to run in this neck of the woods."

Framed in the doorway of the trailer, a long-faced striker stares up at Miller and says, in the deliberate way of men in these parts, "I swear to you, I'd soona vote for the blackest nigga in the State of Virginia than for a Byrd man. Hope to die if that ain't true. They took us for granted because they could ignore us, and we took them for granted because we didn't know any betta."

With all due respect to the O'Sullivan strikers, they could win no more than a footnote in any balanced account of contemporary America if they represented only themselves. But in January, 1956, the employees of Machinery Overhaul Corp. at Palmdale, California, voted 65–28 to be represented by the International Association of Machinists. After protracted negotiations the union struck, and after the required year's wait, the company, having in the meantime hired a shop full of strike-breakers, demanded decertification of the union: all too predictably, the strike-breakers voted 90–1 against the union. Again all too predictably, the NLRB found thereafter that the IAM, by continuing picketing, had committed unfair labor practices in violation of good old Section 8(b)(1)(A). In April, 1958, the strikers were ordered by the NLRB to cease and desist from picketing the shop where they had formerly constituted two-thirds of the employees. All of these strikebreaking decisions, it should be noted, stem from last year's startling *Curtis Brothers* decision, which reversed past precedent favorable to unions, and which dissenting NLRB member Murdock characterized in these words: "The majority's erroneous interpretation of Section 8(b)(1)(A) seems to be prompted in large part by its desire to censure the union's conduct and find some section which can be utilized to ban it."

Forty-five million unorganized workers in the United States can never better themselves through organization by such unions as the Textile Workers, Retail Clerks and the white-collar unions as long as Taft-Hartley remains as law and is interpreted as it is being interpreted by the NLRB. These workers are simply not organizable; and the lawyers and union staffers in the plush Washington offices, whose job is to thread their way through the mazes of NLRB decisions and administrative rulings, are by and large almost as frustrated and furious as the workers of Winchester, Virginia. Let us examine some of the reasons why.

First of all, there are the provisions of Taft-Hartley itself. We have already seen how some of these have changed the hitherto quiet lives of Palmdale, California. In Toledo, Ohio, the Retail Clerks International Association had been bargaining with four stores together, which called themselves Retail Associates. In November, 1957, the union struck one of the stores, Tiedtke's, which promptly withdrew from the employer group and settled with the union. Thereupon the union struck a second member store, LaSalle & Koch (an R. H. Macy affiliate); this strike continues, but the store is open and, as in Winchester, grandmothers walk the picket line, cherishing their new-found militancy but wondering what goes on inside the store and inside the government.

For now the maneuvering had begun. Retail Associates, acting for its three remaining members, asked the NLRB to hold an election among the employees of LaSalle's, Lamson Brothers and Lion Dry Goods, arguing that the bargaining unit had changed. The strategy was obvious: with the unionized employees of Tiedtke's excluded from the vote, with the 400 striking employees of LaSalle's excluded from the vote, and with the 350 strikebreakers of La Salle's included in the vote, the Retail Clerks union couldn't possibly win. The union thereupon withheld its technically necessary non-Communist affidavits in an effort to keep itself off the ballot and thus forestall an election. It went before the NLRB and argued that it had the same right to withdraw from bargaining with the multi-store group that one of the store group did; and it asserted its right to bargain with the three stores individually.

With extraordinary rapidity, the NLRB ruled against the union, thus condemning it in advance to what the Rubber Workers had already been going through in Virginia. As Joseph A. Loftus narrated the story in *The New York Times* of April 11, the board "took the unusual step of notifying the parties by telegram of its decision less than forty-eight hours after it had heard oral argument." In so doing, the board overturned its own ten-year-old precedent, which forbade a union not technically in compliance with filing requirements from participating in an election; it opened the door to employers who would like to force their employees belonging to such powerful unions as the Mine Workers or the Typographers, to submit willy-nilly to an NLRB election; and it drove the infuriated Retail Clerks to the courts, no less, to seek an injunction against the NLRB election. Sol Lippman, union counsel, bluntly called the decision "a naked effort to break a strike," and went before U.S. District Judge Edward M. Curran to demand injunctive relief.

The NLRB attorney actually pleaded that LaSalle's was losing money because of the strike—a strange argument for a government official in a quasi-judicial position. The Associated Press story of April 22 gave another interesting sidelight on the reasoning of the NLRB attorney:

> Mr. Come argued that it was not certain how the election would come out if held on schedule on a multiple-unit basis. He said some of the LaSalle employees who have replaced strikers might vote for the union.
>
> "You don't think they are going to vote themselves out of a job, do you?" the judge asked.

Thereupon the judge issued the preliminary injunction sought by the Clerks, and the case will now be fought through the courts, while the middle-aged ladies march the picket lines in downtown Toledo.

If it seems strange today that labor unions should go to the courts to demand the aid of what has been for generations one of the most dreaded weapons used against labor—the injunction—that can only be taken as a measure of the extent to which the labor movement has become alarmed, not just about Taft-Hartley itself, but about the erosive effect of recent NLRB rulings.

While some of the most deeply entrenched unions have been howling the loudest in outrage (the International Typographical Union, operating for generations under what have amounted to closed-shop conditions, says Taft-Hartley has already cost its members $30,000,000), the truth of the matter would seem to be that it is the workers in the less powerful unions, and even more so the not-yet organized workers, who are affected most directly by the anti-labor bias of what one lawyer refers to as the National Labor Reversals Board. It costs from $3,000 to $10,000 to pursue a case through the circuit court, with the result that some unions simply cannot afford to contest what this lawyer calls "board law, not worth the paper it's printed on," in a court of law; indeed, he finds it currently so difficult to get a complaint issued by the board that he discourages his clients from filing charges with it at all. It should be noted parenthetically that corporations are legally entitled to list as business expenses the cost of fighting unfair-labor-practice court cases.

What is this "board law"? Here the layman finds his feet sinking into legal quicksand, and as he reaches out frantically for solid objects to cling to in the morass of opinions, precedents (some with names like the "Orkin the Rat Man" case), and administrative responses to changes in the political climate (i.e., the board's swing from a New Deal to an Eisenhower stance), he finds himself grasping at the straws of Latin phrases and at footnotes in which numbers outnumber words. Senator Wayne Morse of Oregon had a go at it on the floor of the Senate back in 1956, delivering himself of a ninety-page oration based in large part on a paper by Mozart G. Ratner, formerly Assistant General Counsel of the NLRB, entitled "Recent Changes in National Labor Relations Board Policies." Both of these documents are well worth reading, and one may surmise that the only reason for their not having a greater impact at the time was their lack of sex appeal as well as general public apathy toward labor problems at a time of full employment.

It would be tempting at this point to narrate some of the cases cited by Ratner and Morse, but a good deal has happened since then, and a good deal continues to happen. Let us mention only the case of the B.V.D. strikers, cited with good reason in both monographs. At Pascagoula, Mississippi, a group of women workers had organized themselves into a home-made union and then sought out the International Ladies' Garment Workers' Union for help. The NLRB denied reinstatement and back pay to thirty-seven strikers on the ground that they had continued to picket after acts of violence had been committed against the B.V.D. property by unidentified third parties. There was no attempt to prove that the women strikers instigated or even participated in the acts of violence; there was no evidence of conspiracy on the part of the strikers or of their having any control over the perpetrators. The board held that these ladies, some of whom were putting their children through school and were the main family breadwinners, were not entitled to get their jobs back because they should either have stopped picketing or dissociated themselves from the violence by "admonishment, denunciation or public pronouncement." This astonishing assault upon a group of innocent women, with all it implied not just for their right to their jobs but for their basic right to picket (and how can you conduct a strike without picketing?), forced the ILGWU to take the case to the courts. No wonder Professor Willard Wirtz, writing in the Northwestern University *Law Review*, commented that "the new NLRB . . . has proceeded to 'reinterpret' the [Taft-Hartley] Act in such a manner as to change its practical application substantially beyond anything seriously considered in recent Congresses."

We have to bear in mind, too, that the layman's notion that you can simply go to court (if you can afford it) and get everything straightened out that has been done to you administratively is more than a little simple. The courts are most reluctant to overrule the NLRB, and because of the "substantial evidence" rule, it is extremely difficult to get the board reversed in court on a question of fact. If you are not prepared to argue law rather than fact against the board, the chances are you will only waste your time and money in the courts. One Washington labor lawyer told me flatly: "If I were an employer lawyer, I could break any union just by using Taft-Hartley and the NLRB."

In this connection, we might take note of a Washington story in *The New York Times* of May 27, 1958:

> The Supreme Court held today that an employee kept out of a plant by the threats of striking union members might sue the union for damages in the state courts instead of going to the National Labor Relations Board for relief.

> Chief Justice Warren, joined in dissent by Justice Douglas, asserted:

> There is a very real prospect of staggering punitive damages accumulated through successive actions by parties injured by [union] members who have succumbed to the emotion that frequently accompanies concerted activities during labor unrest. . . . By reason of vicarious liability for its members' ill-advised conduct on the picket lines, the union [the United Automobile Workers, already defending some twenty-nine other suits totaling $1,500,000 as a result of the Decatur, Alabama, strike] is to be subjected to a series of judgments that may and probably will reduce it to bankruptcy.

This brings us to the tricky question which some Washington attorneys regard as the greatest draw back of the present NLRB: its narrow definition of its own jurisdiction. Without going into the complex details, we may say only that several years ago the board drew an arbitrary line and refused—presumably for reasons of budget and work load—to take jurisdiction in cases where the employer was basically "local" in character, as determined partly by the dollar value of business inflow or outflow. NLRB member Murdock promptly pointed out that there was neither a pressing shortage of funds, nor inability to handle case load (which was no higher than it had been five years earlier), nor any serious backlog of cases. He believed that the new jurisdictional standards would eliminate between a quarter and a third of the board's jurisdiction. It was his judgment, fortified by quotations from his more conservative colleagues, that the slash in jurisdiction was motivated by what you might dignify as philosophical considerations: the desire on the part of the board majority to cut back on "federal bureaucracy" and return to the states (most of which, if they have troubled to enact labor legislation at all, have adopted only "right to work" laws and similar employer aids) as much authority as possible on labor questions.

Labor lawyers like Arthur Goldberg and Elliott Bredhoff, counsel for the Steelworkers Union, claim that by thus taking itself out of the picture in such a substantial proportion of cases, the board has cut off the application of federal labor law from those working for hard-core employers and from marginal areas where workers are most in need of government protection. If you have been wondering where the individual human being re-enters the picture, think for a moment of the saleslady in a store or the chambermaid in a hotel, neither of whom can now turn to her government for protection if she wants to unionize—unless she happens to work for a "big" employer.

However, it must be noted that the Supreme Court has complicated matters by refusing to grant the states jurisdiction over some of these cases, thereby creating a "no man's land" for several million workers; that the Florida hotel cases are currently before the Supreme Court; that Congress is very likely going to have to do something about the "no man's land" area; and, indeed, that some labor lawyers in Washington are currently far more exercised about matters other than the board's refusal to take jurisdiction in many cases.

What are these other matters? Some of them are pretty ugly. Plato E. Papps, attorney for the International Association of Machinists, in a bitter article in the University of Detroit *Law Review*, entitled "The Aluminum Workers—Revisited," charges that

... It is hardly risky speculation to ferret out the true motives of the presently-constructed National Labor Relations Board. ... It is patently obvious that NLRB changes in policy have invariably been in favor of management. The cumulative effect of the many small shifts has been considerable. Curtailment of the economic power of labor organizations is but one of a categorized array of anti-labor policies. And even where no explicit change in policy can be garnered from administrative rulings, the "Eisenhower Board" analyzes facts in such a way as to find fewer violations of the Act by employers in contrast to unions. It is necessary to explore only the dissenting opinions of Member Murdock to ascertain how "Republican political facts of life" form the keystone of board persuasion. The recent expiration of Member Murdock's term on the board brings to an end, incidentally, the irritable reminders that Congress did not intend the Taft-Hartley Act to be the manipulative bauble of the National Association of Manufacturers.

In support of these conclusions, Mr. Papps quotes the following comments from articles in the Utah *Law Review*, the *Labor Law Journal*, the Columbia *Law Review*, and the University of Chicago *Law Review:* "... Substantial changes have been made in the NLRB decisions since the advent of an Eisenhower majority...." "The recent decisions of the board have tended ... to favor the employer's interests over the union...." "The recent major policy decisions reveal a total disregard for the fact ... that Congress declared it to be the policy of the United States to encourage unionization for the purpose of restoring equality of bargaining power between employers and employees."

The most comprehensive and devastating summary of what these changes have actually involved is to be found in an article called "Labor Law Upside Down: The NLRB and Member Rodgers," written by Joseph E. Finley and to be published as a pamphlet by the Public Affairs Institute. Mr. Finley, a labor lawyer who makes no bones about his bias, traces the turnabout in labor law to the appointment to the board in 1953 of Philip Ray Rodgers, a Taft protégé. Most particularly since then, he claims, the NLRB has been curtailing union organization, resorting to injunctions, making inexcusable rulings against unions, suppressing union activities over broad areas, and making a feeble defense of its pro-management rulings.

For one thing, in the minds of the NLRB a *threat* has now become a *prediction*. If your boss tells you that he'll have to close down his plant if you vote for a union, or if he tells you that he won't bargain with the union, he's not threatening you—he's merely "predicting" what he may be forced to do, and therefore is not guilty of an unfair labor practice. The lawyers call this "prediction of a legal position."

Moreover, sophisticated employers, thanks to the new board, have now discovered that the realm of permissible campaign propaganda has been vastly enlarged. Finley cites the case of the Zeller Corporation which, after bombarding its employees with mailings and anti-union publications, sent them a copy of a letter from one of its customers which inquired about the company's labor relations. Employees, the company pointed out to its own workers, "can readily see how we can retain customers and secure new business without the presence of a union." This, although it was a misrepresentation, was ruled by the board to be permissible propaganda.

Worse than either of these—at least in the opinion of this writer—is the extraordinary latitude given to employer "expressions of opinions" in the sacred name of "free speech." The cases that Finley cites are bad enough, in all conscience; but there are others he does not cite, particularly in the backward areas that the Textile Workers Union has been trying almost fruitlessly to organize, that are so heartbreaking as to make anyone except the most case-hardened want to weep.

These are not the thirties, we are reminded over and over. These are the fifties, unions are strong (too strong, even some liberals are saying), workers are not deserving of any special sympathy. Yet today women who earn 85 cents an hour waiting on you in stores vote against having a union to defend their rights because they are frightened by their employer, or lied to by him, and have no government agency which will defend them against threats or lies made in the name of free speech. Today, throughout the South, thousands of men and women who work in textile mills at below-standard wages, in below-standard conditions, vote against unions because they are showered with racist propaganda of the lowest kind.

For some weeks now [1958], John W. Edelman, Washington Representative of the Textile Workers Union, has been fruitlessly appealing to Senator McClellan, Chairman of the Select Committee—not on Labor Racketeering, as it has become known—but "to Investigate Improper Activities in Labor-Management Relations." He has asked for the opportunity to show that in Gaffney, South Carolina, in Alexander City, Alabama, in Tallapoosa, Georgia, in Stuart, Virginia, and in other towns throughout the South, there exists a pattern of anti-union violence and obstruction.

Back in 1950 a Senate subcommittee found that:

> The extent and effectiveness of the opposition in the Southern Textile industry is almost unbelievable.

In stopping a union-organizing campaign, the employer will use some or all of the following methods: surveillance of organizers and union adherents; propaganda through rumors, letters, news stories, advertisements, speeches to the employees; denial of free speech and assembly to the union; organizing of the whole community for anti-union activity; labor espionage; discharges of union sympathizers; violence and gun play; injunctions; the closing or moving of the mill; endless litigation before the NLRB and the Courts, etc. . . .

It is Edelman's claim that substantially the same conditions prevail today, in 1959, but so far Senator McClellan has shown no desire to divert the committee's attention from the more eye-catching exposures of venal union officials. We may legitimately ask what has happened to the national sense of proportion, of the fitness of things, when the misdeeds of a handful of loathsome slobs are deemed more worthy of our moral indignation than the deprivation of millions of Americans.

How do Taft-Hartley and the NLRB fit into this picture? Between 1943 and 1946, almost 50,000 Southern textile workers were brought under Textile Workers' labor agreements; since Taft-Hartley, this union's organizing drives have been for the most part dishearteningly unsuccessful. Take the case of the Burlington chain. Burlington is the largest single textile company in the United States, employing about 50,000 workers in about a hundred plants in this country alone. This is no backwoods outfit. It is also not above being involved in the distribution of anti-Semitic and anti-Negro propaganda, in having its supervisors tell employees that the union is 100 per cent for racial integration, in having its plant managers tell employees that the union has given large sums to the NAACP, in informing its employees that white workers would have Negro shop stewards if the union got in. Why not? The NLRB has already ruled that employers have the right to "free speech," and that if employer-subsidized Chambers of Commerce and clergymen peddle anti union race hate during organizing drives, there is no "proof" that the employers are using them as anti-labor "agents" to commit unfair labor practices.

But free speech seems to be a one-way street. In the T.W.U.'s futile effort to organize the workers of the Chatham Manufacturing Company in Elkin, North Carolina, all meeting places within an area of thirty miles were denied to Chatham workers: the Elkin YMCA, the local movie theatres, the Elkin school, the Benham school, the Boonville school, the Boonville movie house, the Surrey County Court House. Meanwhile, the workers were being bombarded not only by the local clergy and the local press, but by a hate sheet called *Militant Truth*. The Elkin *Tribune* was not above reprinting such paragraphs as the following from this hate sheet:

> The boys who head the CIO and would control the policy go under such names as Rieve, Baldanzi, Belanger, Shupka, Jueter . . . Rosenberg, Rubenstein . . . Stetin, Tullar, etc. Where do you think these men come from? Are their backgrounds, their beliefs, their faith anything like yours and ours?

The union lost the election. The union is still losing elections. Let me repeat that there are 45,000,000 unorganized workers in the United States. As Joseph Finley points out in his pamphlet, there are by now "numerous cases where unions have gone into election campaigns with far more than a majority of the employees signed to membership cards, then have received the brunt of an employer's 'predictions,' 'opinions' and 'permissible propaganda,' and have come out losing by margins of three and four to one."

I only wish it were possible for me to elaborate on some of the other points made by Finley—his charges that the NLRB has been suppressing union activities over a broad area, including secondary boycotts, on-the-job union rights, seniority rules, union security, collective-bargaining rights and protection against discriminatory discharges. But space permits mention only of his final pages on the record of NLRB member Philip Ray Rodgers, who voted against unions in every single case cited by Finley, including those labeled by federal judges as "far-fetched," "irrational" and "unjust and intolerable." Finley has compiled a little chart of the voting record of Mr. Rodgers which reveals that, in 1955, he cast sixty-six votes for management and two for labor; in 1956, forty-nine for management and one for labor; in 1957, forty-five votes for management and none for labor: "When a man votes for management 98 per cent of the time over a three-year period in critical cases, the conclusion is inescapable. He is no longer a judge, but a partisan adversary."

Well, the conclusion would seem inescapable, too, that if we are going to have investgations of union skulduggery, we ought to have an investigation of whether honest unions are getting a fair shake at the tribunal of the National Labor Relations Board. The N.A.M. is deeply impressed by the fact that complaints to the NLRB of workers against their *unions* have zoomed upward recently, spurred no doubt by the recession and the anger of laid-off workers at all officialdom; the rest of us ought to be deeply concerned whether the rights of unorganized workers to form unions and bargain collectively are being adequately protected by a board which has been so zealously protecting employers' rights of "free speech," "permissible propaganda" and "predictions" of catastrophes in the event of union victory.

Meanwhile, the observer who compares the lean and quizzical faces of the O'Sullivan strikers with the somewhat better-fed faces in the sleek halls of labor in the nation's capital, may be pardoned for wondering just how much American workers, and the American people in general, have gained from the labor leaders' ostentatious effort to keep up with the Joneses in Washington, only to find themselves a minor vote-trading power bloc in a city of really big power blocs. Perhaps the leaders really belong back with the led—from which independent base they might begin to understand for the first time what the potentialities of power *really* mean.

TVA: THE UNLEARNED LESSON / LLOYD ARMOUR

Twenty-six years separate the historic legislation creating the Tennessee Valley Authority from the latest important TVA measure [1959]: a new method of financing the continuing work of the agency. In that time, a new generation has grown up without knowing what it was like in the days before TVA. And an older generation has had time to forget.

This is a fitting time, then, for a new look at the reality of a dream, at an experiment that has become a $2 billion going concern. How does it justify its costs to its owners, the people of the United States? What has it done for the people of the Tennessee Valley? Is it "creeping socialism," as some have claimed, or is it "democracy on the march," as others describe it? Does the Valley use the agency as a lure to uproot industry elsewhere? Does TVA steal pennies from the pockets of taxpayers elsewhere to subsidize cheap power? Does it build steam plants as an excuse for continuing its work, now that the task of developing a river is all but complete?

These are some of the questions raised by a continuing barrage of criticism against TVA. For the answers, it is necessary first to go back, briefly, beyond the TVA era to some far-sighted statesmen such as Theodore Roosevelt, Gifford Pinchot and Senator George Norris. These were men who pondered long about ways of conserving and developing the nation's resources. From their thinking, and that of others, emerged the concept of total development of river valleys. In the depression years, a small band of men in Congress began a long fight for such an experiment in the Tennessee Valley.

From almost any standpoint, the choice was an excellent one. The South as a whole was underdeveloped, and it was labeled by some as the nation's No. 1 economic problem; and in the South, no region presented a greater problem than did that valley washed by the deceptively passive Tennessee River. For each spring, this sleeping tiger awoke and became a roaring, rampaging flood. Residents fled in terror to the high ground as the water swept away crops, homes and land. Millions upon millions of tons of topsoil vanished in hours. Businesses were wiped out, and with them sources of taxation.

The region depended upon a one-crop economy. "Balance" in agriculture was a phrase of the professors. There was little industry and much poverty. Malaria, tuberculosis and malnutrition left their marks upon the people and the burial places.

But the sickness that sapped the region most was one for which no doctor could prescribe. It was the sickness of fear. There was fear of the river, fear of the land that produced less and less. There was fear of the future. And in the beginning there was fear of TVA.

But the building of dams meant jobs and a flow of money. As the mighty dams took shape, hope rose. There was a new look about the land. Ears began to listen to what the experts of the fledgling TVA had to say. Eyes began to see help, as in mosquito control. There were specialists looking at the land, testing it and finding the need for fertilizers of a particular type. Since the type wasn't being produced, TVA began to make it.

Quickly, the Valley learned something about the TVA: it would help, but there had to be cooperation. Soon the Valley farmers, guided by their extension services and county agents, began to apply lime and phosphates to jaded land in the first of many, many thousands of farm-test demonstrations. They began to learn about soil needs, about contour plowing, about the importance of trees as windbreaks and erosion curbs. In a few seasons, the barren, soil-scalped hillsides were green, the valleys below them lush.

As research and production details were worked out and TVA-born fertilizers developed fully, the agency turned over its data and its processes to private industry—free of charge. In addition, industry got another gift—a ready-made market. Since research, introduction and promotion of any new fertilizer is costly, the industry moved slowly. But here TVA was doing the whole job with its research, demonstration plots, fertilizer schools and educational programs for the farmer.

Today, the farmer in Wyoming or New York, as well as in Tennessee, benefits by the TVA fertilizer program (which is paid for by appropriations from Congress). Minnesota farmers saved almost $750,000 from 1949 to 1954 by using TVA-developed and promoted "4-16-16" and "5-20-20" fertilizers.

It may be noted here that a chemical paradox—the fact that nitrogen is both a life-giving plant food and an ingredient of powerful explosives—makes it possible to turn the TVA fertilizer development center from peacetime to wartime use in a day.

As TVA was helping to promote a new and more productive farm economy, it was also having an effect on commerce and navigation. The series of high dams which canalize the Tennessee created a long, deep waterway over which freight traffic moved in increasing tonnage. Tows hauled automobiles from the industrial North to the Alabama plains, saving more than $10 a car. Ferro-alloys moved from Muscle Shoals, Alabama, to Pittsburgh $5 a ton cheaper.

What does this mean to shippers? On 12.1 million tons of traffic in 1958, they saved more than $24 million. Deducting the annual cost of the waterway—$4.2 million—there was a net transportation benefit of $19.8 million. This is a 14.5 per cent return on the $136 million net investment in a navigation system which contributes to inter-regional commerce and strengthens the whole nation.

It is axiomatic that navigation development and industrial growth go hand in hand. Since 1933, private industry has invested nearly a billion dollars in more than 130 terminals and plants along the river. All in all, more than 3,000 new industries have come to the TVA region.

This growth has prompted many critics of the agency to raise cries of "industry piracy" on the part of the Valley. But the vast majority of new plants represent branches and subsidiary operations of industry which still have their headquarters elsewhere. In a recent survey by TVA, it was found that during a nineteen-year period only twenty-five plants pulled up roots elsewhere and relocated in the TVA area. During this time, nine much larger plants left the region. The twenty-five incoming plants represented 3,800 jobs; the nine outgoing, 2,000: net gain for the Valley, 1,800 jobs.

The truth is that while industrialization in the Valley has been rapid, it has lagged behind the nation as a whole, and the cry of "industrial piracy" is absurd.

Originally, cheap electric power was considered among the less important objectives of TVA. It was viewed merely as a by-product of river control that would allow for increased rural electrification and encourage a moderate expansion of industry. But with the coming of World War II, the picture changed. A "secret" installation known as Oak Ridge needed power in enormous quantities. Opportunities for increasing hydro-power were limited: new dams might justify their costs in power terms, but not, at the time, in other ways. Besides, a huge dam is not an overnight project. In 1940, TVA turned to a much quicker method of adding to generating capacity: the steam plant. First to be built was the Watts Bar plant, with a capacity of 240,000 kw.

After World War II, and with the beginning of the Korean conflict, it became increasingly clear that more sources of quick power were needed. Not only were farms, homes and factories demanding more current, but entirely new energy-devouring installations were entering the area: atomic-energy plants, the Arnold Engineering Development Center and the Redstone Arsenal, where the Army was building missiles.

By fiscal 1958, the atomic-energy plants and other federal defense agencies in the area were using 51 per cent of all TVA power—more than 29 billion kwh. This is more power than was sold last year in any of the states outside the Valley except four.

So TVA became a defense weapon. But it had an extra meaning for taxpayers in that it provided very large savings on the government's electric bill. Perhaps this will show how much:

From 1953 to 1958, TVA delivered 129.8 billion kwh. of power to Oak Ridge and Paducah, Kentucky, atomic facilities. This cost the government $590 million. If there had been a one-mill per kilowatt-hour increase in this cost, the bill would have been $130 million more—about the cost of the U.S. share of the St. Lawrence Seaway.

Now compare the average cost of producing and marketing electric power by TVA with that of privately owned utilities. Last year, the operating cost for TVA was 5.21 mills per kilowatt-hour; the corresponding cost of privately owned utilities was about 10.09 mills. At that rate, the government's $590 million electric bill would have been almost doubled.

But, say the private utilities, TVA doesn't pay taxes. It's a subsidized operation. True, TVA doesn't pay taxes in name, but it makes payments to state and local governments in lieu of taxes. In 1958, these payments (from TVA and its distributors) totaled $13,751,000. Excluding federal agencies, about 6.3 per cent of the electric bill of all TVA consumers was paid to state and local governments. Corresponding taxes of private utilities in neighboring areas ranged from 5.1 per cent to 11.8 per cent.

In addition, the law requires TVA to repay to the Treasury, from its power revenues, the entire investment in each power facility within forty years. To date, payments of $250 million put the agency well ahead of schedule. The payments exceed the entire federal investment in the first thirteen dams TVA built.

There are other money savings involved. Millions of electricity users in other parts of the nation are paying lower electric bills because of TVA's rate policies—the so-called "yardstick" of power. Electric rates, according to Federal Power Commission data, are lowest in the TVA and Bonneville areas, and grow progressively higher as the distance from these public-power facilities increases. Before TVA, rates in a semicircle through parts of Texas, Oklahoma, Iowa, Michigan and New York were $10.08 for each 250 kwh. In 1958, rates for the same area averaged $7.10.

The power companies nearest the Tennessee Valley have made the greatest reductions in retail rates. Nevertheless, their earnings have increased at a rate substantially greater than the average of all the large utilities in the nation. From 1937 to 1957, according to published Federal Power Commission figures, earnings available to the common stockholders of the larger privately owned utilities multiplied three and one-quarter times; similar earnings of companies bordering the TVA increased eight times.

So much for power. To many people a more important objective of TVA is flood control. The Valley is now protected by ten major multiple-purpose dams providing six million acre-feet of storage for flood waters.

Were there no TVA dams, a flood stage of 57.9 feet in the Tennessee River today would cause $100 million in damage to low-lying Chattanooga. The total estimated annual average value of flood regulation by the reservoir system is $11 million. Over twenty-six years, this annual sum more than equals the annual cost and total investment combined of the system's flood-control facilities.

TVA's extensive experience in mapping, advising and aiding in engineering studies of flood control is being put to work in many sections of the country. One of the agency's special interests now is the tributary watershed program—away from the rivers, back among the creeks and branches where flooding is also destructive, though less so than on the rivers. This program seeks to establish ways by which, under state leadership, communities can organize themselves, study their problems and apply solutions through their own agencies and their own resources.

Critics charge that the citizens of the Valley are the helpless victims of an autocratic project. How well have these "helpless victims" done with the help of the TVA? In 1933, only 3.4 per cent of the total federal income-tax collections came from the seven states of the TVA region. By 1958, the percentage had more than doubled. From 1933–56, total collections amounted to $21,900,000,000. If we assume a rate of gain based on the 1933 percentage, TVA has meant an extra $10 billion in federal tax revenues—almost five times the entire cost of the project.

At the same time, the Valley has become a vast market for goods produced outside. From 1934 to 1958, TVA alone purchased $1.1 billion worth of outside goods. Users of TVA power spent $1.8 billion for electrical appliances. Still another billion has been spent on automobiles, boats, motors and other products.

These figures should not lead anyone to envision the Valley as more prosperous than any other section of the nation. It is far from that. It lags the national averages in almost all economic measurements. Twenty-five years ago the per capita income was only 45 per cent of the national average; despite a sizable gain, it is only 63 per cent today.

There is a great deal yet unaccomplished. The balance between agriculture and industry is short on the industry side. Too great a portion of the region's youth leave each year because there are not enough jobs. Farms are too small and too many. An estimated 2.7 million acres need to be reforested.

The demand for electricity is growing at a rate of 800,000 kilowatts a year. People are just naturally using more power—the air conditioner, for example, is a big sales item where it once was a rarity. Business expansions, new industry, demand more—and the Valley must have these if it is to continue to progress.

So TVA must have new funds merely to keep abreast of demand. That is why its supporters have fought for a self-financing measure (a method, incidentally, first suggested by the Eisenhower Administration). TVA will be lucky if the $750 million made available by the latest TVA legislation can adequately provide for needed facilities in the Valley. The pattern of progress has been set, and there can be no slackening off without harm to the region.

The great irony of TVA is that its value is given more recognition abroad than in the United States. It is the one great American project that draws a steady stream of potentates, students, engineers and politicians from every corner of the globe. It is the one great idea we have exported with success. Eight foreign countries now have big projects based on TVA—countries ranging from India to tiny Lebanon.

Efforts have been made to establish TVA-type authorities in the valleys of other American rivers: the Missouri, Rio Grande, Colorado. A new Columbia Valley Authority bill—the Neuberger bill—is before Congress. None of these efforts has thus far succeeded.

The TVA was an experiment at a time of national economic distress when the public was receptive to daring innovations. The electric utility interests, natural enemies of such an enterprise, were themselves in trouble. These interests, reviving, have since fought the spread of the TVA idea with a rising fear. While keeping TVA under carping attack, they have sown widely and nurtured well a confusion that restrains the people of other sections from emulating a valley program that is, nevertheless, the outstanding example of a people's ability to make the most of a natural environment.

PLANNING FOR THE YEAR 2000 /
J. BRONOWSKI

A specter is haunting the Western world—yes, today as in 1848. But it is no longer the one that was paraded in the Communist Manifesto. Today [1958] the name of the specter is automation.

In every industrial country, men are looking with alarm at the installation of new automatic machines. They see the machines taking over work which, until a few years ago, seemed to need the most delicate human judgment. For the new machines do not merely replace the brute power of the muscle—machines have been doing that for nearly 200 years, ever since first the water wheel and then the steam engine were brought into the factory. The new machines are beginning to replace a gift which is neater and more specifically human: the ability of the eye to measure, of the hand to adjust, of the brain to compare and to choose. When the Luddites smashed factory engines in 1811, they were fighting, hopelessly, against their mere physical power, which dwarfs the strength and with it the output of a man. But the specter of automation points its long shadow at his intellect.

In the United States as in England, and in most industrial countries, the automatic control of machine operations has gone farthest in the making of motor cars. This may be because, whenever anybody wants a car, everybody wants one; and alas, it is equally true that whenever anybody does not want a car, then all at once nobody wants one. That is, the motor industry is peculiarly sensitive to good times and to bad times; and in England, it was putting in automatic machines just when the times turned abruptly from good to bad. The result was panic among employers, a bitter but divided strike by the workmen, and bewilderment (heavily lathered with platitudes) in the Government. No one is clear whether the dispute reached back to automation, or was merely a by-product of the credit squeeze; and was the strike a protest against *any* dismissal of workers, or only against their sudden dismissal?

Questions like these are never answered in the day-to-day of politics. A compromise is reached, a crisis is settled for the moment; and when the next crisis comes, we suddenly find that what had been a midnight compromise has become a permanent principle. For example, the strike of Britain's auto workers was settled by paying some of them compensation for the loss of their jobs. This is a new principle in English industry. Is it really good government, is it good sense, to invent such a principle on the spur of the moment in order to get on with the export of motor cars?

There are political thinkers who believe that it *is* good sense, or at least that it is inevitable, that issues are decided in this way. They say that all acts of state are particular acts, and that they do not conform to a principle but rather, one by one, combine to form the principle which wise historians read into them after the event. It is useless, these thinkers say, to ask statesmen in advance whether men who are displaced by machines should or should not be paid compensation: that will be decided at the historical moment when the change comes, almost by accident, by the strength of the two sides, and by the social backing they can muster.

But surely it is possible for men, even if they are historians, to be wise before the event. I think that there are some changes in the structure of our society which can be foreseen now. It can be foreseen that in the year 2,000 more people will do one kind of job and fewer will do another; that one kind of thing will be valued and another will not. That is, we can draw now the bony skeleton of any industrial society in the year 2,000. It may be a world society or a city state; it may live in a settled peace or still under the threat of war; it may be democratic or totalitarian. Whatever it is, I believe that life in it will have certain large features.

First, it is of course plain that everyone will have at his elbow several times more mechanical energy than he has today. The population of the world must be expected nearly to double itself by the year 2,000. But the rate at which energy is being added, particularly in the industrial countries, is much faster than this. The four billion people who will be alive in the year 2,000 will not all have the energy standard of Western Europe today, where every inhabitant commands the mechanical equivalent of about five tons of coal a year. But they can be expected to average about half this standard—say, the equivalent each of two tons of coal a year.

The use of energy per head is closely linked with the standard of living, and the rise that I have forecast is therefore in itself the mark of a massive advance in living standards. But more than the crude figures, it is the whereabouts, the distribution of this energy that is significant. Most energy of this kind is generated in electric-power stations, and today these stations run, nearly all of them, on coal. The real difficulty in getting energy to Central India or Northern Australia or the Copper Belt in Africa is the difficulty of carrying coal there. In the year 2,000, the greater part of the world's electrical energy will be generated from nuclear fuels. A nuclear fuel such as uranium or heavy hydrogen is over a million times more concentrated than coal; one ton of it does the work of more than a million tons of coal. Therefore it will be possible to carry the fuel, and to generate the energy, wherever it is wanted. There will no longer be a reason for the great industrial concentrations in the Ruhr, in Northern England and in the Eastern United States. And what is as important, it will at last be as simple to have energy for agriculture as for industry.

Second, there will be advances in biological knowledge as far-reaching as those that have been made in physics. For fifty years now, we have been dazzled by a golden rain of exciting and beautiful discoveries about matter and energy—the electron, the quantum, relativity, the splitting of the atom, the proton, the neutron, the mesons—the bright list seems to have no end. But do not let us be blinded by them to the work which has been done in the last twenty years in the control of disease and of heredity. We are only beginning to learn what happens when we use a selective killer of weeds or breed a new strain of corn, when we feed anti-biotics to pigs or attack a cattle pest. That is, we are only beginning to learn that we can control our biological environment as well as our physical one. For the year 2,000, this will be critical. Starvation has been prophesied twice to a growing world population: by Malthus about 1800, by Crookes about 1900. It was headed off the first time by taking agriculture to America, and the second time by using the new fertilizers. In the year 2,000, starvation will be headed off by the control of the diseases and the heredity of plants and animals—by shaping our own biological environment.

And third, I come back to the haunting theme of automation. The most common species in the factory today is the man who works or minds a simple machine—the operator. By the year 2,000, he will be as extinct as the hand-loom weaver and the dodo. The repetitive tasks of industry will be taken over by the machines, as the heavy tasks have been taken over long ago; and mental tedium will go the way of physical exhaustion. Today we still distinguish, even among repetitive jobs, between the skilled and the unskilled; but in the year 2,000, *all* repetition will be unskilled. We simply waste our time if we oppose this change; it is as inevitable as the year 2,000 itself—and just as neutral.

But its implications go very deep. For it will displace the clerk as well as the fitter; and the ability to balance a ledger will have no more value, or social status, than driving a rivet. This is the crux in the coming of automation, that it will shift the social standing of those who do different kinds of work. And this is why these speculations about the year 2,000 are in place: because the shift is already going on, and it is our business to foresee now where it is certain to take us.

In themselves, the changes I have described will not determine whether by the year 2,000 Africa will become industrialized, whether the nations will still be testing bombs, or whether we shall live under totalitarianism or under democracy. They will not even determine whether we shall live in large communities or small ones.

The last point is odd and easily overlooked, but I think that it is important. For 200 years now, it has been the rule that, as a nation has grown in industrial strength (and with it in industrial complexity), so more and more of its workers have had to move together into large cities. In the sixteenth century, Queen Elizabeth I of England passed laws to prevent the growth of London, yet today Greater London houses nearly one-fifth of the population of Britain, and carries on about a quarter of all her industries. The same process of industrial concentration has been at work in France, in Germany and in America.

There are several forces which prompt this process. One is the hunger of industry for power; and in the past, power has been cheap only where it has been made on a massive scale. A second force has been the growing specialization of agriculture. And a third has been the sheer physical need to have large numbers of people to handle manually semi-finished goods through the many stages of manufacture.

Not one of these reasons need have force fifty years from now. The atomic-power plant need not be large; if it can reasonably drive a submarine now, it can reasonably power a community then. In the same way, biological control of the heredity and the disease of plants and animals will make it possible in the year 2,000 to grow our food in smaller units. But potentially the most powerful influence on the size of future communities, of course, is the coming of automatic machines. They make it possible for a few men to take a complex product such as a drug or an engine through all the stages of its manufacture. By using automatic machines, quite small communities can live in the elaborate world of industry; and they can do so either as the makers of some one product for a nation or, what is more difficult, as units which are self-contained and self-sufficient.

I have stressed the change which is possible in the size of the community, because this happens to be an historical subject as well as a critical one. Back in the 1820's, the pioneer of an idealistic socialism in Britain, Robert Owen, insisted that the industrial revolution of his day ought in the end to lead to smaller, not larger communities. He hoped that societies of between 1,000 and 1,500 people, working co-operatively, could survive, and he actually founded some in America. In the setting of his time, Robert Owen was premature; but he was not wrong. There are now industrial developments which open the way to smaller communities, if we choose to take that way. Atomic energy and automation are among them; and so are the radio-telephone and the helicopter and the microfilm, because they all help to make it possible for the man in the village to be physically and intellectually as well equipped as the man in the metropolis. The size of the future community really depends only on the rarest skill which it needs to support on the spot—the surgeon, the brilliant teacher, or the matinee idol. Fifty years from now, a community of 10,000 may well be large enough to afford that.

But what such a community cannot afford is the unskilled worker. The atomic-power plant, the agricultural station, the automatic factory— none of them has a place for him. In the small community, each unskilled man is a heavy burden.

In a profound sense, therefore, the choice ahead of us is this: If between now and the year 2,000, we can, step by step, turn the men who now do our repetitive work into men with individual skills, then we have a prospect of living in small and homogeneous communities. But if we remain with a large reservoir of unskilled men, then society will continue to move towards larger and larger concentrations.

To my mind this is a profound political choice; it is the choice which we must make now, every day, in a hundred tiny actions. We are about to have introduced, day by day, here and there, another and another automatic machine. One will do the work of ten typesetters, another will displace a hundred auto workers; and soon, a third will take the place of a thousand clerks. I have said repeatedly that automation today is coming to do the work of the brain, and therefore is taking the place of the white collar worker. If these men are permanently reduced to unskilled work, they will become the material for a new army of Brownshirts. Hitler's squads were recruited in just this way, from unemployed men whose collars had once been white.

That is already the danger in the short term. And it remains a danger in the long term, too, threatening the generations ahead of us. If we allow the survival of a permanent reservoir of unskilled workers, then we do two things: we insure that our cities will get larger and larger; and we connive at a permanent war in society between the skilled and the unskilled. It seems to me most likely that a society of this kind, concentrated in large units and divided between top dogs and under dogs, will fall into a totalitarian form of government. I do not need to look to the year 2,000 for that; George Orwell looked only so far as 1984, and saw it.

Technical foresight is a necessity; our political actions depend on it. And they do not depend on taking the short view; they depend on the long view, on looking far beyond the years of which we can speak positively—they depend on seeing the large features of a future whose detail is still unformed. We cannot escape the large bony features: atomic energy, biological control, automation. But the body of society is not all bone; a good many different bodies clothe that skeleton. It is possible on that skeleton to have either a totalitarian or a democratic society. I think that it can be foreseen that the future society will be totalitarian if it contains many unskilled men working in large cities, and will be democratic if it consists of skilled men working in small communities.

Changes toward one or another of these future schemes are not brought about by some instant illumination, a thunderclap of universal conversion. They are brought about by our small daily acts, if we know in what direction we are trying to act. And I have given two general directions to which we should bend whatever we do, whenever we have the choice.